VALLEYS of the POETS

The Author

Ray Jones was born in Whitegate, Wrexham, and attended the Victoria Primary and Grove Park Grammar Schools. After leaving school he joined the Post Office as a trainee telephone engineer but after six years left to train as a teacher. He gained his Teacher's Certificate at Chester College (now University College, Chester) and began his teaching career in West Sussex.

Whilst living in Sussex, he gained a first degree in geography and a higher degree in historical geography at Birkbeck College, University of London. He subsequently held lecturing posts at colleges in Sussex, Merseyside, Warwickshire and Derbyshire. As Assistant Principal of High Peak College in Derbyshire he set up local history research groups in Buxton and surrounding villages as part of the college outreach programme. He edited histories of the villages of Peak Dale and Hartington and a study of the early Victorian tourist industry in Buxton.

In 1987, he was appointed as Senior Adviser for Post 16 Education in the City of Liverpool and went on to become Head of Inspection and Advice Services in the city. In 1994, he took early retirement following the onset of a serious eye condition. In the following year he accepted the offer of a Fellowship at the University of Liverpool and subsequently worked as a freelance education consultant, lecturer and writer.

Ray is married with two children and lives in Chester. He maintains a keen interest in landscape history and is currently chairman of the Chester Society for Landscape History which meets at University College, Chester.

VALLEYS of the POETS

A History of the Landscapes and People of the ELWY and ALED Valleys

Ray Jones

Marlston Books, Chester

Valleys of the Poets

A History of the Landscape and People of the ELWY and ALED Valleys

Copyright: R. J. Jones, 2005

All rights reserved. No part of this publication may be reproduced, stored in a retrieval system, or transmitted in any form or by any means electrical, mechanical or otherwise, without prior permission of the copyright holder.

Published by: Marlston Books, 115, Lache Lane, Chester. Cheshire. CH4 7LT .

British Library Catalogue-in Publication, Data.
A catalogue record for this book is available from the British Library

ISBN 0-9549705-0-0

Printed and bound by Antony Rowe Ltd., Chippenham, Wiltshire. SN14 6LH

This book is dedicated to my nain, Mary Jane Jones
Born Nant-y-Ffrith 1896 died Wrexham 1978

CONTENTS

List of Illustrations	7
Preface	11
Acknowledgements	18
1 The Physical Landscape	20
2 The Landscapes of the Paleolithic and Neolithic	35
3 The Bronze Age Landscape	48
4 The Iron Age	63
5 The Impact of Roman Occupation	76
6 "Celtic" Monasticism and the Early Church	83
7 Medieval Churches in the Landscape	97
8 The Medieval Political Landscape	127
9 The Evolution of Rural Settlement and Agriculture in the Medieval Period	145
10 The Late Middle Ages: Upheaval and Change in the Landscape	172
11 The Making of the Present Day Landscape	179
12 Land Ownership and the "Great Re-building" from 1575	208
13 Industry and Transport	234
14 The Landscape of Religious Change 1750 – 1910	254
15 The Influence of the Part in the Plans of Present Day Villages and Hamlets	279
16 St. Asaph (Llanelwy) – The City of the Valley	326
Index of Places	345
List of Abbreviations	348

LIST of ILLUSTRATIONS

Maps

Location map of Elwy River Basin	10
1 Physical Landscape	27
2 Prehistoric Sites	43
3 Mynydd-y-Gaer Hillfort	69
4 Medieval Sites	137
5 Parish Boundaries	165
6 Pennant & the Upper Cledwen valley	181
7 Ffrith Uchaf c1880	184
8 Pant-y-fotty	187
9 Upper Aled Valley	188
10 The Great Rebuilding 1575-1675	209
11 Industrial Sites 1550-1900	236
12 Elwy Basin c1830	252
13 Religious Change 1750-1910	256
14 Gwytherin c1880	280
15 Llangernyw 1880	284
16 Llanfair Talhaearn c1880	291
17 Llannefydd c1880	295
18 Llansannan c1880	301
19 Henllan c1880	306
20 Bontnewydd 1880	314
21 Cefn Berain c1880	315
22 Bryn-Rhyd-yr-Arian c1880	321
23 St. Asaph 1610 (after Speed)	329
24 St. Asaph c1880	335

Black and white plates

1 Dedication page: Cotton grass Moel Bergam	5
2 Llansannan Monument	9
3 Llyn Aled	21
4 The mouth of the Cledwen Gorge	22
5 The Elwy Valley at Cefn Rocks	23
6 The Aled Valley east of Llansannan	25
7 The Cledwen Valley south of Pennant	30
8 Gwytherin Church	98
31 Leat, Elwy valley, Wigfair	247
32 Restored sluice, St. Asaph	248
33 Early chapels in the vernacular style	261
34 Early chapels with common design	252
35 Chapels extended after religious revivals	268
36 Capel-y-Cwm, Llangernyw	270
37 Late chapels (built after 1850)	271
38 Architect-designed chapels 1845-1910	273

9 Inscribed stone Gwytherin churchyard	101	39 St. Mary's Church, Cefn Meiriadog	273
10 Llangernyw church	107	40 St. Thomas' Church, Bylchau	276
11 Inscribed stone, Llangernyw	109	41 Doorway arch, Ebenezer chapel, St. Asaph	278
12 Ancient yew tree, Llangernyw	110	42 Site of smithy, Gwytherin	281
13 Llanfair Talhaearn Church	114	43 Ty'n-y-llan, Gwytherin	282
14 St. Asaph Cathedral	116	44 Lion Inn, Gwytherin	283
15 St. Kentigern's Church, St. Asaph	120	45 Llangernyw from the west 1880	285
16 St. Sadwrn's Church, Henllan	121	46 Bridge Inn, Llangernyw c1881	287
17 Llansannan Church	123	47 Llanfair Talhaearn from churchyard	289
18 Llannefydd Church	124	48 National School (1836) Llanfair Talhaearn	290
19 Cross stump, Llannefydd Churchyard	125	49 Morris Street, Llanfair Talhaearn	293
20 Motte near Llangernyw	139	50 Llannefydd from churchyard	296
21 Medieval ridge abd furrow, Bontnewydd	150	51 Hawk and Buckle Inn, Llannefydd	297
22 Abandoned farm, Glan-y-gors, Llansannan	191	52 Llansannan: Saracen's Head Inn	302
23 Windbreak, Glan-y-gors	192	53 Llansannan church and Afon Aled 1880	303
24 View across Upper Cledwen Valley	198	54 Henllan, Ty Coch Street	308
25 Aled Isaf Dam	207	55 Henllan, former alms houses	314
26 Galltfaenan House	214	56 Henllan, Capel Seion	312
27 Hafodunos Hall (before 2004 fire)	223	57 Pennant from the south	319
28 Wigfair Hall	225	58 St. Asaph: former alms houses, High Street	331
29 Waterwheel, Llanfair Talhaearn Mine c1898	238	59 Elwy Bridge, St. Asaph c 1880	334
30 Pont-yr-allt-goch watermill	246	60 St. Asaph: 18th century town houses, High St.	336

Colour Plates:
I The Elwy at Llanfair Talhaearn (watercolour)   IV Garthewin (watercolour)   VII Cledwen headwaters
II : Aled headwaters   V : Pont Newydd (watercolour) :   VIII Aled: Bryn rhyd yr arian
III St. Mary's chapel and well, Wigfair   VI: Gwytherin & Henllan churchyards

Plate 2 : **Monument to local writers, Llansannan by Sir William Goscombe John (1860-1952)**

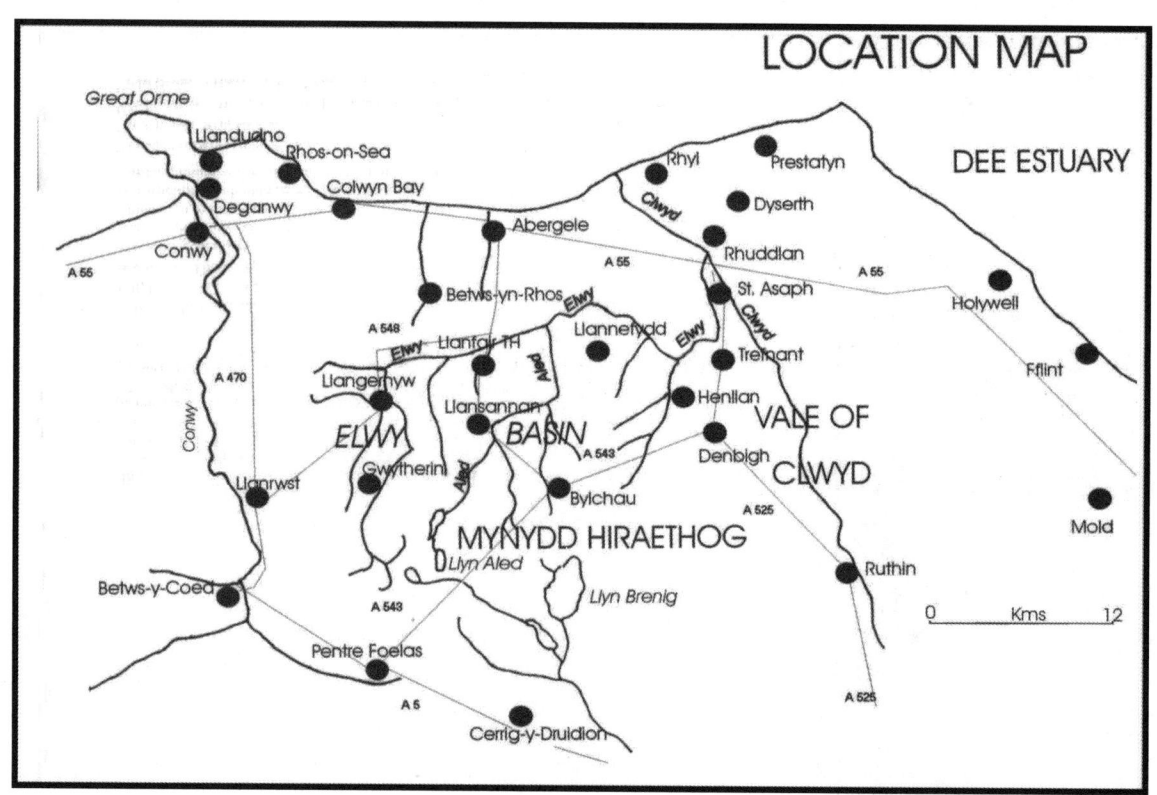

PREFACE

"Observe yon verdant fields, and shady bowers,
Wherein I've passed so many happy hours;
See, too, yon rugged hill, upon whose brow
Majestic trees and woods aspiring grow."

".....These lovely prospects, how they cheer my soul,
With what delight and joy I view the whole!"

Felicia Hemans "Written in North Wales" [1]

The scenery along the valleys of the River Elwy and its tributaries is one of North Wales' best kept secrets. The river basin lies between the valleys of the Conwy and the Clwyd the Elwy being a left bank tributary of the latter. This tract of countryside has been described as one of those parts of Wales *"that invites you to believe you are an explorer"*[2] I myself first discovered this area one beautiful summer's day when staying on holiday with my family on a farm near Glascoed. I had planned a walk to the summit of a hillfort I had spotted on the Ordnance Survey map

---

[1] Felicia Dorothea Hemans "Poems - England and Spain, Modern Greece" Garland Publishing, New York (1978) p5
[2] Trevor Fishlock : "Fishlock's Wild Tracks" Poetry Wales Press, Bridgend (1998) p133

labeled *Mynydd y Gaer*. My route took me along a series of track ways and hollow-ways until I reached a narrow bridge over a beautiful stream overhung by trees in full leaf through which a dappled light played on the surface of the stream as it gurgled and splashed its way through its boulder-strewn bed. The stream was the River Elwy and over succeeding years I visited its valley on many occasions never ceasing to be stimulated by the stunning waterside scenery, the delightful villages along its course and its long and fascinating history. What follows in this book is a history of the people and landscape of not just the River Elwy but also the many tributaries that make up its river basin.

The choice of a river basin rather than a political unit such as a county or former cantref as the area of study is based on the fact that a river basin - the area of land drained by a river and its tributaries, is a permanent feature in the landscape unlike our seemingly ever changing political units. Its boundaries are clearly marked by the high hill summits and ridges that separate it from neighbouring river systems. These are known as "watersheds" or, in the case of tributary streams, "interfluves". Significantly, earlier inhabitants of the area also saw the value in using rivers and watersheds as the basis for political frontiers. The Elwy itself formed the boundary between the medieval cantrefs of Rhos and Rhufoniog, while the watersheds of streams frequently mark the boundaries of many late medieval townships and parishes.

The River Elwy, described by the antiquarian Thomas Pennant in 1790 as " *a most turbulent stream*" flows for some 42 kilometres (26 miles) from its source in a peat bog on the western slopes of the upland area known as Mynydd Hiraethog (Denbigh Moors) to its confluence with the River Clwyd 3.2 kms (2 miles) north of St. Asaph (Llanelwy). The Elwy valley is largely by-passed by today's tourists hurrying west on the A55 trunk road or along the Conwy Valley. Yet, this small, rather isolated river valley has a long and fascinating history of human occupancy. In Pontnewydd Cave located where the Elwy has carved a steep gorge through the underlying Carboniferous limestone rocks, relics of Neanderthal man have been uncovered representing the oldest evidence of human occupancy in Wales. Evidence of later occupation of the river basin during the Mesolithic, Neolithic, Bronze and Iron Ages has also been discovered. The Elwy basin is also home to what may be Wales' oldest living organism - a 4000 year old tree!!.

The valley landscape has changed only marginally since the eighteenth century. In 1772, Jinny Jenks, an Enfield gentlewomsn, visiting homes of the gentry in the area, described the scenery on a coach journey between Denbigh and Garthewin, Llanfair Talhaearn... Miss Jenks described

"a perpetual change and transition from one delightful scene to another as you pass from hill to hill, from the tops of which you look down on the most beautiful cultivated vales or landscapes in miniature, and then up to the enclosed hills with hanging woods or grassy slopes with flocks and herds on them". [3]

Little has changed today over 230 years later. The Elwy river itself has also changed little since 1790 when Thomas Pennant, the Welsh antiquary and topographer described the course of the river south of St' Asaph as

"Running west and then north along most romantic dingles, varied with meadows, woods and cavernous Rocks".

---

[3] "A Tour of North Wales by Jinny Jenks, 1772" Nat. Library of Wales MS 22753B p25

The sylvan beauty of the lower valley was recognized by the eminent English poet Gerald Manley Hopkins (1844 - 1889). The valley scenery inspired at least three of his poems of which *"In the Valley of the Elwy"* is the most apposite containing the lines:

> *"Lovely the woods, waters, meadows, combes, vales,*
> *All the air things wear that build this world of Wales"*

The scenery of the lower Elwy valley also provided poetic inspiration another eminent English poet of international repute: Felicia Dorothea Hemans (1793 - 1836), lived in St. Asaph (where she had spent the latter part of her childhood) from 1825. She enjoyed considerable popularity in pre Victorian Britain, her work was much admired by William Wordsworth. Today, her work as one of the "romantic" school of poets is still held in esteem, particularly in North America.

If the lower valley of the Elwy provided stimulus to English poets, then it comes as no surprise that the captivating scenery along the upper Elwy and its main feeder stream, the Aled, also inspired local poets writing in their native Welsh. John Jones (1810-1869) of Llanfair Talhaearn was awarded bardic status at the Welsh National Eisteddfod at Bala in the year of his death. He wrote under his bardic name of *"Talhaearn"*. There was a lively community of eminent Welsh poets living in the village during the mid nineteenth century. They are said to have met regularly at Jones' mother's inn in the village known as the "Harp". It is now a private house near the church known as *"Hafod y Gan"*.

Other eminent Welsh literary figures were born in the valleys of streams that feed the Elwy River. Iolo Goch (c. 1325 - c. 1398), born at *Llechryd* near Henllan, was essentially a "praise" poet who frequented the courts of the wealthy writing poems in their honour. He was not solely a client of Welsh gentry since he also wrote poetry praising Edward II and an eminent marcher lord, Roger Mortimer, one time lord of Denbigh castle. Some 400 years later, in a house close to Iolo Goch's birthplace, Thomas Edawrds (1739-1810), better known as *"Twm o'r Nant"* (Tom of the Dingle) one of Wales' best known dramatists and poets, was born at a farm known as *Penporchell Isaf* near the village of Llannefydd. [4] In the same area, Robert Parry (c1560-1612) was born at *Tywysog* near Henllan. He is best known as a diarist, whose works give an insight into life in Tudor Denbighshire[5]. His work paints a vivid picture of the violence still afflicting the area around Denbigh in the late sixteenth century despite the stability allegedly brought about by the coming of the Tudors.

The Aled valley was home to and no doubt inspired some other leading Welsh writers and poets of their day. Tudor Aled (1465-1525) was the earliest, taking his name from the valley of his birth. In the nineteenth century, the village of Llansannan was the birthplace of another holder of a bardic chair, William Rees (1802 - 1883) alias *"Gwilym Hiraethog"*. Rees, a Nonconformist minister in Denbigh, wrote in a number of genres and edited a local newspaper. In the centre of Llansannan, a bronze sculpture by Cardiff-born Sir William Goscombe John (1860-1952) was erected in 1899 to celebrate the lives of writers born in or near Llansannan (see Plate 2)

---

[4] See R Morris Roberts "Thomas Edwards" in Clwyd Historian No, 47 Autumn 2001 pp14-15.

[5] See Dewi Roberts "The Extraordinary Diary of Robert Parry" Clwyd Historian No. 36 Spring 1996 p20

The upper reaches of the basin are still relatively sparsely populated but in early medieval times, following the withdrawal of Roman troops, must have been even more remote. This isolation attracted several early Christian hermits to the valley. Notable among these were St. Winifred who settled in Gwytherin near the head of the valley after her recovery from beheading in Holywell!. The valley is also associated with St. Digain, a son of the ruler of Dumnonia (modern Cornwall) who possibly settled in the present day village of Llangernyw.

The Elwy and Aled rivers have their sources high on an area of moorland that has been recently given the designation as the *"Creigiau Llwydion" Historic Landscape Characterisation area* by the Clwyd and Powys Archaeological Trust. This 18 kilometre square area lies on the northern edge of Mynydd Hiraethog and lies at an altitude of between 290 and 465m above sea level[6]. Mynydd Hiraethog is still one of the loneliest places in North Wales where one can wander on ancient track ways in a virtual wilderness within a few minutes of leaving the main A543 road that has crossed this moorland since 1825. The writer and poet AG Bradley was inspired by the ghostly silence of this landscape and described the moors in 1898 as a

"Purple tableland, the silent wilderness of the Hiraethog where fairies dance beside the bank of lonely lake and belated travellers see uncanny Sights".[7]

---

[6] CPAT : "Historic Landscape Characterisation - Mynydd Hiraethog: Creigiau Llwydion HLCA 1102" Welshpool (2001)

[7] A G Bradley "Highways and Byways in North Wales" McMillan London (1898)

The landscape of an area of countryside has been compared to a palimpsest, a piece of parchment from which the original writing has been removed in order that it can be used again. Likewise, the landscape is subject to similar changes in which earlier landscapes are obliterated, at least in part, by man's activities which in an area like the Elwy river basin might include the removal of woodland cover, the ploughing up of upland pastures, creating a resevoir or enclosing areas of common land. Such activities mean that sometimes only traces of earlier landscapes survive or are identified only through the application of techniques such as the analysis of aerial photography, the radio-carbon dating of organic remains or the analysis of pollen grains within peat bogs...[8] In the following pages, we will examine the physical landscape of the area drained by the river Elwy and its tributary streams and the evidence on the ground of man's activity through time which has contributed to the landscape we see today in this exceptionally beautiful little valley. The springtime beauty of the Elwy valley no doubt helped inspire Felicia Hemans, to write the following lines of poetry:

> *"Sing them upon the sunny hills,*
> *When days are long and bright,*
> *And the blue gleam of shining rills*
> *Is loveliest to the sight!*
> *Sing them along the misty moor,*
> *Where ancient hunters roved.*
> *And swell them through the torrent's roar,*
> *The songs our fathers loved! "*   Felicia Hemans[9]

---

[8] See David R Wilson "Reading the Palimpsest: Landscape Studies and Air Photography" Landscape Studies Vol. 9 (1987) p5

[9] From *"Song of Our Fathers"* : "Poems" - Felicia Hemans, The Co-operative Publication Society, New York (1914) p 321

ACKNOWLEDGEMENTS

My thanks are extended firstly to my brother-in-law, Paul Sumner without whose help this book would never have been finished. When failing eyesight led to me having to stop driving, there was still much field work to be completed. Paul stepped in and drove me to the remotest corners of the Elwy river basin. He accompanied me on many walks following the headwaters of the Elwy and its tributaries. His opinions on what we were seeing were always most valuable.

Thanks also go to my wife Margaret for valued advice on the presentation of the book and for her watercolour pictures. Thanks too to my wife's kinsfolk, Emyr and Marie Thomas of Colwyn Bay for introducing me to the Upper Cledwen valley which inspired the initial interest that led to the writing of the book. Thanks also to my children Richard and Katherine Jomes for their help with IT. problems.

I am also indebted to many people for their help in the research stages. These include the staff of Chester and Wrexham public libraries, the University of London Library, Senate House and at the Denbighshire County Record Office in Ruthin, I also acknowledge the valuable information on the poetry of Felicia Hemans that I received from Dr. Naomi Sweet of the University of Missouri, St. Louis and my cousin Dr. Hugh Jones of Ball State University, Indiana. Thanks also to Gwynne Griffiths of CADW for information on Garthewin and other parks and gardens in the valley and to Jeff Spencer and Richard Phipps of CPAT for information relating to the survey of Mynydd Hiraethog. Permission to publish archive photographs was kindly given by Llyfrgell Genedlaethol Cymru, Aberystwyth. Information on the history of Roman Catholicism in the Vale of Clwyd was supplied by my sister, Marian Sumner.

Landscapes do not make history, men and women do"

Professor Gwyn. A. Williams 1988

CHAPTER 1 : THE PHYSICAL LANDSCAPE

The Drainage System: The Elwy river basin, that is the area drained by the river Elwy and its tributaries, covers about 207 square kilometres (80 square miles). The entire basin and its main streams are shown in Figure 1. The section of the stream above Llangernyw, which represents the stream's headwaters, flows roughly northwards from its source to a point just to the north of the village of Llangernyw. This section of the stream is known confusingly as the Afon Cledwen. At Llangernyw, the Cledwen is joined by two other tributaries, the Gallen and the Collen which combine here to form the River Elwy. The Elwy and its major tributaries have their source on Mynydd Hiraethog (also known as the Denbigh Moors) at a height of between 370 and 450 metres above sea level. It is very unusual that all the main tributaries join the right bank of the Elwy with little drainage emanating from the left bank with the main river flowing eastwards close to the northern rim of its basin throughout its middle section that extends from the great bend just to the north of the village of Llangernyw to where the stream enters the Vale of Clwyd around 3 kilometres south of St. Asaph. Its final phase is again northwards flowing close to the western edge of the Vale of Clwyd roughly parallel to the River Clwyd which flows on the eastern side of the vale. The two rivers combine 3 kms north of St. Asaph.

Geomorphology: The headwaters of the Elwy and its major tributary the Afon Aled, together with most of the eastward flowing middle section of the Elwy valley flow on rocks dating from the Lower Palaeozoic era. The majority of these rocks are represented by sedimentary mudstones, shales, grits and sandstones dating from the middle Silurian period (about 400 million years ago). These produce scenery typified by smooth rounded slopes with small escarpments forming where the sandstones are hard and resistant to erosion. The sources of the Elwy and most of its tributaries lie on the northern slopes of Mynydd Hiraethog which are carved into distinctive landscape blocks that lie between the upper courses of these streams. These landscape areas have been subject to glacial action in past ice ages and much of the area has a covering of glacial till - deposits left by the ice as it melted, in which small lakes such as Llyn Aled, the source of Afon Aled, (shown right) and Llyn y Foel Frech are found.

Plate 3

The highest sections of the valleys of the Elwy and its major tributary the Aled are shallow broad valleys through which the streams flow very sluggishly. However, at an altitude of around 353 metres (1150 feet), the streams dramatically change their character and flow rapidly through steep gorges which, in the case of the Derfyn and the Aled are entered via spectacular waterfalls. Rhaeadr y Bedd on the Aled is probably the most spectacular of these falling from a height of around 25 metres. The creation of these gorges is the result of river erosion rather than glacial action. The streams acquired much greater erosive power through a process known as "rejuvenation" often triggered by sea level change increasing the down-cutting power of the streams. Such changes in sea level have occurred frequently in recent geological times.

At the end of the middle section of the valley, the Elwy river flows through a steep sided gorge, at its most spectacular at Cefn Rocks (GR 025705), as it passes through the relatively narrow strip of younger (340 million years old) Carboniferous limestone rocks that runs from Colwyn Bay to Ruthin and form a major geological unconformity. The limestone exposure which dips eastwards at an angle of 20 to 30 degrees and forms a westward facing escarpment that overlooks the Elwy basin. These rocks contain several large caves that played an important part in the early settlement of the area. The most significant caves in this section of the river basin are those known as Pontnewydd, Cefn (Old and New), Galltfaenan, Brisgyll (Nant y Gaer), Plas Heaton and Cae Gronw caves. The Tudor topographer John Leland noted their presence in his description of the area written around 1538.

Plate 4

The spectacular and distinctive scenery along the Elwy as it passes through the underlying limestone rocks together with the long history of human occupation of this section of the Elwy valley has now been formally recognised. The Lower Elwy Valley has been designated as an *"Historic Landscape"* area in the Register of Landscapes of Historic Interest in Wales published in 1998.[10] The title "Lower Elwy" is a little confusing in that the river continues to flow northwards for over 5 kms after emerging from the gorge.

Plate 5: Elwy Valley at Cefn Rocks

After its emergence from the gorge, the river

---

[10] CADW/CCW/ICOMOS "Register of Landscapes of Historic Interest in Wales" Cardiff, (1998)

turns northwards as it enters the broad Vale of Clwyd through which it continues its northerly course having been diverted by the hills of boulder clay north of Trefnant that mark the southernmost extent of ice from the Irish Sea during the last Ice Age. This period ended with the melting of the last Welsh ice sheets some 14000 years ago. A ridge of these boulder clays (known as a terminal moraine) separates the river from the River Clwyd. (See Fig.1) On this ridge stands the small cathedral city of St. Asaph and probably the former Roman base of Varae (sometimes spelt Varis). Beneath the glacial clays in this part of the valley lie Coal Measues whose narrow coal seams were once the subject of plans for a mine near Llannefydd

Landscape: Mining has also occurred in the Silurian sedimentary rocks which yielded small quantities of copper and lead as a result of mineralisation along the lines of the many geological faults that underlie the area... These ores were exploited commercially on a small scale between Llanfair Talhaearn and Llansannan until the early tears of the 20th century. Similarly small scale (probably part time working) of lead and zinc ores occurred throughout history in the Carboniferous limestone section in the parish of Cefn Meiriadog on the north side of the valley.

Plate 6

The actual courses taken by the present day streams within the Elwy basin have been strongly influenced by the positions of geological faults within the underlying strata A strong case has been made for concluding that at one stage in the geological history of the area, streams such as the Cledwen and the Aled once flowed northwards directly to the Irish Sea (see Fig.1). What subsequently occurred

Aled Valley east of Llansannan

was a process known as "river capture".[11] The Elwy, once a small side tributary of the Clwyd, was able to cut back its headwaters by wearing away the shattered rocks along an east - west geological fault in the earth's crust known as the Elwy Valley Fault. As it did so, it extended its headwaters westwards "capturing" the northward flowing Aled and Cledwen rivers. Thus the rivers Dulas and Gele which now flow northwards from beyond the northern rim of the river basin are "beheaded" streams, the remnants of the former Cledwen and Aled rivers. The courses occupied by the former courses of the Cledwen and Aled are represented by "wind gaps," parts of the valleys abandoned when the headwaters of the streams were diverted. These gaps lie between the headwaters of the rivers Dulas and Gele and the Cledwen and Aled respectively. The great bend in the course of the Elwy north of Llangernyw is the point of capture and the bend itself can be described as an "elbow" of capture.

---

[11] C. Embleton "The Elwy River System, Denbighshire" Geographical Journal Vol. 126 London (1960) p.318

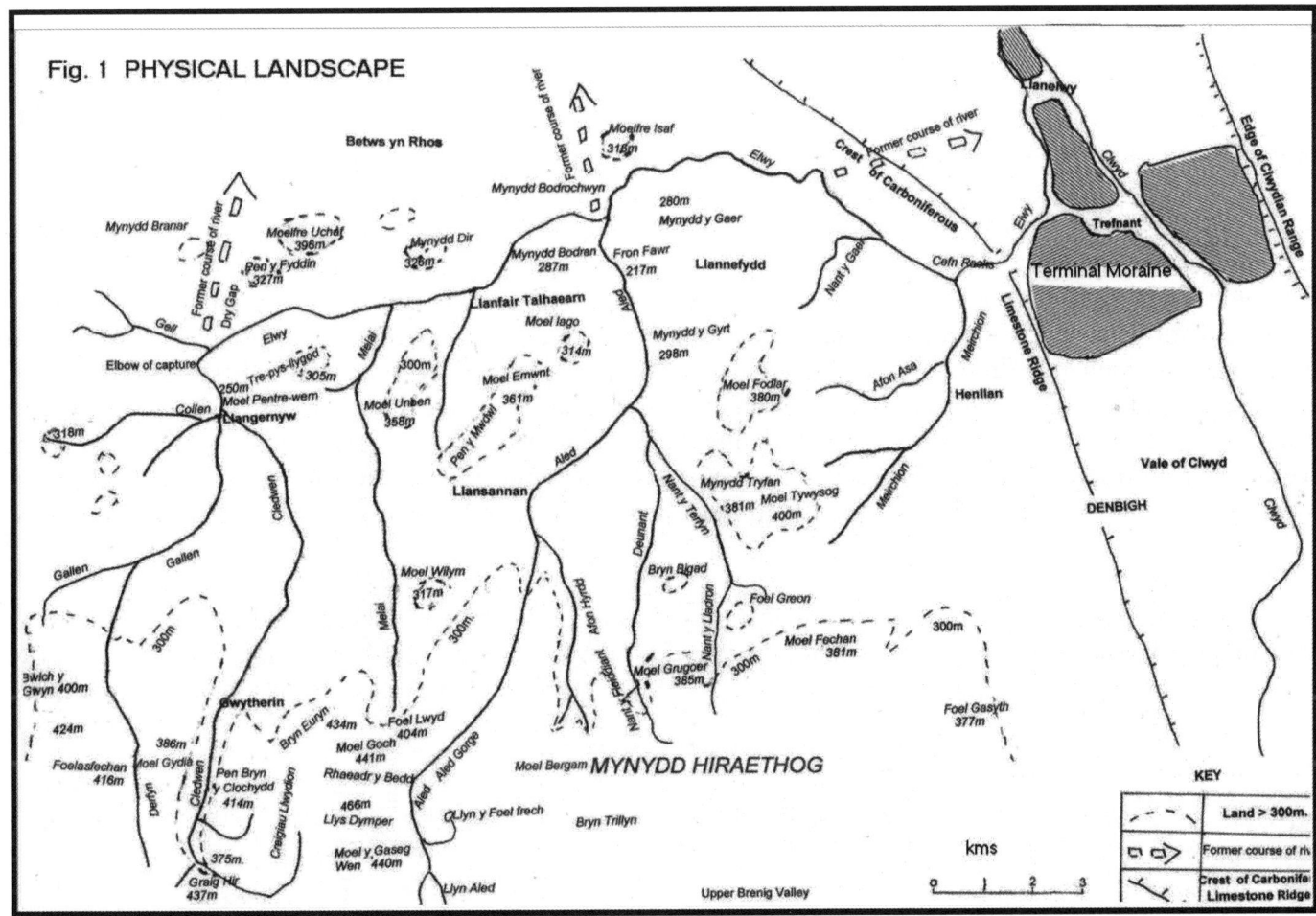

Climatic Change and the Landscape: The present day physical landscape of the Elwy river basin owes much to shaping by forces associated with climatic changes over the past 1.8 million years in the geological period known as the Quaternary. This has been a period that has seen invasions of ice at around 100,000 year intervals although only three phases of glaciation are still identifiable in the present landscape of the area[12]. In these ice invasions, ice accumulated and pushed eastwards from Snowdonia, the Conwy valley or possibly north from small ice fields to the south on Mynydd Hitaethog. The direction taken by the moving ice can be deduced from the alignment of small hills of glacial material known as drumlins of which there are many within the Elwy river basin. These streamlined mounds are shaped like half an egg and have their long axes parallel to the direction of ice flow. In the Elwy basin they are mostly aligned in a south west - north east direction and are particularly evident on the northern slopes of Mynydd Hiraethog area where the Elwy and Aled rivers have their sources. The lower section of the valley was also affected by much thicker ice moving southwards from the Irish Sea that left a thick covering of red boulder clays over the area.

These glacial episodes were separated by interglacials when climatic conditions may have been similar to those in the area today, or, immediately after the retreat of the ice, close to those in the Arctic tundra. Ice action was responsible for some deepening and to a lesser extent widening the valley of the Elwy and its major tributary the

---

[12] H H Lamb "Climate and Landscape in the British Isles" in S R J Woodell 2The English Landscape" OUP, Oxford 1985 p150

Aled. However, only the upper valley of the Cledwen above Gwytherin (see Plate 7) and the upper Gallen valley show signs of being modified by ice action to give the typical U-shaped valley cross sections.[13]

The ice also plastered the floors and sides of the valley with boulder clays. The boundary between Welsh ice and Irish Sea ice fluctuated according to the relative strengths of the respective ice sheets but a clue to the dominant ice mass at any point can be gleaned from the nature of the boulder clay deposited by the ice. Those glaciers emanating from Welsh source areas to the west and south have left deposits of blue-grey boulder clays while those moving southwards from the Irish Sea have deposited reddish boulder clay derived from the floor of the Irish Sea. An early glaciation of the area from the Irish Sea left deposits on the floor of Pontnewydd Cave that have been dated to 250,000 - 300,000 years ago. The meltwater from retreating ice together with lower sea levels and isostatic adjustment (the earth's crust rising in response to the reduction in weight upon it following the melting of ice sheets), had a significant impact upon the landscape by increasing the erosive power of the Elwy and its tributaries so deepening the valleys considerably. These "pro-glacial" streams also left deposits of sands and gravel in terraces in parts of the middle section of the Elwy valley.

---

[13] C. Embleton (ibid) 1960 p323.

Plate 7

It has been asserted by some authorities[14] that glacial meltwater flowing at the margins of Irish Sea ice during an early glaciation diverted the course of the Elwy from its former course across the Cefn Meiriadog limestone ridge east of Ddol to its present gorge-like section between Ddol (982727) and Cefn rocks (025705) where the stream emerges from the limestone section of its gorge. This diversion of the stream must therefore pre-date the deposits found on the floor of Pontnewydd Cave, which opens on to the new course, that are up to 250,000 years old which

Cledwen Valley south of Pennant

---

[14] Boswell (1949) and Embleton (1960 & 1970)

would place the diversion and the creation of the Cefn Rocks gorge in the Middle Pleistocene period..

In the last 14,000 years there has been significant climatic variation. As has already been noted, the immediate aftermath of the ice ages was a period when tundra-like conditions would have prevailed. The surface layers of soils would have been frozen during winter then melted to form a watery sludge during the summer season. These water laden soils when located on slopes could move downhill in a mass movement known as "solifluction".[15] They were then deposited near the base of the slopes as deposits known as "head". These processes would have particularly affected the warmer south facing slopes of the middle section of the Elwy valley during the Late Pleistocene period.

The Quaternary epoch is made up of two geological periods, the "Pleistocene" that lasted about 1.8 million years and ended about 10,000 years ago with the onset of a period of global warming that caused the final retreat of the ice sheets. This ushered in the period known as the "Holocene" that makes up the last 10,000 years of our geological history and still continues. The Pleistocene was a time of major advances and retreats of ice sheets across Europe. At least nine can be identified over the last 800,000 years. The conditions experienced during the Holocene represent those of a warmer interglacial period. We await the onset of the next "glacial" phase!

---

[15] D K C Jones "Shaping the Land, the Geomorphological Background" in S R J Woodell (ed) "The English Landscape" OUP, Oxford (1985) p 41

It has been asserted that the climatic changes during the Quaternary had a stressful impact on both flora and fauna which were forced to migrate northwards or southwards in response to fluctuations in climate between 15,000 and 10,000 BC.[16] Most species of flora survived the changes but underwent little evolution. Several species of animal failed to survive the last ice age in Britain notably the mammoth, woolly rhinocerous, lion and bison but man was accompanied in his re-occupation of formerly glaciated areas by other more successful species such as red deer, bison, wolves, beavers and bears. It may be the case that man's activities had an impact upon the extinction of some of the larger mammals such as the bison and reindeer that lived in a largely treeless landscape prior to colonisation by tree species such as birch, Scot's pine, alder and finally elm and oak.

Human Colonisation: A leading authority on prehistoric settlement has claimed that the fluctuations in climate that affected Britain are a key element in our understanding of human occupation in Britain.[17] Certainly the earliest post-glacial human occupation probably relates to settlers moving into Britain from the continent of Europe via the land bridge that existed until around 6500 BC when it was destroyed by rising sea levels.

Human settlement continued throughout the Quaternary and the settlers were able to modify the environment to suit their own purpose. In the Mesolithic period (8500 - 4000 BC) the sea level was much lower than it is at present and no doubt many sites dating from this period now lie below the sea. In the climatic phase from 7000 - 5000 BC

---

[16] S. Campbell and D Q Bowen "Quaternary of Wales" Geological Conservation Review Vol.2, Nature Conservancy Council, Peterborough (1989)

[17] Nicholas Barton "Stone Age Britain "Batsford/English Heritage London (1997) p25.

known as the "Boreal", it was between 36m. and 52m. lower than at present. However, over the period as a whole sea levels must have been rising slowly bringing about the most significant physical outcome of climatic change in the Quaternary, the separation of Britain from continental Europe[18]. From around 5000 BC there was some stabilisation in sea level to levels within 2 metres of present day conditions[19] (although slow change is still occurring).

Vegetation History: During the "Atlantic" climatic phase between 5,000 and 3,000 BC, average temperatures were about two degrees Centigrade warmer than those of today. Pollen analysis has shown that at that time the only areas of Britain that were not forested were the 5% of the country that lay above a height of 500m[20]. No part of the Elwy river basin reaches that altitude therefore we can assume that the primeval vegetation of the whole area consisted of forest dominated by the sessile oak *(Quercus Petraea)* with some sub-dominant alder *(Alnus glutinosa)* and hazel *(Corylus avellana)* trees [21] and possibly limes *(Tilia)*. From around 3000 BC a climatic phase known as the "Sub Boreal" began in which changing climatic conditions gradually deteriorated becoming cooler and wetter which

---

[18] S. Minden "Hunter-gatherers of the Mesolithic" in J Hunter and S Ralston "The Archaeology of Britain" Routledge, London (1999) p35

[19] Robert Bewley "Prehistoric Landscapes" Batsford/English Heritage, London (1994) p 35

[20] Neil Roberts "The Holocene ; An Environmental History" Blackwell, Oxford (1989) p 144

[21] Delia Hooke "Place Names and Vegetation History as a key to understanding Settlement in the Conwy Valley" in Edwards N. "Landscape and Settlement in Medieval Wales" Oxbow Oxford 1997.

caused the decline of the oak and alder forests. This phase of climatic change brought an increase in heather moorland along the northern side of Mynydd Hiraethog. Pollen analysis from peat bogs on Cefn Mawr close to the sources of both the Elwy and Aled rivers indicate a steady increase in heather moorland in this area from around 200 BC, this vegetational change continued into the present day,[22]

In the lower Elwy valley an area of ancient broad leafed deciduous woodland known as *"Coedwigoedd Dyffryn Elwy"* (Elwy Valley Woods) has been designated a "Special Area of Conservation" (SAC). The 83 ha site (GR 020691) is located on a series of steep slopes, screes and ravines on the exposure of Carboniferous limestone. It has been so designated owing to it forming an example of well preserved *Tilio-Acerion* (ravine forest). Within the woods, the ash *(Fraxinus excelsior)* is the most prolific tree although a few small-leafed limes *(Tilia cordata)* are in evidence along with wild service trees *(Sprbus torminalis)*. Below this canopy are strata containing lime-loving plants known as *calcicoles*. These include some rare *bryophytes* (mosses and liverworts).[23] Part of this woodland area can be seen on Plate 5.

On the eve of man's permanent occupation of the lands of the Elwy river basin in Neolithic times, he was confronted with a heavily wooded landscape reaching to all areas in the catchment area, even on to the lower slopes of Mynydd Hiraethog that marked the southern rim of the river basin.

---

[22] CPAT : "Historic Landscape Characterisation - Mynydd Hiraethog: Creigiau Llwydion HLCA 1102" Welshpool (2001)
[23] JNCC Site details of SAC UK0030146 (2000)

CHAPTER 2: THE LANDSCAPES OF THE PALEOLITHIC AND NEOLITHIC

The first human occupants: Only a tiny fraction of the valley's primeval and early prehistoric landscape has survived the impact of time and we must therefore approach the subject with caution, realising that what survives today may not be truly representative of the landscape of the time. The first known occupants of the Elwy valley were early Neanderthal people who lived in the Pontnewydd Cave system (GR 015711) about 230,000 years ago[24] Excavations in the cave found bones of an adult and three children. The remains were fragmentary owing to them being located in secondary deposits on the floor of the cave. These deposits represented debris flows within the cave system. The remains are Lower Paleolithic in age and date from a warmer interglacial phase. Other finds included hand axes, spear points and flakes suggesting the manufacture of tools on site. The raw materials for these implements were locally derived with both flints and volcanic pebbles being available in deposits left by the ice and glacial meltwater.

The cliff face containing the cave has been worn back by erosion in the last quarter of a million years and the hearths of the hunters who lived at the mouth of the cave have been destroyed by flows of debris from beneath the cliff face running into the cave itself in a saturated condition. The excavations show that the occupants of the cave entrance were hunters and gatherers who hunted the open woodland that characterised the landscape of this area during the long interglacials. The cave has yielded the bones of characteristic fauna of such an environment which includes wolf, bear, narrow nosed rhinocerous and wood mice. The upper layers of cave debris provided evidence of

---

[24]CADW/CCW/ICOMOS "Register of Landscapes of Historic Interest in Wales" Cardiff, (1998)

the succeeding cold phase of climate heralding the onset of a new "Ice Age". These include the bones of bison, Norwegian lemmings, hyaena and northern voles. There is no firm evidence of human occupation of any of the caves in the valley in the Upper Paleolithic period following the retreat of ice when Britain was once again colonised by humans crossing the land bridge from Europe from around 11,000 BC. Pontnewydd is not the only large cave in this section of the river valley, Cefn Cave (GR 021704), some 750m south east of Pontnewydd Cave, has yielded some flint blades but little else, suggesting that human occupation of this cave was only temporary.

The Mesolithic Period: There is evidence of the Elwy river basin being occupied in the Mesolithic period (8500 - 4300 BC) from substantial lithic collections dating from around 6000 BC made from the site of the Aled Isaf reservoir (GR913595) on the upper reaches of the Aled valley on Mynydd Hiraethog[25]. Mesolithic stone implements were also uncovered during excavations on Mynydd Hiraethog in the upper Brenig Valley, 6 kms ESE of Llyn Aled Isaf. In Henllan parish, an unworked blade or flake, probably dating from Mesolithic times was excavated in a cave at Plas Heaton (GR 032691)[26].Evidence from elsewhere in Britain suggests that it is possible that Mesolithic people may have cleared woodland by burning to facilitate easier hunting of the herds of wild red deer[27]. Mesolithic

---

[25] K Brassil "Llyn Aled Isaf, Mynydd Hiraethog" Archaeology in Wales Vol. 29 (1989)

[26] See E Davies "Plas Heaton Cave" Proceedings of the Llandudno and District Field Club (1931)

[27] CPAT Project 761"Historic Landscape Characterisation - Mynydd Hiraethog" Welshpool, (2000)l

settlements dating from c6700 BC has been discovered in the lower Clwyd Valley at Rhuddlan[28] and along the coast near Prestatyn.[29] The stone implements recovered from the Mynydd Hiraethog moorland were of a distinctive black chert from the Carboniferous limestone hills east of Prestatyn may provide a link between Mesolithic occupance of the moorlands and the coastal sites 30 kms to the north east. It is possible that the artifacts from Mynydd Hiraethog were left from seasonal occupation of the uplands by Mesolithic hunters following deer herds that migrated to the more open upland pastures in summer.[30] It is also possible that there may have been some permanent movement migration of Mesolithic people from coastal and estuarine areas as sea levels rose relatively rapidly between 7000 and 4000 BC. This coincided with climatic change as the "Atlantic" phase brought warm, wetter conditions to North Wales. The late Mesolithic site at Tandderwen in the Vale of Clwyd near Denbigh may reflect a more permanent occupation of inland sites.

The fact that sea levels were much lower in the Mesolithic period means that some evidence of human occupance may lie beneath the Irish Sea. It should also be borne in mind that a conservative estimate has put the total Mesolithic population of Britain as only about 20,000.[31] It is now believed that the earliest limited clearance of

---

[28] S. Minden "Hunter-gatherers of the Mesolithic" in J Hunter and S Ralston "The Archaeology of Britain" Routledge, London (1999) p43

[29] Robert Bewley "Prehistoric Settlements" Batsford/English Heritage London (1994) p34

[30] Ian Brown "Discovering a Welsh Landscape – Archaeology in the Clwyd Range" Wingather Press, Bollington 2004 p40

[31] Robert Bewley (1994) ibid p40

forest by fire to create woodland glades can be dated to the Mesolithic period. This impact upon the landscape has led one of Wales' leading historians to describe the Mesolithic settlers as the "earliest makers" of Wales.[32]

The Neolithic Period: It is now believed that some elements of the Mesolithic lifestyle were carried forward into the succeeding Neolithic period, namely the social trait of sharing resources, and the use of fire to modify the environment such as the preservation of woodland clearings in order to attract grazing game[33]. There was no invasion of new people bringing with them a culture displaying an ability to domesticate both animals and plants and build monuments as was once widely believed to be the case.[34] Although the first woodland clearance can be dated to the Mesolithic period, the demands of pastoralism and crop production led to an expansion of clearance during the Neolithic period, particularly after 3000 BC as population expanded. In some cases, the delicate woodland ecosystems of upland areas such as the fringes of Mynydd Hiraethog experienced irreversible change by about 2000 BC. It has been suggested that many areas cleared in that period remain as upland heath or moorland The Graig Llwyd stone axe factory near Penmaenmawr developed to serve the demand for axes from this time.[35]

---

[32] John Davies "The Making of Wales" Cadw/Alan Sutton, Stroud. (1996) p12

[33] I.G. Simmons "Ecology into Landscape : some English Moorlands in the Later Mesolithic" Landscapes Vol.2 No.1 (2001) p43

[34] A. Whittle "The Neolithic Period c4000 - 2500/2200 B.C" in J Hunter and S Ralston "The Archaeology of Britain" Routledge, London (1999) p59

[35] John Davies "The Making of Wales" Cadw/Alan Sutton, Stroud. (1996) p14

There is only thin evidence to support the occupation of the Elwy river basin in the early Neolithic period that began around 4000 BC. Canon Ellis Davies[36] describes a cave in Llannefydd parish on the opposite side of the Elwy River to Pontnewydd Cave. This cave is located about 0.8 kms WNW of Bont Newydd in a gorge known as Nant y Graig that leads into the Elwy valley. In fact, the gorge contains a series of nine caves on both sides of the valley about 70m SSW of Fron Hill. (GR 005713) One cave was explored by local amateur archaeologists Mrs Williams-Wynn and a Colonel Mainwaring in 1871. Professor Sir William Boyd Dawkins (1837-1929), curator of the Manchester Museum, gave an account of their findings in a book "Cave Hunting" published in 1874[37]. The cave was called "Brisgyll Cave" in the book although it is also known as the Nant y Graig cave. The finds included a flint arrow head, flint flakes and cores and bones of horse, goat, ox and dog together with some human bones. This may constitute evidence of Neolithic occupation, although no recent evaluation of the finds has taken place. A further dig at the cave in 1946 revealed further human and animal bones together with some Romano-British pottery and later shards of the 14th and 17th centuries showing a degree of continuous occupation...[38]

In the light of this inconclusive evidence, it must be accepted that no confirmed sites dating from the Early Neolithic (4000- 34/3300 BC) have yet been identified in the Elwy Valley. This period saw the first farmers carrying out herding, growing some cereals and clearing woodland. These activities would have been supplemented by hunting

---

[36] Canon Ellis Davies "Prehistoric and Roman Remains of Denbighshire" (1929)

[37] W Boyd Dawkins "Cave Hunting" Macmillan, London (1874) p 160

[38] E Tankard "Notes on Finds in a Limestone Cave at Nant y Graig" Arch. Camb. Vol. 99 (1946) pp 119-122

and gathering. The Early Neolithic population in Britain was relatively mobile and constructed the first monumental architecture: long barrows and megalithic chambered tombs and cairns. These early settlers in North Wales cultivated light soils with a thin woodland cover and used stone axes for clearance.

Evidence of Neolithic activity in the Elwy Valley comes from the Middle Neolithic period (34/3300 - 3000/2900 BC) with the chambered tomb in the parish of Cefn Meiriadog dating from this time. Professor Boyd Dawkins was also associated with the excavation of this, the valley's only Neolithic structure which is important in that it possibly represents the first evidence of permanent settlement and woodland clearance in the lower reaches of the Elwy valley on the outcrop of Carboniferous limestone The chambered tomb is located in a field known as Tyddyn Bleddyn (GR 006724) on Tan y Graig farm The structure is .described by Ellis Davies as a "long cairn." The remains contained two "cistfaen" (stone chests covered with stone slabs). The cairn was 26m long, 12m wide and 0.8m high. The tomb was "discovered" in 1869 when the rector of the parish was informed by the farmer that he had come across human bones whilst carting away limestone from the site of the cairn to repair a road. The limestone blocks removed by the farmer were the capstones from one of the cists under the cairn. One of the upright base stones had also been broken by the farmer. The site was "excavated" by two clergymen who removed sand within the cist to expose human remains including several skulls. The burials appeared to have been made with those interred in a crouched position. Similar Neolithic crouched interments have been discovered in caves and rock shelters in the Clwydian Range. Professor Boyd Dawkins examined the human remains and found them to be of mixed age groups and considered that the interments had taken place over an extended period of time which indicates continuous settlement of the area.

In 1871, one of the clergymen (Rev D R Thomas, Rector of Cefn Meiriadog) returned to the site and found a second cist within the cairn, this is no longer visible today. An excavation followed involving the two clergymen and Professor Dawkins. The second cist was roughly triangular in plan (1.8m by 0.6m) accessed via a narrow long passage only 0.6m wide. The second cist and the access passageway contained numerous human remains deposited in a crouched position. The cist also yielded a small flint and bones from a roebuck, goat, dog and pig. The male bones indicated that the people interred were short in stature, around five feet tall. The bones were re-buried in the local graveyard although two skulls were retained by the owner of Plas yn Cefn Hall, one of the Williams-Wynn family.[39]

Only the first cist discovered in 1869 survives. It has been suggested[40] that such sites may have had a dual purpose: firstly as a burial site but also as a means of underlining a community's claim to the lands they occupied[41]. They may, as such, have had some significance in ritual proceedings. These monuments have been given the generic term *"cromlechi"* and it has been estimated that there are some 150 in Wales as a whole[42]. Such sites are therefore relatively rare, there are others in the Dee and Conwy valleys, Breconshire and south west England. It may be that

---

[39] Canon Ellis Davies (1929) ibid

[40] W.J. Britnell : "The Neolithic" in J Manley et al "The Archaeology of Clwyd" 1991 p.61

[41] Andrew Hayes "Archaeology of the British Isles" Batsford, London (1993) p66

[42] John Davies "A History of Wales" Penguin, London (1993) p9

they are rare because in other areas, they may have been of timber rather than stone construction. Such monuments have been classified as *"Cotswold/Severn"* in type displaying strong links with similar monuments in Brittany. Indeed, there is evidence of a culture of monument building along the whole western Atlantic seaboard from Spain, Brittany, Ireland and the western coasts of England and Wales. This may indicate that Neolithic farmers arrived in this area at a later date than in coastal areas such as Anglesey and Pembrokeshire[43] and that the spread of technological advances came into this part of North East Wales from the west rather than the east.

The loss of this site is indicative of the problem surrounding relict features from the Neolithic landscape in North Wales. The 19th century Enclosure Acts created an instant demand for large quantities of stone for farmers to enclose their field boundaries. Consequently stone slabs from megaliths were broken up and standing stones removed to field boundaries. An examination of farm boundary walls frequently reveals the presence of exceptionally large blocks of stone, some of which may have originated as Neolithic structures. The farmers concerned cannot be condemned for their actions, value systems were different and farming in the Welsh uplands during the later 19th century was an economically precarious activity.

---

[43] Clwyd-Powys Archaeological Trust (CPAT) "Prehistoric Funerary and Ritual Monuments in North East Wales" 2000

Fig. 2 Prehistoric Sites

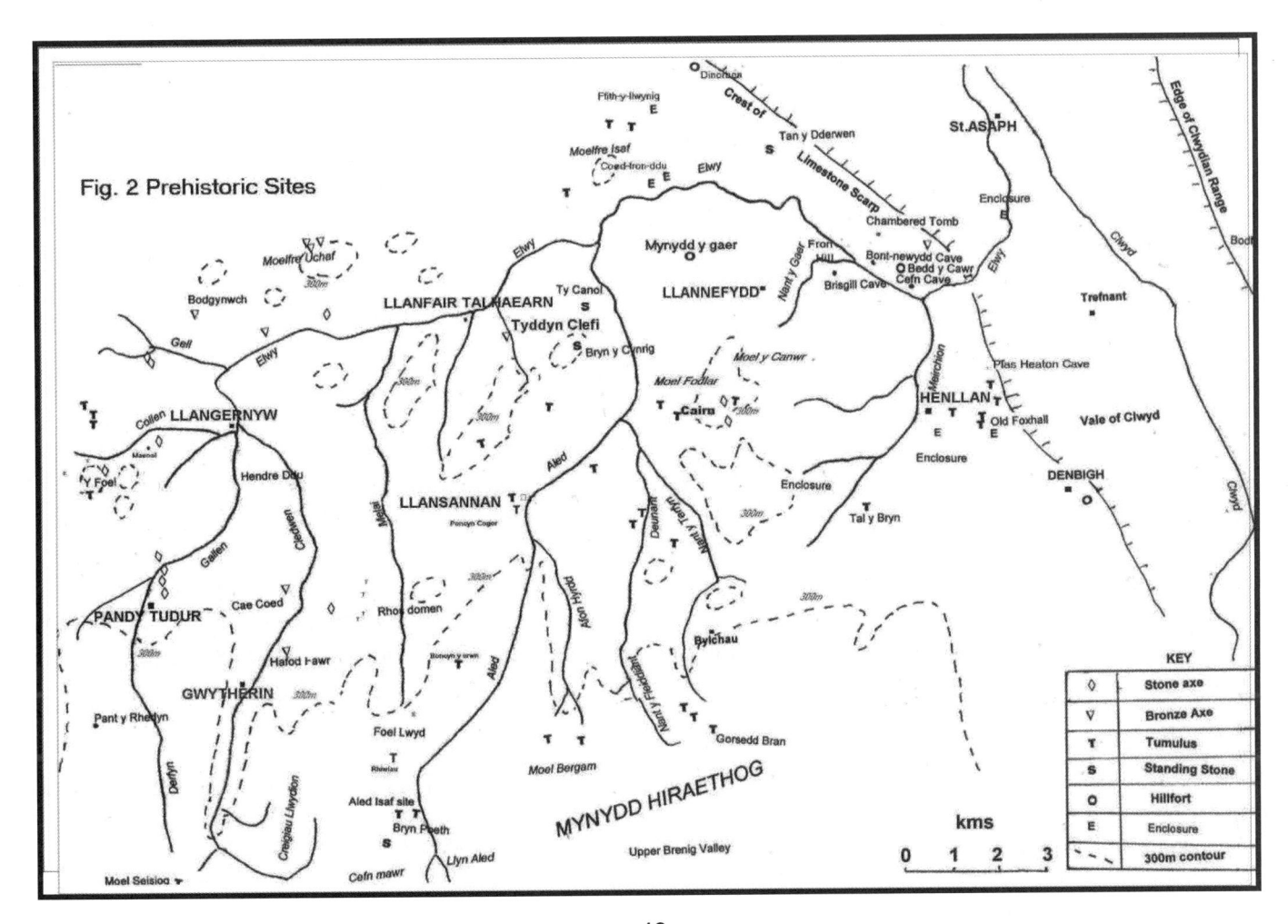

43

A few lines of a poem by John Ormond reflect on the fate of such ancient monuments:

> *"Sometimes they keep their privacy*
> *In public places, nameless, slender slabs*
> *Disguised as gate-posts in a hedge; and some,*
> *For centuries on duty as scratching posts,*
> *Are screened by ponies on blank uplands."*[44]

The charm of Canon Ellis Davies' work on prehistory and indeed its strength lies in his pursuit of oral evidence. His diligent enquiries made in conversations with local farmers in their native Welsh about the discovery of artifacts in their fields led to a record being made of finds and the locations in which they were found even though in many cases the artifacts have subsequently disappeared. Such was the case in his recording of two stone axes allegedly of flint, discovered in a field during the 1890s, that were placed in an outbuilding on a farm close to the Afon Cledwen. The farm concerned was *Hafod Fawr* (GR 891639) in the parish of Gwytherin, sadly, the artifacts subsequently disappeared. Local farmers found such objects of interest, hence their memory of them (the farmer described the

---

[44] John Ormond *"Ancient Monuments"* from R Garlick & R Mathias "Anglo-Welsh Poetry 1480 - 1980" Poetry Wales Press, Bridgend (1984) p 249

finds to Davies in 1925) but obviously had no insight into their historical significance and thus they were sometimes laid aside in outbuildings.

The importance of axes is that they possibly indicate the location of areas where woodland clearance was proceeding in Neolithic times (see Figure 2) although they also could have just been lost by their owners as they passed through an area along an ancient track way. However, it is now also thought that axe heads themselves may have had some ritualistic function within Neolithic society and may have been deliberately buried in certain places by their owners.[45]

On another occasion Davies was able to recover an artifact that would otherwise have been lost. This occurred at a farm known as *Plas Isaf*, 2.4 kms northeast of Llangernyw church where a stone hammer was discovered in a pile of quarry waste in the 1890s. The farmer deposited the hammer in an outbuilding on the farm. When Davies visited the farm to make enquiries regarding its whereabouts in 1925, he was told by the farmer's wife that it had disappeared but the persistent researcher discovered it lying on the ground in the farmyard. It was subsequently deposited at St Asaph Cathedral. The hammer was made of green augite/dolerite and probably originated from the east of the former county of Caernarfonshire. A second smaller, oval-shaped stone hammer was discovered on the same site in the 1890s but has been lost.

---

[45] A. Whittle "The Neolithic Period c4000 - 2500/2200 BC" in J Hunter and S Ralston "The Archaeology of Britain" Routledge, London (1999) p65

Stone artifacts such as these provide some evidence of Neolithic occupation of the Elwy river basin in the Late Neolithic period (34/3300 - 25/2200 BC) although the use of stone tools continued into the Bronze Age. Ellis Davies records six stone tools found within the river basin in the parishes of Llannefydd, Gwytherin and Llangernyw, Three of these were probably manufactured at the Graig Llwyd axe factory near Penmaenmawr, indicating at least some short distance trade. Most of these finds were made in river valleys or on close to hill top track ways such as the one that ran north-south to the west of Llangernyw. (See Fig.3)

Recent use of pollen analysis from peat deposits[46] has shown that the process of woodland clearance was underway in uplands some 15 kilometres west of Llangernyw on the west side of the Conwy valley. The analysis indicates that the vegetation of land in North Wales at around an altitude of 300m. was originally open oak and alder woodland and that clearance began in early prehistoric times. Similarly, pollen analysis of peat bogs in the upper Brenig river valley just across the watershed of the Elwy river system has shown that during the Neolithic period, the upland area of Mynydd Hiraethog was dominated by grassland vegetation with rushes and reeds in poorly drained hollows[47]. More recent pollen analysis of peat from Cefn Mawr in the upper Aled river valley has there is evidence of human

---

[46] Delia Hooke "Place Names and Vegetation History as a key to understanding Settlement in the Conwy Valley" in Edwards N. "Landscape and Settlement in Medieval Wales" Oxbow Oxford 1997.
[47] CPAT : "Historic Landscape Characterisation - Mynydd Hiraethog" Welshpool (2001)

activity in the area in Neolithic times from around 3000 BC.[48] This late Neolithic pastoral activity, like the earlier Mesolithic hunting and gathering culture, may have modified the existing woodland ecosystems of the higher parts of the river basin but over the Elwy basin as a whole, their impact was only slight.

---

[48] CPAT : "Historic Landscape Characterisation - Mynydd Hiraethog : Creigiau Llwydion HLCA 1102" Welshpool (2001)

CHAPTER 3   THE BRONZE AGE LANDSCAPE

Copper-based metallurgy was well developed in Europe long before its appearance in Britain in the Early Bronze Age (2600 - 1600 BC). The first use of this technology in Britain was probably in Ireland. This period saw the continued use of monuments and barrow burials although all such monuments now tended to be round and smaller than their Neolithic predecessors. It has been argued that this change reflected a new social structure with the advent of a hierarchical structure within society with a ruling individual.[50] The new society flourished, enjoying the benefits of a more favourable climate that was significantly warmer and drier than today. This allowed settlement and associated agriculture to flourish at a much greater altitude with new centres of population developing just to the south of the Elwy river basin high on Mynydd Hiraethog.

The use of copper metallurgy from c2400BC on the mainland of Britain was contemporaneous with "Beaker" burials containing red earthenware beakers thought to imitate copper together with other grave goods in the new burial tradition such as jet buttons and daggers. A beaker burial has been excavated on the edge of the Elwy river basin at Henllan. Barrows and cairns from the later part of the Early Bronze Age frequently contain cremation urns indicating a departure from the beaker tradition. Urns were discovered when a barrow at *Hendre Ddu* (GR 878665)

---

[50] Clwyd-Powys Archaeological Trust (CPAT) "Prehistoric Funerary and Ritual Monuments in North East Wales" 2000

in Llangernyw was cleared for agriculture in 1856. Sadly neither the whereabouts of the urns nor the exact site of the barrow are known.

Trade in Stone and Bronze Axes: Interior communications probably developed in North Wales from the first half of the 2nd millennium BC. One authority[51] suggests that in the Bronze Age, there was a much greater degree of contact between this area of North East Wales (the old county of Clwyd) and adjoining regions to the west and north east. This is evident from the distribution of artifacts and burial practice. The prehistoric routes used for inter-regional trade are often difficult to identify today although travel was still mostly local, many longer distance routes must have developed to cater for the demand for specialised items such as axes. Graig Llwyd axes from a volcanic plug of augite granophyre quarried near Penmaenmawr were exported across the country with examples being found in Derbyshire Peak District, Yorkshire and the Midlands - suggests the use of overland routes.

Neolithic and Early Bronze Age ridge-top tracks continued to be used but a number of holloways developed serving more lowland areas. The locations of finds of ax whether of stone or bronze may indicate the path of an ancient trade route[52]. If this is the case, the routes across the Elwy Valley in prehistoric time tended to have a north west - south east alignment reflecting trade from Ireland and the western sea routes. (see Fig.2)

---

[51] Frances Lynch "The Bronze Age" in J. Manley, S. Grenter, F. Gale (ed) "The Archaeology of Clwyd" Clwyd CC. Mold 1991 p65.
[52] Richard Muir The New Reading the Landscape" Univ. of Exeter Press (2000) p 113

A long distance trade developed in bronze axes with axes manufactured in Ireland passing through the Elwy basin en route to markets to the south east. The *Moel Arthur* hoard of Irish flat axes found in 1962 in a col on the eastern side of the Vale of Clwyd dates from the Early Bronze Age An analysis of the copper found in the axes (bronze is 90% copper and 10% tin) indicated that they had almost certainly been made in Ireland. This design was superseded c1700 BC by palstaves made with a more advanced two piece mould. Bronze axes of an unusual design were found close to the northern rim of the Elwy river basin at *Moelfre Ucha*, Betws yn Rhos. These are thought to have been an experimental design known as "protopalstaves" precursors of the true palstaves. The *Acton Park hoard* found on the northern outskirts of Wrexham contained true palstaves possibly using copper mixed with lead from Halkyn Mountain.

No North East Wales site for the production of bronze axes has yet been identified, However, some authorities believe that some production occurred in this region. and may have been located close to Halkyn Mountain where small deposits of copper ore exist alongside the more ubiquitous lead and zinc. Alternatively, they could have been manufactured close to the Great Orme copper mines where local copper could be blended with tin imported by sea from Cornwall. Products from this unknown source are found across north Wales. The prosperity generated may have been responsible for the magnificent gold cape found in Mold in 1833 alongside the skeleton of a young man. The cape is now in the British Museum. Other hoards containing valuable gold items have been recovered from the Clwydian Range supporting the thesis that wealthy local elite existed whose wealth was derived from trade and possibly industrial production.

Bronze Age Settlement: In a phase of extensive excavation on Mynydd Hiraethog during the construction of the Brenig reservoir in the mid 1970s, evidence of extensive Early and Middle Bronze Age settlement was revealed. This area, just to the south of the Elwy river basin in the upper Brenig valley, was settled by arable farmers. Pollen analysis has revealed that both wheat and barley were grown at an altitude of around 500 m.

Recent investigations show that some form of Bronze Age settlement existed within the upper reaches of the Elwy and Aled river basins. Pollen analysis of peat from *Cefn Mawr* (GR 910573) 0.5 kms west of Llyn Aled, shows a decline in woodland species and a rise in grasses and herbs between 1900 and 1000 BC indicating that clearance was underway. Between 200 BC and AD 60, the first evidence of cultivation is apparent together with evidence of burning which may reflect attempts to control the spread of heather[53]. Thus settlement in this area took place later than that in the nearby upper Brenig basin. The presence in the Elwy river basin of other relict features in the landscape dating from the Bronze Age support the hypothesis that settlement of the upper parts of the Elwy river basin was taking place during the Middle Bronze Age. One may also speculate that copper mining and smelting may also have been carried out in the Elwy and Aled valleys. The rocks underlying the area between Llanfair Talhaearn and Llansannan had been subject to mineralisation and contain small workable deposits of copper, zinc and lead. There is, however, no evidence to support the exploitation of these ores in the prehistoric period although a bronze axe head was discovered at *Tyddyn Clef* copper mine near Llanfair Talhaearn in the late nineteenth century.

---

[53] CPAT : "Historic Landscape Characterisation - Mynydd Hiraethog: Creigiau Llwydion HCA 1102" Welshpool (2001)

Local Discoveries of Bronze Age Artifacts: The *Tyddyn Clefi* axe head was uncovered while a pond was being dug for the mine in 1890. It was presented to St Asaph Cathedral Museum in 1918. This is one of several Bronze Age axes have been found in the Elwy basin. A Middle Bronze Age palstave was discovered at *Bodgynwch*, a farm in Llangernyw parish (GR 884699), about 3 kms NNE of the village church - this was seen by Ellis Davies at the Llangernyw School in 1928. (The finder had presented it to the school after finding it close to his farm). Its present whereabouts are unknown. A palstave of similar age was found during ploughing in Gwytherin parish at *Cae Coed* farm (GR 886641) in 1910. This is now housed in the National Museum of Wales in Cardiff. All three of the above finds were found in valley bottom sites and may be indicative of woodland clearance that began in late Neolithic times proceeding in these areas during the Middle Bronze Age. Davies records two other bronze axes being discovered in Cefn Meiriadog parish but both have disappeared[54].

Related Regional Developments: Bronze horse harness and jangles were found at *Parc y Meirch* hill fort close to Dinorben just to the north of the Elwy valley. These were of French design and dated to around 900 BC. Copper for the manufacture of bronze certainly came from the *Great Orme* mines where it was present as a visible green malachite. This mineral is found in a band of dolomitised limestone and is easily mined even with bone implements. The Bronze Age mines were over 70 metres below the surface and extended for 8 kms[55]. Radio carbon dating of charcoal from the mine galleries shows a date of 1800 - 600 BC. It is not yet clear as to whether the ore was smelted

---

[54] Ellis Davies ibid

[55] Tony Hammond "New Discoveries at the Great Orme Copper Mines": lecture to Chester Archaeological Society 21st February 2004.

close to the mine although this seems to have been likely. Refined Great Orme copper deposits may have figured in trade along track ways to the Clwyd valley that passed through part of the Elwy valley en route to Denbigh and the Vale of Clwyd.

During the Middle Bronze Age (1600 - 1200 BC), long distance trade continued to prosper but around 1300 BC there was considerable upheaval throughout Europe including North Wales accompanied by the onset of a cooler, wetter and probably windier climate. There is a rise in votive offerings in damp places perhaps to assuage the gods bringing deteriorating climatic conditions. These include gold torcs in Anglesey and a gold encrusted shale bowl depicting a boat from a bog below Caergwrle Castle, a prehistoric hilltop site. The decoration on the bowl is thought to be of North European design indicative of the complexity of trade links.

Late Bronze Age Developments: Climatic deterioration continued into the Late Bronze Age (1200 - 700 BC.) with a much more marked onset of cooler and wetter conditions from c 1000BC There is evidence that this climatic deterioration made agricultural production in upland areas less efficient which is reflected in a rise in the growth of peat bogs between 1200 and 1000BC. It has been claimed that many of the settlements established at altitude were abandoned[56] and that more protected lowland settlement sites became much sought after perhaps leading to inter-

---

[56]C. Burgess "Bronze Age Settlements and Domestic Pottery in Northern Britain: Some Suggestions" in I. Kinnes & G. Vandell (ed) "Essays on British and Irish Pottery for Ian Longworth" Oxbow, Oxford (1995) pp145-158.

tribal conflict since this period was also one of sharp population growth.[57] However, recent research has cast doubt on the "abandonment" theory, and suggests that some upland sites remained in occupation despite climatic deterioration in the Late Bronze Age.[58] This period saw establishment of the tribal groupings that were well established by the time of the Roman invasion, fixed territorial ideas and permanent settlements and fields.

Agriculture became more intensive and complex reflected in the use of oxen for draught purposes, the use of wool as a textile and the expansion of arable activity producing spelt, barley beans and rye. There was some development in the building of granaries or pits for storage of grain. The salt trade also developed with the demand for salt for the preservation of meat. Deep mined copper from the Great Orme and the bronze manufacturing industry in North Wales appears to have entered a recession in this period. It is significant that this decline was synonymous with a rise in the use of imported decorative Irish and European gold and bronze work.

The Late Bronze Age also saw what has been described as "the most complex technological achievement of the Bronze Age," [59] namely the invention of the wheeled vehicle and ploughs. We do not know much about their design or use but if wheeled vehicles were used in the long distance trade in copper, bronze, salt and grain, a key feature of

---

[57] Peter J. Fowler "The Farming of Prehistoric Britain" CUP Cambridge (1983) p33
[58] Richard Tipping "Climatic Variability and "Marginal" Settlement in Upland British Landscapes a Re-evaluation" Landscapes Vol.3 No.2 (2002) pp10-28.
[59] Timothy Champion "The Later Bronze Age" in J. Hunter and I Ralston "The Archaeology of Britain£ Routledge, London (1999) p109

the Bronze Age, they would most certainly have contributed to the many hollow ways that abound running across the Elwy valley from north west to south east. A leading writer on the geography of ancient roads has pointed out that old trading track ways such as these are important in that they allowed virtually every other feature of the landscape such as settlements, stream crossing points and defensive positions to develop.[60]

The Early Hill Forts: The first hill forts date from this period perhaps reflecting tensions associated with pressure to control land in favourable locations with the possible retreat of settlement from the higher slopes as climatic conditions worsened. (although, one authority has suggested that some hillfort sites may have their origins even further back in the Neolithic period)[61]. Otherwise, there was little impact by settlement on the physical landscape which meant many sites from the Late Bronze Age have remained undiscovered. Typical funerary arrangements included cremations without grave goods or monuments in small cemeteries behind settlements. There is no evidence to date of occupation of the limestone caves of the Elwy valley during the Bronze Age.[62] The wooden houses of the period have left little trace and finds are by chance and inferential rather than hard evidence of settlement such as the flint implements exposed by ploughing at *Maenol*, Llangernyw adjacent to a hearth of blackened stones some 1.5m in diameter. This may be a Bronze Age settlement site **(GR 856669)**[63]

---

[60] Paul Hindle Medieval Roads and Tracks" Shire Archaeology, Princes Risborough" (1982)
[61] James Dyer "Hillforts of England and Wales" Shire Archaeology, Aylesbury (1981) p 26
[62] F. Lynch "The Bronze Age" in J. Manley, S. Grenter, F. Gale (ed) "The Archaeology of Clwyd" Clwyd CC. Mold 1991
[63] CPAT SMR 100431

Bronze Age Barrows: The commonest relics of the Bronze Age in North Wales are round barrows of earth, turf or stone. It has been claimed that 547 such sites exist in the old county of Clwyd[64]. These are described on OS maps as "tumuli" or "cairns" depending on the material used in their creation. Tumuli are made of earth and cairns of loose stone. The known sites of tumuli and cairns are shown in Fig. 2 which indicates that most tumuli and cairns in the Elwy river basin were located on hill summits and along the ridges that separate tributary streams. In recent years, researchers have put forward the hypothesis that both cairns and tumuli were built to be seen and would have been sited on ground that had been cleared of woodland and thus represent important indicators of the extent of woodland clearance in an area by this period in an area's history.[65]

On the hilltop of *Gorsedd Bran*, (GR 975603) which forms part of the southern watershed of the river basin, is a distinctive barrow cemetery. These barrows are visible from lower slopes around Bylchau to the north. It has been suggested that these barrows were built by a Bronze Age community perhaps based in the valley of *Nant y Lladron* which made use of both upland and lowland resources in this area.[66] Similarly the tumulus known as *Boncyn y Crwn* (GR 919622) would have been visible to communities occupying *Dyffryn Aled* The presence of these tumuli, together with that of clearance cairns west of Llyn Aled Isaf on Mynydd Hiraethog, also supports the hypothesis that

---

[64] Frances Lynch "The Bronze Age" in J. Manley, S. Grenter, F. Gale (ed) "ibid (1991) p67
[65] R Young "Barrows Clearance and Land Use some suggestions from the North East of England" Landscape History Vol. 9 (1987) pp 29-
[66] CPAT "Historic Landscape Characterisation - Mynydd Hiraethog: Sportsman's Arms. HLCA 1109" Welshpool (2001)

upland sections of the Elwy and Aled river basins may well have supported a significant population in the Middle and Late Bronze Age.[67]

Ellis Davies pointed out that in the old county of Denbighshire; many cairns had disappeared owing to the use of the stones for building purposes, particularly in the 19th century. Their former existence is sometimes recorded in the names of fields or farms containing the elements *"carn"* or *"carnedd"* Some tumuli are surrounded by a circle of stones, sometimes these are standing stones. Davies held the view that these may have served as retaining walls at the base of the mound. He also warned that some "tumuli" or "cairns" are merely abandoned piles of dug peat turfs or piles of stones picked from the fields by farmers.[68]. Recent investigations have shown that Davies himself sometimes mistook a peat mound for a tumulus as was the case with a mound on *Moel Seisiog* (GR 864575) part of Mynydd Hiraethog. Similarly, tumuli identified by Davies at *Foxhall* (GR 033674) have turned out to be spoil heaps from building and quarrying.[69]

Surviving tumuli in the former county of Denbighshire mostly occur in elevated areas although examples are found in the wider valleys such as the Clwyd and on the lowlands near Wrexham. Examples of ridge top sites of tumuli in the Elwy basin include the two tumuli on *Moel Fodlar* (GR 977681) located at an altitude of 390m, thirty metres

---

[67] CPAT Project 761 "Historic Landscape Characterisation : Mynydd Hiraethog" Welshpool (2001) p41
[68] Canon Ellis Davies "Prehistoric and Roman Remains of Denbighshire" 1929 pp 4-5
[69] CPAT SMR 100578/9

apart in the extreme south of Llannefydd parish close to the parish boundary with Llansannan parish. A further group of four tumuli have also survived almost midway between Llansannan and Gwytherin on either side of the main road. They are known as the *Rhos Domen* tumuli (GR900640) Two of the mounds are 2-3 metres high and the others about 4m high. *Boncyn Crwn* (GR 919622) in Llansannan parish is only 1.8m high but like many others in the river basin (see Fig. 2) occupies the top of a ridge separating two valleys and has intervisibility with other ridge-top barrows.[70]

Tumuli are rare in narrow valley bottoms such as those of the Elwy and its main tributaries. This may partly reflect the fact that many tumuli have been destroyed by agriculture while of those surviving, most have been tampered with. The few tumuli that are known to have occupied valley bottom sites such as the "*Gorsedd*" and "*Poncyn Cogor*" (GR 933652) tumuli in Llansannan that may have been erected close to routes across the valley bottom linking sections of ridge-top route ways. A valley bottom tumulus is also known to have been located in Llangernyw parish at a farm to the south of the village known as *Hendre Ddu*(GR 878665) This was a large tumulus located in a field 300 metres north of the farmhouse. There is no longer any trace of the tumulus or its contents illustrating the difficulty in mapping prehistoric data on the basis of just field evidence and of different value systems among local inhabitants through time Evidence of Bronze Age tumuli are also concealed by twentieth century landscape changes.

---

[70]Helen Burnham "A Guide to Ancient and Historic Wales - Clwyd and Powys" HMSO CADW, London (1995) p23

During a period of low water levels in the summer of 1989, several small cairns were identified on the western side of *Llyn Aled Isaf* reservoir below the normal water line. (GR 013596)[71]

In Llansannan parish, in the basin of the Elwy's largest tributary, the Afon Aled, a tumulus shown on the OS map close to a farm known as *"Rhiwiau"* (GR 944607) yielded two funerary urns around 1830, their present whereabouts are unknown. The tumulus is close to a lane leading along a ridge to Llyn Aled. This is one of several tumuli set on high points of ridges or close to lanes on the north facing slopes of Mynydd Hiraethog in Llansannan parish. Clues to the existence of tumuli lie in place and field names Those relating to tumuli include *"Tomen"*; *"Gorsedd* (throne or meeting place)"; *"Poncyn"*; *"Crug"*; *"Twmpath"*; *"Gwyddfa"* and *"Bedd"*.

Cairns have survived mainly of hilltops particularly those of Mynydd Hiraethog where it was found that those of prehistoric dates had a single upright stone at their core.[72] At lower altitudes they have been destroyed through the use of their stone for buildings and walling. Stone from the cairn at *Poncyn Cogor*, (GR 933652) was removed in 1924 to repair the bridge known as *"Pont y Faen"* at Llansannan just one kilometre away. Davies describes the site of a former cairn in Llannefydd parish in the township of *Tal y bryn* at GR 005657. The cairn was located close to a public footpath (described by Davies as an old lane) just to the east of the turning to *Bryn Isa* farm. There is some historic basis for the former existence of a cairn at this point in Llwyds' "Parochlia" of 1688 describes a "carnedd"

---

[71] K Brassil "Llyn Aled Isaf, Mynydd Hiraethog" Archaeology in Wales Vol. 29 (1989) p46
[72] W G Owen & R J Silvester "The Mynydd Hiraethog Survey, Clwyd" CPAT (64) Welshpool (1993) p4

in the township where "*a man was buried with an arrow*".[73] It would seem that the cairn's disappearance is in keeping with the view that many cairns were removed for their stone in wall building operations. In this case, the cairn and its contents were obviously removed at an earlier date than 1688.

It is significant that the cairns just described was located close to a public footpath since several cairns on Mynydd Hiraethog were located close to track ways that may be of prehistoric date. There is a pre-Christian tradition of graveyards being located close to route ways. Such an association has been noted between the lines of ancient route ways and the location of round barrows.[74] This may indicate a very ancient origin for the public footpaths concerned. Other links have been suggested between the location of early inscribed stones in graveyards and nearby route ways that may represent a continuation of this ancient tradition into Christian times. If this is the case, does it indicate the existence of an ancient route way close to the church sites of Llangernyw and Gwytherin which both have inscribed Stones?[75]

Standing Stones: Standing stones also frequently date from the Bronze Age. These features are of uncertain function and may, in certain circumstances, be the sole remnants of larger structures such as stone circles or burial chambers. Other single standing stones marked graves or boundaries. In Celtic Brittany, standing stones themselves

---

[73] R H Morris (Ed) "Edward Llwyd's Parochlia" reprinted in Archaeologia Cambrensis 1911.
[74] C.A. Gresham & H.C. Irvine "Prehistoric Routes Across North Wales" Antiquity 37. 1963
[75] C.A. Ralegh Radford "Early Christianity and the Emergence of Wales" in "Ancient Monuments of Wales" HMSO London 1973 p48

were objects of worship[76] Ellis Davies described two erect stone pillars close to the site of the chambered tomb in Cefn Meiriadog.[77] He stated that they were located in a field 140 m. south east of *Tan y Graig* farm adjacent to the road. He also describes a standing stone in Llannefydd parish which he termed the *Ty Canol* Standing Stone (GR 950706) this was about 2m high and formerly stood in a field known as *Cae Garreg* (field of the stone) on Ty Canol farm. Around 1900 it was removed and dragged by three3 horses to the lower edge of the field where it was seen by Davies in 1918, evidence that the destruction of relict features from past landscapes was still underway in the early twentieth century. Sometimes only field names give a clue to the sites of former standing stones as at *Bryn y Maen Ucha* (Highest hill of the stone) in Llansannan parish. Today, no trace of a stone remains. Such stones can often be seen incorporated into field walls or as gate posts to fields throughout the river basin. Such is the case of the *Tan y dderwen* stone in Cefn Meiriadog parish (GR 991739). This 0.9m high stone stands at the end of a wall. The stone is tapered at the top and has twelve deep lined cuts up to 13 cms long possibly forming part of a radial design.[78]

Since Ellis Davies' time, several other less spectacular standing stones have been identified in field archaeology surveys of the area. The upland area to the west and south west of Llansannan village is the location of several of these. A group of three small standing stones has been identified on *Nant Bach* to the west of the Aled reservoir (GR 903595), In the same area, the *Bryn Poeth* standing stone is a wedge shaped monument high on the hillside. (GR

---

[76] A Whittle: "The Neolithic Period" in F. Lynch, S. Aldhouse-Green, and J.L. Davies "Prehistoric Wales" Sutton, Stroud. 2000.
[77] Canon Ellis Davies "Prehistoric and Roman Remains of Denbighshire" 1929
[78] CPAT SMR 101980

904604). The *Foel Lwyd* stone is located a little further north ay GR 909613. Also in the north of Llansannan parish, the *Bryn Cynrig* stone is located about 120m from a Bronze Age tumulus at GR 948696.

CHAPTER 4 :   THE IRON AGE

The Iron Age is the term given to the period from the late 8th century BC until AD100. The climatic deterioration that began in the Late Bronze Age continued through the Early Iron Age until around 400 BC and may have caused the continued retreat of settlement from upland areas into favored valley sites. The transition from the Bronze Age to the Iron Age was gradual. Bronze continued to be used for items such as ornaments and horse decorations. Initially, metallurgical skills were primitive with only cast iron goods being produced. The techniques of forging were not well established until around 300 BC.[79]

Iron Age Small Enclosures: During this period the dominant form of settlement was the single enclosed (or open) farmsteads[80], with each farmstead being enclosed in an area of between 0.2 and 1.2 ha (0.5 - 3 acres). These "small enclosures" varied in plan, but most dwellings within them were circular. Such settlements are thought to have been occupied by families of lower social standing. [81] Many such sites in Wales have possibly been destroyed by cultivation and those that are known tend to be in hilly areas where building stone was in good supply. Many others have been identified from crop marks in aerial photography. Currently known sites in the Elwy basin are shown in Fig. 2.

---

[79] Helen Burnham "A Guide to Ancient and Historic Wales: Clwyd and Powys" HMSO London 1995. p50
[80] Colin Haselgrove "The Iron Age" in J. Hunter and I Ralston "The Archaeology of Britain£ Routledge, London (1999) p117
[81] J.L. Davies and F. Lynch in "Prehistoric Wales" Sutton, Stroud. 2000 p162

Two examples have been identified close to the watershed of the Elwy river basin at *Old Foxhall* in Henllan parish (GR 035674). In the best known example, a low bank marks the perimeter of this circular enclosure which is about 60m in diameter. The bank survives to a height of c 80 cms. Its entrance had an elaborate 35m long entrance passage that may indicate that the site could be defended since it is sited on a slight rise that gave good views to all sides across a fairly flat landscape. There is no trace of any other structures in this enclosure.[82] Close to this site another enclosure has been identified from aerial photography (GR 033673) on the limestone plateau. The earthwork is very vague but appears to be of an elongated oval shape .There is a trace of a circular tumulus within the .enclosure disturbed by two trees[83].

The Elwy River basin contains several other earthworks that may be survivors of Iron Age farming practice; in addition other sites may be represented by crop marks revealed in aerial photography in the past twenty years. The upland area to the west of Llangernyw village contains numerous tumuli and may have been a north-south ridge top route way in prehistoric times. Close to this ridge top route, about 1.4 kms west-south-west of Llangernyw church stands an earthwork whose original function is still something of a mystery. This is the *Pant y Rhedyn* earthwork (GR 841663) that is shown on the 1:25000 OS map of the area. The earthwork is a crescent shaped embankment about 0.5m high with a ditch to the outside and a causewayed entrance. The embankment is around 65m long. There

---

[82] Helen Burnham "A Guide to Ancient and Historic Wales: Clwyd and Powys" HMSO London 1995. p55
[83] P Frost "Clwyd Small Enclosures Rapid Survey" CPAT, Welshpool (1995)

is no trace of any eastern extension that may have completed a circular or oval shaped plan although an enclosure may have been completed using timber. [84] On the same ridge, aerial photography in 1972 revealed a crop mark that indicated the site of another possible Iron Age enclosure at *Y Foel, Caledeira* (GR 839668)

Another largely unexplained earthwork has been recorded in Llannefydd parish, this being known as the *Moel y Canwr* earthwork (GR 977689). This stands in an area well served by footpaths and lanes once known as *"Mynydd y Llan"*. ("mountain enclosure".) The earthwork is not recorded on the OS maps and is a 200m crescent-shaped length of bank about 0.6m in height It has an adjacent ditch and apparently forms part of an oval shaped structure Inside the crescent is a hollow some 10m across surrounded by a small bank [85]. It is described in Llwyd's "Parochlia". Its function can only be guessed at but its plan is broadly similar to that of the *Pant y Rhedyn* and one of the *Foxhall* enclosures and presumably relates to pastoral activities.[86]

An aerial photograph taken in 1987 identified another possible Iron Age enclosure at *Coed Fron Ddu* (GR 962730). The enclosed area is 0.25 hectares in size and occupies a non-defensive site overlooking the Elwy on the south east slopes of Moelfre Isaf. A second irregular rectilinear enclosure was discovered nearby in the early 1990s. This is

---

[84] CPAT SMR 100424

[85] CPAT SMR 100533

[86] R H Morris (Ed) "Edward Llwyd's Parochlia" reprinted in Archaeologia Cambrensis 1911.

known as "*Ffrith y Llwynog*" enclosure (GR 962735).[87] Aerial photography has identified other crop marks that identify possible enclosures in Cefn Meiriadog on a south facing slope on the north side of the Elwy valley and near *Plas Coch* on a site close to the lower Elwy (GR 038719) Some 4 kms to the south west near *Tywysog* (GR999668) in Llannefydd parish, a further possible enclosure has been located on a gentle east-facing slope.[88]

Most of the smaller enclosures with sites of less than 0.5ha, often located on sloping ground had slight defences and are associated with pastoral communities. Such settlements were contemporaneous with hill forts but the social and economic relationships between the two forms of settlement are unclear. A recent piece of research has indicated that in North West England and North East Wales, the social elite occupied the larger hillfort sites while their sub-ordinates occupied smaller enclosures such as those at *Old Foxhall* and *Bedd y Cawr* perhaps as Late Iron Age entrepreneurial independent landowners exploiting new lands,[89]

Hill forts: At the other end of the scale were hill forts with the potential to be occupied by several hundred people. Some settlement sites in the uplands were only occupied seasonally; this was particularly true of some hill forts. The origins of hill forts as a feature of the landscape is unclear, a few hilltops were defended in the Neolithic period[90]

---

[87] CPAT SMR 104566/7

[88] J F Manley "A Preliminary Survey of Some Small Un-dates Settlements in North East Wales" Arch. Camb. Vol.139 pp22-55 (1990)

[89] See K. J. Matthews "The Iron Age of North West England" Journal of the Chester Archaeological Society Vol. 76 2000-01 p 34

[90] Robert Bewley "Prehistoric Settlements Batsford/English Heritage London (1994) p94

and in the Welsh Marches, many hill forts are thought to have Late Bronze Age origins[91] with the earliest hill forts dating from c800 BC to 550 BC on the point of transition between the late Bronze Age and the Iron Age, during a period of more adverse climatic conditions. This cooler and wetter climatic phase known as the "Sub- Atlantic" phase nay have affected yields of food crops. Some retreat of settlement from higher altitudes may have caused greater dependence on pastoralism in upland areas, possibly conflict associated with cattle raiding and a need to exercise control over the best land.

It has also been suggested that the prevalence of raiding for slaves in the late Iron Age may account for the concentration of hillfort sites in the North Wales marches[92] Hill forts may therefore have had a role in protecting both people and their cattle from raiders in areas such as the Elwy valley and on the North Wales coastal limestone escarpment immediately to the north. Many of these hill top sites clearly had a defensive function and often have elaborate bank and ditch defences and complex gate defences. This was not the case in the valley's main hillfort at *Mynydd y Gaer* in Llannefydd parish (GR 973718) where the defences were relatively simple.(see Fig. 3) It may be that this hillfort is of early date since early examples of the 6th or 5th centuries BC had a single rampart and relatively simple entrances. Many hill forts were abandoned after around 350 BC suggesting some form of

---

[91] L Laing "Celtic Britain" Routledge Kegan and Paul London 1979.
[92] Nicholas Higham "Rome, Britain and the Anglo Saxons" Sealy, London (1992) p19

concentration of power[93]. Those that survived became "dominant" hill forts in their area and received more elaborate defences.

It may be the case that the fort at *Dinorben*, alias *Parc y Meirch* (GR 967757), less than 5 kms north of *Mynydd y Gaer*, became the "dominant" hillfort of the area. Radio-carbon dating for *Dinorben* dated the palisade surrounding the fort to 770-400BC, this succeeded earlier palisades making the site an early example. In fact, two leading authorities place the hill forts of North East Wales as a whole in the earliest phase of hillfort construction.[94] In the area surrounding the Elwy Valley is a cluster of 5 hill forts: *Mynydd y Gaer, Bedd y Cawr, Dinorben, Castell Cawr* and *Pen y Corddyn*. Successive extensions and modifications to gates in the north east Wales hill forts (including *Dinorben*) may indicate successive phases of occupation as perceived physical threats to the community were realised, these were interrupted by phases of abandonment. Other hill forts in relatively close proximity include *Bryn Euryn* (Colwyn Bay); *Deganwy*; *Conwy Mountain* and *Pen y Gaer* in the Conwy Valley together with the forts of the Clwydian range to the east.

---

[93] C. Haselgrove "The Iron Age" in J. Hunter and I Ralston "The Archaeology of Britain£ Routledge, London (1999) p132
[94] J.L. Davies and F. Lynch in "Prehistoric Wales" Sutton, Stroud. 2000

Fig. 3

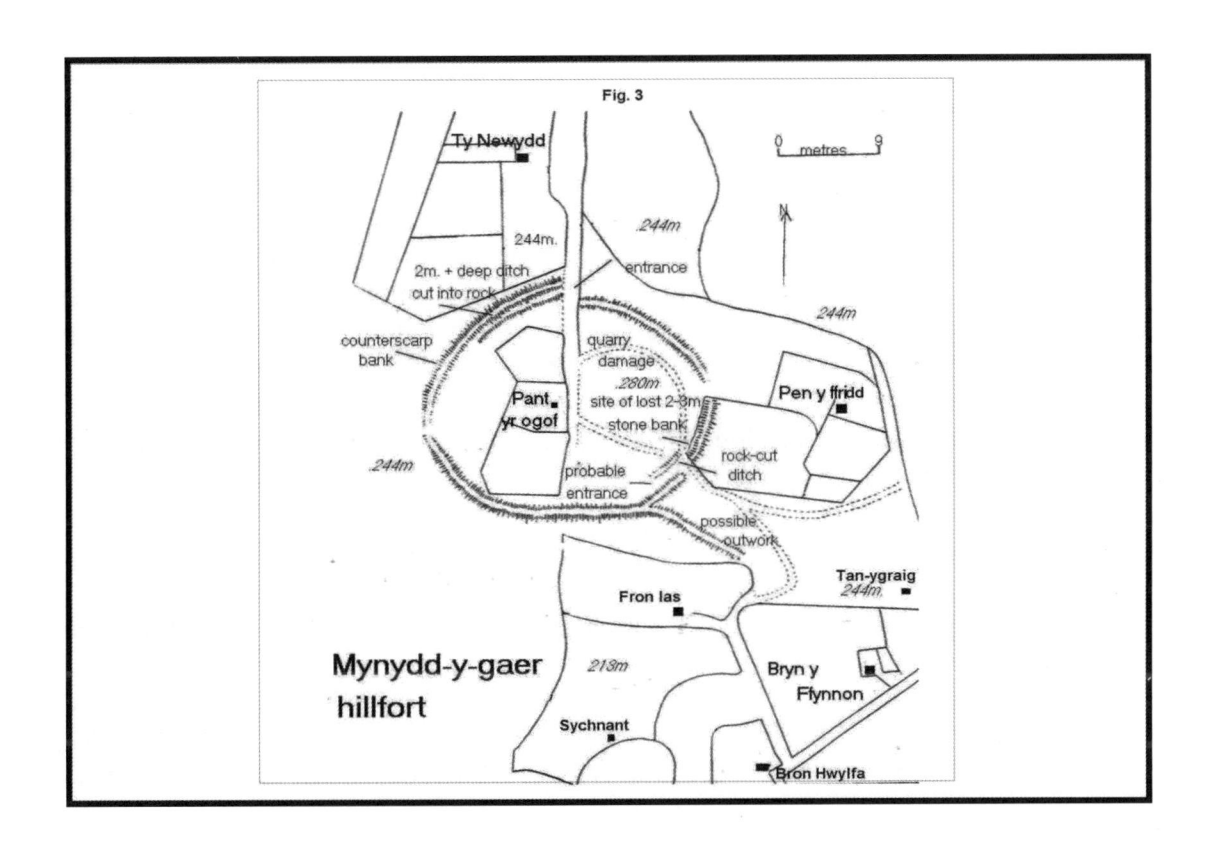

Mynydd-y-gaer hillfort

Mynydd y Gaer: *Mynydd y Gaer* represents the main relict feature of the Iron Age (it is possibly earlier) in the Elwy Valley. It is located about 1.6 kms (1 mile) north west of Llannefydd church on a steep sided conical hill that reaches an altitude of over 280 metres. The site occupies the whole hill top and is 4 ha in size (10acres) but has been damaged by quarrying and farm improvements. The site is shown in Figure 3. The hillfort stands high above the River Elwy but why was it constructed here? The lower Elwy itself has never provided a through route from the Clwyd valley into the heartlands of North Wales because the limestone gorge section is too narrow for such a route. Other questions can be raised such as what then was the fort protecting? Could it be the copper and lead deposits of the Llanfair Talhaearn area? This is an unlikely explanation and it is more likely that the fort controlled an important prehistoric route way passing through present day Llannefydd linking the Clwyd Valley at Denbigh with the Conwy Valley and the copper producing area of the Great Orme. The route would have passed close to the foot of the hill on which the hillfort stands. It is possible that goods from Ireland also passed along this route. A nearby bridge over the River Elwy is known as "*Pont y Gwyddel*" (Bridge of the Irishman) (GR 953718} It may therefore be the case that at one stage in its history, *Mynydd y Gaer* acted as a re-defended distribution centre for goods from Ireland, north west Wales and perhaps salt from Cheshire.

The hillfort presents evidence of significant local co-operation (or coercion) in its construction phase regardless of how long it was subsequently occupied. It reflects considerable control of local human resources perhaps under a Late Bronze Age warrior aristocracy. As can be seen in Figure 3, the defences appear for the most part to have been a single bank and ditch. On the north west side, the ditch is cut into the rock and is still over 2m deep and has a counterscarp bank of excavated material. On the south and south west sides the ditch is also cut into solid rock. Ellis

Davies, using oral evidence, claimed that there was once a rampart of stones on the inside of the ditch about 2-3 metres in from it on slightly higher land. In 1920, when Davies last visited the site, traces of the stones were still visible in situ on all sides except the east side. Davies spoke to local old people who indicated that the stones from the rampart were removed for building purposes during the course of the 19th century.[95] Today, a line of small stones still marks its line. The fort has never been excavated and no traces of hut emplacements are discernible although the ramparts housed a working farm in recent times.

Bedd y Cawr: The Elwy Valley has one other hillfort in its basin, the *Bedd y Cawr* hillfort in Cefn Meiriadog parish (GR 014720). This small promontory fort controlled the limestone gorge section at mouth of valley and is located at an altitude of 150m (487 feet) at the southern end of the limestone ridge known as Cefn Meiriadog. This ridge may have formed part of a ridge top route leading from the Clwyd Valley along the North Wales coast since three other larger hill forts were located further west along the ridge *Parc y Meirch (Dinorben), Castell Cawr* and *Pen y Corddyn*. The defences were simple; a man-made bank of small stones runs across the end of the ridge from west to east, its maximum height is 2.43 m. The fort had a simple single entrance and had good views on all sides except the north west where it is dominated by higher ground. This infers that danger was felt to emanate from the east and south. Two trenches were excavated by the owner of nearby *Plas yn Cefn Hall*, Mrs Williams-Wynn, in 1875 but nothing was discovered.

---

[95] Canon Ellis Davies "Prehistoric and Roman Remains of Denbighshire" 1929

Other Possible Hillfort Sites: From time to time, historians have speculated upon other possible hill fort sites in the river basin, particularly in the upper reaches of the valley to the west. Sites for hill forts have been postulated for *Moel Pentre Wern*, Llangernyw (GR882672); *Gwytherin churchyard* (GR 876614) and the appropriately named *Bryn Castell* (GR 885634) also near Gwytherin, All three sites have defensive potential but to date no convincing supporting evidence for a hillfort on the sites has been forthcoming.

The Role of Hill forts: There has been considerable debate among archaeologists about the role of the hillfort in Iron Age society. Some have questioned the defensive role assigned to hill forts; one study based on Herefordshire evidence suggested that they had the role of independent villages.[96] Another view prominent in the 1980s was that they had a territorial significance as distribution and re-distribution centres.[97] Finally, there has been some return to the view that hill forts were purely military structures.[98] The truth probably lies in a more flexible approach whereby most, if not all, hill forts were multi-functional. Archaeological research on hill forts is progressing so rapidly that one writer was led to observe that detailed "definitive" studies fall out of date faster than they are written[99]

---

[96] S.C. Stanford "The Function and Population of Hillforts in the Central Marches" in F. Lynch and C. Burgess (ed) "Prehistoric Man in Wales and the West"(1972)

[97] Barry Cunliffe." Iron Age Communities in Britain" Routledge Kegan and Paul; London 1992

[98] R. Bradley "The Social Foundations of Prehistoric Britain" (1984)

[99] A.H.A. Hogg : ""A Guide to the Hillforts of Britain" Paladin, London 1984

It seems likely that some sites in southern Britain were permanently occupied and had "proto-urban" roles acting in peacetime as agricultural or administrative centres or could be places for organising procurement of slaves that could be defended in times of war, the prototypes of the walled towns of the medieval period. In Wales, some forts such as *Tre' Ceiri* were occupied only in summer months except when danger threatened in which case they would be used as temporary refuges. They nevertheless represented a considerable outlay in terms of labour in their construction and thus may reflect coercion by a ruling body that controlled the fortification and the surrounding area. [100] The elaborate defences of some hill forts may indicate that status of the ruler was as important as defence in their construction.[101]

The *Mynydd y Gaer* hilltop may have been continuously occupied for much of the period since the Iron Age. *Bedd y Cawr*, on the other hand, is at a much lower altitude but is no longer occupied and may have had a different role to that of *Mynydd y Gaer*. Until these sites can be investigated by archaeologists their functions can only be speculated upon. *Bedd y Cawr* enclosed only 0.8 ha (2 acres) and may have been a family farm or temporary refuge. The promontory site, defended only by a single bank could be easily outflanked and attacked from higher ground to the west. *Mynydd y Gaer* on the other hand, possibly had its own spring and was well located to resist attack. The site is large enough to have housed a population of 240 (at a density of 60 persons per hectare)[102] If this was the case, then

---

[100] GRJ Jones "The Earliest Settlers in Britain" Geographical Magazine Vol XLII No 5 February 1970
[101] Colin Hasel grove "The Iron Age" in J. Hunter and I Ralston "The Archaeology of Britain" Routledge, London (1999) p132
[102] A.H.A. Hogg "A Guide to the Hillforts of Britain" Paladin, London (1984) p57

the available workforce could have made the hilltop defensible in a period of 2 - 4 months, a significant feat of organisation.

Other Iron Age Relict Features: Other relict features of the Iron Age landscape include field systems, track ways and linear boundaries. The period has left few visual burial sites. There were regional variations in agricultural practice and the impact of this on the landscape. Analysis of bone deposits from Iron Age sites indicates that agriculture was mixed, the principal livestock kept were cattle and sheep but also some pigs, small horses and domestic fowl were kept. Pollen analysis has revealed that the main crops grown included spelt wheat, barley, beans and rye. Crops were grown in what have been termed "Celtic" fields but these would be better described as "native" fields for the sake of accuracy. The cultivable land of pre Roman Britain continued to be worked in much the same way during the Roman occupation giving a direct continuity between Early Iron Age and Roman field systems. However, one researcher has claimed that in northern Britain, Bronze Age field systems persisted until Roman times when new systems were introduced[103].

The late Iron Age was one which brought about significant change in the landscape of upland Britain with the help of a climate that was more helpful to agricultural production than had been experienced for a millennium. This was conducive to increased agricultural output, falling mortality and population growth and supported an expansion of

---

[103] S. Applebaum : "The Pre Roman Heritage" in HPR Finberg (ed) The Agrarian History of England & Wales , Vol1 (ii) AD43 - 1042; CUP 1972 (pp18-19)

both settlement and agricultural production[104] and there can be little doubt that such changes also impacted upon local landscapes in the Elwy Valley. The rise in agricultural activity was accompanied by further clearance of woodland for agricultural purposes. Pollen analysis has shown that the period of 1,000 years from 500 BC was the most active period of woodland clearance in history.[105]

---

[104] Nicholas Higham "Rome, Britain and the Anglo Saxons" Sealy, London (1992) p18.

[105] N. Roberts "The Holocene - An Environmental History" Blackwell, Oxford (1989) p149

CHAPTER 5 : THE IMPACT OF ROMAN OCCUPATION

Invasion and Conquest: In the mid first century BC the heartland of Celtic power in mainland Europe lay in Gaul. Here, Roman conquest was leading to the "Romanisation" of the population bringing new lifestyles to the upper middle class elements of Celtic society together with urban developments, taxation and more intensive agricultural production. One hundred and fifty years later, these processes were under way in Britain[106] although it is doubtful if the native population of the upper and middle Elwy river basin ever noticed much difference.

The Romans invaded Britain in AD 43. It has been suggested that the Romans initially may have had no intention to conquer Wales[107] but support for dissidents such as Caractacus, who led a troublesome revolt by the Silures of south east Wales in AD47/48, together with the mineral wealth of Wales in terms of lead, copper and gold, changed this policy. It seems likely that the tribes of North Wales supported the Silures. The Deceangli tribe occupied the area between the Conwy and the Dee that was, according to the description of the events by Tacitus, attacked by Roman troops in AD 48.[108] There followed an attack on their neighbours, the Ordovices, part of whose territory lay to the south of that of the Deceangli in southern Denbighshire. The successful domination of the lands of these two tribes cut Wales off from the support of the Brigantia tribes of northern England. Anglesey was captured around AD 61

---

[106] John Davies "The Celts" Cassell, London (2000) p100
[107] Helen Burnham "Clwyd and Powys" HMSO London (1995) p 78
[108] John Davies "A History of Wales", Penguin, London (1993) p1

but consolidation of these territorial gains was hampered by Boudiccan revolt that drew away troops from the area to put down the dissident queen. A campaign to re-conquer Wales began in AD 74.and was completed by AD 77. By AD 84, Roman structures of political and economic control were being put into place.

Roman Roads: Control was obtained through a linked system of legionary fortresses joined by road to forts that served as forward units. Thus the key legionary fortress controlling the Elwy valley area was that at Deva (Chester). This was linked via a series of forts that included *Canovium* in the Conwy Valley and *Rhyn Park* on the north Shropshire border. Other settlements were established at *Varae* and Prestatyn although it is not known if these were forts. The site of Varae mentioned in the *Antonine Itinerary for Britain*, a list of Roman road stations produced during the second century AD. This document describes fifteen roads in Britain Part of the document known as itinera. *Iter XI* relates to the route running along the North Wales coast, from Chester to *Segontium* near Caernarfon on the Menai Straits. The route passed through *Canovium* in the Conwy valley. No known Roman road ran through the Elwy basin itself although no doubt existing track ways remained in use.

Varae: The location of Varae is still uncertain but is thought to lie on the ridge between the Clwyd and the Elwy rivers either within or close to the bounds of the present day small city of St. Asaph (Llanelwy) where coins, pottery and tile finds are indicative of Roman occupation. It has been noted that the Latin verb *varico* 'to straddle' may relate to the site of Varae which, if located at St. Asaph, straddled the narrow ridge between the Elwy and Clwyd rivers. The actual site of Varae has been narrowed down to three possible sites in St. Asaph, either on and around the site of the cathedral, beneath the H.M. Stanley Hospital (GR 043737) or to the south of the city at *Bryn Polyn*. (GR

047731)[109]. The second named site is well aligned with the Roman road from the Conwy Valley and the first century AD fort at Canovium. There have been claims that Varae may have been sited at either Prestatyn or the Iron Age fort at Bodfari which certainly has place-name connections, but neither site has the road alignments with the Roman route.

Political Control: The Romans established tribal capitals (*civitates*) to act as administrative centres for the conquered tribal areas drawing on the native population's own conception of their territorial units. The Deceangli easterly neighbours, the Cornovii tribe, who occupied what was later the northern Welsh marches, had their *civitates* at Viroconium (Wroxeter) while the formerly troublesome Silures had their *civitate* at Vemta Silurum (Caerwent). Yet, the Deceangli were never granted a *civitate* of their own despite their territory being one of significant industrial importance through the production of lead and probably copper and silver. It may be that the legionary fortress of Deva (Chester) administered their territory which presumably remained within the military zone throughout the Roman occupation. The *civitates* were designed to encourage the population to adopt Roman ways and thus the lack of such an urban centre in North Wales may have contributed to the low level of Romanisation in the region.

The *Deva - Segontium* Road: The Roman road linking Varae to Canovium ran west and lay to the north of the Elwy Valley. Its route from St Asaph followed the modern B5381 for some distance with both later parish and

---

[109] Kevin Blockley "The Romano-British Period" in Manley et al "The Archaeology of Clwyd" Clwyd CC., Mold. 1991.pp117

former county boundaries following part of its course.[110] At GR 945744, the Roman route diverges from the modern road but its course has been traced in some detail across fields, along bridle paths and through overgrown coppices to the point where it crossed the River Conwy near *Tal y Cafn* before passing on west via *Bwlch y Ddeufaen*[111]. A secondary route ran south westwards to forts at *Bryn y Gefeiliau* and *Tomen y Mur*. It should also be remembered that well surfaced roads such as those just described were the top-status routes in the hierarchy of Roman communications which no doubt intersected with unsurfaced pre-existing track ways that remained in general use by the rural population[112]. Such a route may have been the ancient ridge-top route running along the watershed between the Elwy and Conwy river basins to the west of Llangernyw.

Occupation of Hillfort Sites: Until archaeological investigations can be carried out, we will not know if the occupation of the Elwy valley hillforts at *Mynydd y Gaer* and *Bedd y Cawr* continued after the Roman conquest. We do know however, that at *Tre'r Ceiri* hillfort on the slopes of *Yr Eifl* in Gwynedd, the Ordovician tribe's Iron Age village within the ramparts continued to be occupied well into the Roman period. More significantly, the hill fort at *Parc y Meirch (Dinorben),* just north of the Elwy valley on the limestone ridge above the coast, was also occupied in Roman times and has been described as a fairly well-to-do farmstead in the late 3rd and 4th centuries Over 250 Roman coins have been found on the site testifying to the farm's involvement in day to day commerce possibly with

---

[110] I. D. Margary "Roman Roads in Britain" Baker, London. (1973) p 349.
[111] Edmund Waddelove "The Roman Road between Varis and Canovium" Archaeologia Cambrensis Vol.132 pp95-106 (1983).
[112] Richard Muir "The New Reading the Landscape" University. of Exeter Press (2000) p100

Roman garrisons at *Segontium*, *Varae* and *Canovium* together with the Romano British settlements at Prestatyn, Rhuddlan [113] and along the Dee Estuary. The coin total found at *Dinorben* compares well with those obtained from villa sites in lowland Britain[114]. The series of coins ends in 353 AD perhaps marking a permanent disruption to the trading process.

The Impact of Rome in the Elwy Basin: It has been noted that the upland area to the west of the Clwyd valley, which includes the middle and upper Elwy valley, has been virtually devoid of archaeological finds dating from the Roman period[115]. Thus, one leading authority has suggested that North Wales received only the thinnest veneer of Roman culture.[116] In the absence of direct archaeological evidence, we can only speculate upon the human occupance of the middle and upper Elwy valleys during the Roman occupation drawing upon evidence from adjacent areas and developments elsewhere in the Highland Zone of Roman military occupation in northern Britain. Pollen analyses from peat bogs in upland areas of Wales reveal that in the Roman period the continuing mild wet climate of the sub-Atlantic epoch supported the development of heathland vegetation and peat bogs above an altitude of 300m. This reflects the impact of continued forest clearance and the burning of vegetation prior to

---

[113] Kevin Blockley "The Romano-British Period" in Manley et al "(1991).pp117-126.
[114] G.C. Boon "The Roman Occupation" in "Ancient Monuments of Wales" HMSO London (1973) p 46
[115] Kevin Blockley "The Romano-British Period" in Manley et al ibid p117
[116] John Davies "The Celts" Cassell, London (2000) p101

seasonal grazing. These processes had their origins well before the arrival of Roman troops[117] and continued after their departure.[118]

The rural economy would have been highly localised and insular with the chief cash product probably being leather, an important raw material in that period. Arable production, even on a limited scale, would have been essential to provide food grains for the indigenous population. This production was presumably centered on more favourable sheltered locations on lower valley slopes. The type of settlement involved in these activities may well have been small nucleated hamlets of small circular huts of wood or stone possibly surrounded by an enclosing bank. These enclosures may have been similar to those found elsewhere in highland Britain dating to this period[119]. No such sites have yet been positively identified within the Elwy valley although the *Old Foxhall* Iron Age site at Henllan and other small enclosures may have continued to have been occupied in this period. Thus the economy of regions such as this would have exhibited more traits of Iron Age culture than Roman.

The low levels of productivity with the resultant impoverishment, together with possible hostility to Roman influence, would have served to reinforce the rejection of Romanised lifestyle leading to cultural isolation. As a result of this, the local population almost certainly continued to speak the ancient Brythonic Celtic language

---

[117] F.V. Emery "Wales" in "The World's Landscapes" ed. J.M. Houston Longman, London (1969) p24
[118] N. Higham "Rome, Britain and the Anglo Saxons" Sealy, London (1992) p78
[119] Robin Hanley "Villages in Roman Britain" Shire, Princes Risborough, (1987) pp13-17

throughout the Roman period and well into the medieval period. Thus the relative isolation of the Elwy valley in Roman times contributed to the maintenance of strong indigenous pre-Roman native traditions.[120] Even today, around 60 per cent of the population of the former parishes of Llanfair Talhaearn, Llangernyw and Gwytherin are Welsh-speaking.

---

[120] N. Higham "Rome, Britain and the Anglo Saxons" Sealy, London (1992) p87

CHAPTER 6   "CELTIC" MONASTICISM AND THE EARLY CHURCH

The Roman Legacy: Christianity has been described as one of the most decisive elements in the shaping of early medieval society[121]. The religion first flourished in Britain during the late Roman period[122] having been legitimised by the emperor Constantine in 313 AD. The religion was almost certainly introduced by Roman troops. One leading scholar takes the view that Christianity would have been well established in Britain by the late 4th century and that a diocesan structure had emerged by this time.[123] It is possible that this organisational structure for the church may have persisted until the 7th century although in Roman times, Christianity was almost certainly confined mainly to the urban areas. By the late 5th and 6th centuries, it seems that monasticism was emerging as an alternative structure for Christianity in Britain[124] although some form of diocesan system appears to have survived in Wales.

Early Monasticism: Monasticism had its roots in late 3rd century Egypt when early Christians retreated into the desert to live as hermits. These "Desert Fathers" were later joined by others who formed communities of monks and nuns who devoted their lives to Christ.[125] Monasticism appears to have reached Britain from the eastern

---

[121] M. Green and R Howell "Celtic Wales" University of Wales Press, Cardiff. (2000) p83
[122] C. Thomas "Christianity in Roman Britain to AD500" Batsford, London (1981) p240
[123] Lloyd Laing "Celtic Britain" Paladin/Granada St. Albans (1981) p200
[124] Leslie Alcock "Arthur's Britain" Pelican, Harmondsworth. (1973) p134
[125] Mick Aston "Monasteries in the Landscape" Temple, Stroud (2000) p29.

Mediterranean and southern Gaul and had taken a hold before the 6th century. Wales appears to have been among the first areas of development with monasteries in place by AD 500. In addition to the groups of gathering together for common observances in monasteries, there were much smaller establishments, hermitages where one, two or three men (or women) could lead a solitary existence in their communion with God.

Early Welsh Monasticism: It is possible that many early Celtic ascetics seeking the "desert life" deep in the Welsh countryside during the 5th century were trained in Gaul and arrived in Wales via the Western seaboard. The movement is thought to have subsequently spread to northern England during the 6th century. However, it is too simplistic to accept the model of a "pan-Celtic" monastic church organisation throughout Wales[126]. It seems probable that in the post Roman period, paganism still flourished in many parts of the Welsh countryside. One writer has claimed that paganism was still in "excellent health" in Britain at the end of the 4th century[127]

Politics and the Early Church: The Welsh church, with its roots in the late Roman period, was clearly part of the political establishment[128] It has been suggested that ecclesiastical office was regarded as one of status and profit in

---

[126] Wendy Davies "The Myth of the Celtic Church" in N Edwards and A. Lane (ed) "The Early Church in Wales and the West" Oxbow Monograph 16, Oxford 1992 p12
[127] N. Higham "Rome, Britain and the Anglo Saxons" Sealy, London (1992) p65 and p97
[128] .W. Davies "Wales in the Early Middle Ages" Leicester (1982) p140

the recently established British kingdoms of sixth century Britain.[129] The patronage of the church by the ruling dynasties gave them an institutional dimension for their control over local society.[130] This may have found expression in the dedication of the early church of St Digain in Llangernyw to the son of the prince of Dumnonia in the West Country. St. Elerius (Eleri), the traditional founder of the church and monastery at Gwytherin, was the son of the ruler of the *Selgovae* people of Southern Scotland. The dedication of other North Wales churches to the descendants of Cunedda, a shadowy figure reputed to have driven Irish settlers from North Wales around the turn of the fifth century. Cunedda was responsible for a key political dynasty in post Roman Gwynedd with many chiefs of embryonic Welsh kingdoms in the fifth century claiming direct descent from him in order to give their claim to rule some degree of legitimacy.[131]

The monastic movement may have been expanded as an alternative to the worldliness of the existing politicised church. The rise in popularity of a monastic style of Christianity in Britain is not surprising since a diocesan structure was urban based and with the departure of Roman forces, urban life diminished in importance. British society had reverted to its tribal roots and thus monasticism could better serve this more rurally orientated

---

[129] M. Winterbottom (ed) "Gildas, the Ruin of Britain and other works" Chichester (1978) p52
[130] N. Higham "Rome, Britain and the Anglo Saxons" Sealy, London (1992) p99
[131] M. Green and R Howell "Celtic Wales" University of Wales Press, Cardiff. (2000) p78

population. This change in emphasis from a diocesan to monastic-ascetic form of Christianity appears to have gained ground after AD 500.[132]

Monastic Sites in Roman Forts: The larger examples of early monasteries were set within an enclosing bank and contained the cells of monks set around a central church. Many of the early monasteries had a rectilinear plan perhaps following eastern European traditions or because some were built within the walls of Roman forts as was the case at *Caer Gybi* (Holyhead), *Caerwent* and *Llandaff* in South Wales. It is tantalising to speculate that at *Canovium* in the Conwy Valley, the site of the present parish church of St Mary dating from the 13th or 14th century may have replaced an early medieval church on the site of the Roman fort. Stones from the Roman fort appear to have been utilised in the fabric of the church. An early church on the site would help explain why the church is so geographically remote from the settlement it serves. Could it also be that St. Kentigern's monastery at Llanelwy was located within the defences of the lost Roman site of Varae? To date, no definitive archaeological evidence to support either theory has been forthcoming. Pennant pointed out that the cathedral lay within an ancient township known as *Bryn Paulin (now Bryn Polyn)*, a name, he speculated, that may have its origins in the campaigns of Suetonius Paulinus in AD 58-9 when he is thought to have defeated the Deceangli or AD 60 prior to the capture of Anglesey.[133]

---

[132] John Davies "A History of Wales" Penguin, London (1993) p75

[133] T Pennant "A Tour of Wales 1770 " (Vol II) Bridge Books, Wrexham (1991) p19

Curvilinear Churchyards and the Retention of Pagan Tradition: Foundations with a circular plan soon replaced the rectilinear form, perhaps indicating a resurgence of Celtic tradition of circular boundaries for sacred sites[134]. The circle's boundary separated the religious from the profane and the dead from the living. One may see parallels in the case of henges. Some Bronze Age burial locations continued in use in the Iron Age and Romano-British period and even into medieval times.[135] There are also examples of Christian churchyards being located on the site of earlier pagan graveyards[136].

The use of churchyards for burials was established by the first half of the sixth century.[137] The location of many early inscribed stones in the graveyards of country churches such as Llangernyw and Gwytherin, often close to route ways may also indicate a return to a pre Celtic tradition and an early origin for the church It has been asserted that there are as many as 139 inscribed stones surviving in Wales from the 250 year period following the fall of Rome.[138] The absorbing of ancient Celtic traditions into early Christian practice had a degree of official sanction in that a

---

[134] C. Thomas "The Early Christian Archaeology of North Britain" OUP London (1971) p51
[135] H. James "Early Medieval Cemeteries in Wales" in N. Edwards and A Lane (ed) ibid (1992) p90
[136] Lloyd Laing ibid (1981) p202 also N. Edwards and A Lane (ed) ibid (1992) p6
[137] C.A. Ralegh Radford "Early Christianity and the Emergence of Wales" ibid (1979) p48
[138] John Davies "A History of Wales" Penguin, London (1993) p46

papal instruction to St. Augustine ordered him to convert pagan customs into a Christian solemnity[139], a most pragmatic solution to overcoming pagan resistance to the spread of Christianity.

Monastic Organisation: "Clas" Communities: The larger monasteries have been described as "monastic villages" [140] In North Wales there were some large monastic institutions such as Bangor on Dee and probably St. Asaph but also simple structures consisting of a single hermit's cell, a chapel and graveyard. This may have been the case at Llannefydd and Llangernyw where the saints to whom the sites were later dedicated: Nefydd and Digain were possibly hermits.

The Welsh Laws of Hywel Dda were in use certainly by the 10th century and were probably based upon much earlier precedents possibly going back to the end of the 7th century AD. These laws refer to the existence of "mother" churches that probably began life as monastic institutions since they were under the control of an abbot. Such a clerical community was often termed a *"clas"* a community of Christians living together under the monastic rule of an abbot. The term clas derives from the Latin *"classis"* - a band or body of people. The exact origins, precise nature and functions of the *clas* are obscure and many surviving references are ambiguous. [141] However, we can be

---

[139] Francis Jones "The Holy Wells of Wales" Univ. Of Wales Press, Cardiff (1992) p21
[140] Mick Aston ibid p 30
[141] J. Wyn Evans :"The survival of the *clas* as an institution in medieval Wales, some observations on Llanbadarn Fawr" in N Edwards and A. Lane (ed) "The Early Church in Wales and the West" Oxbow Monograph 16, Oxford 1992 p33

certain that the *clas* communities were not part of any monastic order. These arrangements appear to have formed the basis of ecclesiastical organisation within the Celtic church in Wales, and thus a clerical and non clerical group could settle around a church practising a Christian lifestyle.

The Celtic Church and Rome: The Celtic church thus developed separate practices from those of the continent, particularly Rome itself. At the time of St Augustine's arrival in Britain in 597 AD, there were a great number of Celtic monasteries in existence particularly in Wales and the West. The main differences between the Celtic and Roman churches were the calculation of the date of Easter and the style of tonsure. There are also indications that some Celtic priests were married (St. Sadwrn, founder of the church at Henllan born c485 AD). In some areas there were hereditary rights for both monastic and non monastic offices. This was not uncommon throughout Europe in the 8th - 10th centuries but the ending of priests' right to marry occurred later in Celtic areas[142] with some references to the practice surviving until after the Edwardian Conquest of 1282.[143] As time went by, the system of worship prescribed by Rome was gradually adopted in Britain. The Synod of Whitby in 663 brought about the acceptance of the Roman system throughout Northumbria but the more conservative Welsh church still refused to change until the year AD 768.[144]

---

[142] W Davies "The Myth of the Celtic Church" in N Edwards and A. Lane (ed) ibid (1992) p16
[143] Gareth Elwyn Jones "Modern Wales - A Concise History" CUP, Cambridge 2nd Ed. (1994) p107
[144] John Davies "A History of Wales" Penguin, London (1993) p78

A "Clas" at Gwytherin?: Even as late as 1334, tenants in Gwytherin held their lands from the "abbot" indicative that some archaic elements of the Celtic monastic system, probably those of the *"clas"*, were still influential. well into the medieval period. The entry for Gwytherin in the Survey of the Honour of Denbigh 1334 states that land was held in the parish from *"the descendants of Canon ap Lauwargh* (Llywarch)".[145] The use of the title "canon" in medieval Gwytherin may, as was the case at Llanbadarn Fawr near Aberystwyth, be a native term for members of the community of a major church indicating that the Gwytherin site may have once held a more important role than that of merely a parish church.[146]. However, to the Normans and the rulers of Wales following the 1282 conquest, the *clas* with its wooden huts, married priests and holders of hereditary offices within the *clas* structure was unacceptable.[147] Thus many former *clas* churches such as Gwytherin and possibly Llangernyw and Llannefydd were given the status of parish churches or chapels of ease.

"Mother" Churches: The *clasau* (plural) often occupied large circular enclosures[148] containing the church, graveyard and cells of the priests. Sometimes, a vallum delineated the boundaries of the clas as at Gwytherin where traces of a defensive vallum are discernible Within the enclosure, buildings were distributed in haphazard fashion

---

[145] P. Vinogradoff and F. Morgan (ed) "A Survey of the Honour of Denbigh 1334" London (1914) p193
[146] J Wyn Evans ibid (1992) p28
[147] John Davies "A History of Wales" Penguin, London (1993) p118
[148] R. Silvester (1997) "Historic Settlement Surveys in Clwyd and Powys" in N. Edwards (ed) "Landscape and Settlement in Medieval Wales" Oxbow; Oxford p115)

unlike the classic monasteries of later medieval times. Inside the monastic enclosure lay hermits' cells, a chapel and subsidiary buildings. There were also homes of lay craftsmen and perhaps slaves on the fringes of the compounds. Later, non clerics could hold land in the settlement that developed. Many of these *"clasau"* became "mother" churches examples from North East Wales included Llanelwy (St. Asaph), Abergele, Llanynys and Bangor Isycoed. Llanelwy may have had some pre-conquest episcopal tradition but the present bishopric was not created until 1141. Other *clasau* remained as small monastic centres, perhaps centred on a hermitage as was possibly the case at Gwytherin founded by St. Elerius, a former monk at St. Asaph..

Archaeological evidence to support a monastic origin for Welsh churches is rare since it is probably buried beneath the foundations of later church buildings. In Clynnog fawr on the west coast of Gwynedd, excavations revealed the existence of an ancient oratory containing a long cist burial, indicative of an early site, beneath a 16th century chapel known as "Eglwys y Bedd" [149]

"Clas" Communities in the Landscape: *Clasau* were responsible for the pastoral care of areas of the countryside. The *"clas"* system persisted in Wales from early Christian times until the Edwardian Conquest following which the system of patrimony dominated clerical appointments[150]. Often the *clasau* were very powerful bodies politically and were wealthy. Individual *clas* settlements were often associated with a hermitage to which members could retire or

---

[149] B. Stalybrass ""Recent discoveries at Clynnog Fawr" Arch Camb. Vol.14 (1914) pp271-296
[150] C.A. Ralegh Radford "Early Christianity and the Emergence of Wales" in "Ancient Monuments of Wales" HMSO London (1979) p49

use as a retreat. Gwytherin may have such an origin, St Winifred reputedly retired here following her ordeal in Holywell. There are Irish parallels of this[151] as well as Tintagel in Cornwall where a bank and ditch separate the *clas* settlement on the rocky promontory. Within the Tintagel are monks' cells, an oratory, farm buildings and graves.

It has been suggested that the size of the ecclesiastical enclosure was an important factor since the larger the enclosure, the more important was the church site[152]. At Llanafanfawr, Powys, the circular enclosure has been revealed by aerial photography and is over 120 metres in diameter The actual area of the occupied by the church and graveyard is relatively small, it has been suggested that the larger enclosure may represent the boundary of the *clas*[153]. The original churchyard at Gwytherin was also unusually large, perhaps this supports the hypothesis that the site once held *clas* status, certainly medieval documentation also supports this theory. Thus the size of many ecclesiastical enclosures is often large in comparison to the burial needs of the community indicating perhaps the original may have even included some agricultural land for the subsistence of the clerics.

"Llan" Names: The names of many early Celtic churches are prefixed with the word *"Llan"* meaning an enclosure. The original *"llanau"* were possibly graveyards for the local Christian community that were later also chosen as the

---

[151] John Bradley "Walled Towns in Ireland" Country House, Dublin (1995) p6
[152] C. Thomas "The Early Christian Archaeology of North Britain" OUP, London (1971) p 38
[153] . C.A. Ralegh Radford ibid (1979) p50

site of a church.[154] Such enclosures frequently had curvilinear boundaries which would certainly date them to pre Norman times. In landscape history terms, these *"llanau"* enclosures represent a network of graveyards created to meet the needs of a scattered rural population. In the former Denbighshire there are 38 *"llan"* names but only 4 in the former Flintshire. The names of the hermit monks may be reflected in dual names of churches where the dedication includes a local saint, perhaps the original dedication, plus the Virgin Mary, in line with the newly-awakened cult of the Virgin Mary popular from the twelfth century, as at Llannefydd and Llanfair Talhaearn. Many early curvilinear churchyards have been subsequently modified in shape by later developments. This is the case at Llannefydd, Llangernyw, Llanfair Talhaearn and Llansannan where traces of the original curved boundaries survive but encroachments by later buildings, particularly public houses, have modified the original shape of the churchyards.

The Sites of Early Churches: The late Professor Emrys Bowen noted that most early medieval Welsh churches were founded at a relatively low altitude in valley locations as is the case throughout the Elwy valley.[155] They were often close to small settlements of bondmen but with the decline of this form of tenural arrangement in late medieval tomes these bond settlements. were deserted leaving the church isolated from its community. This continued until the expansion of trade and settlement took them into the bounds of the emerging present day settlements from the

---

[154] John Davies "A History of Wales" Penguin, London (1993) p75
[155] Emrys Bowen "The Settlements of the Celtic Saints in Wales" Univ. Of Wales Pres, Cardiff (1954).

sixteenth century. Certainly this bears out John Leland's observation in the late 1530s that there was no nucleated settlement in the area other than Denbigh although he did note several parish churches.[156]

In Henllan, Llansannan and Gwytherin, there may have been some nucleation in the form of a bond hamlet near the church in medieval times, but the present nucleation dates only from the sixteenth century or later. At Llangernyw, the church site is some distance from the medieval motte that suggests dispersion of settlement while, Llannefydd, which is not mentioned in the 1334 Survey of the Honour of Denbigh, appears to have been another isolated church which grew from a graveyard enclosure near the cell of St. Nefydd whose holy well is located a short distance from the church.. Wigfair too, has no nucleation close to the medieval chapel. Edward Llwyd's "Parochlia" survey of the late seventeenth century of churches and the settlements they serve confirms that in many cases few houses stood close to many Welsh churches.

Early Celtic churches were often associated with water which had been venerated in religious practice from pre Christian times as is evidenced by the recovery of valuable artifacts left as offerings at watery sites such as Llyn Cerrig in Anglesey, Llyn Fawr in Glamorgan and the bog below Caergwrle Castle, once a hillfort, that produced the "Caegwrle Bowl" an impressive piece of craftsmanship dating from 1200 BC.. This was certainly the case in mid Wales, where most early Celtic church sites have an intimate association with water and are set in valleys, on river

---

[156] Lucy Toulmin Smith " Leland's Itinerary in Wales 1536-1539" Bell, London (1906) pp 93-94

terraces or on spurs above streams[157]. This last named form of location is true of churches at Gwytherin, Llangernyw, Llansannan and Llanfair Talhaearn. Such water-orientated locations are rarer in Anglo Norman church sites.

All such sites have defensive possibilities if the natural slopes to the adjacent streams were supported by a vallum on the more vulnerable sides of the enclosures. There has been speculation that the site of Gwytherin churchyard may occupy that of an earlier promontory hillfort[158]. We know too, that Maelgwn (c480 - c539), ruler of Gwynedd donated the site of the shore fort of Caer Gybi (Holyhead) to St. Gybi setting an early precedence for the re-use of former defensive sites for religious purposes[159]. Maelgwn also allegedly donated the site of the church at Llangernyw to St Kentigern. Could this site too have once been defensive? if not, the presence of the ancient yew and remains of a possible megalithic structure indicate possibly earlier religious use of the site. Certainly visitors to the churchyard of Llanfair Talhaearn cannot fail to note the defensive possibilities of the site.

---

[157] R Silvester ibid (1997) p117

[158] J.W. Evans "The Early Church in Denbighshire" Trans. Denbs, Hist Soc.Vol 35 (1966) p67

[159] See Charles Thomas "Christians, Chapels, Churches and Charters – or "Proto-parochial provisions for the Pious in a Peninsular" (Land's End) Landscape History Vol.11 (1989) p21

Holy Wells: Many early church sites are located close to ancient wells that served to provide a water supply for clerics and were used for baptism. There are 76 holy wells known in former Denbighshire and 51 in Flintshire.[160] Many such wells were holy sites even in pre Christian times and continued to be associated with places of worship even into medieval times when elaborate canopies were sometimes placed over them and chapels such as that of *St. Mary's* in Wigfair, adjacent to the well known as *Ffynnon Fair*. In the valley of the Afon Meirchion, north west of Henllan are the remains of a lesser known holy well complex known as "*Ffynnon Wen*" (GR 020688. The name translates as "holy well" since "*wen*" can mean "holy" as well as white. The site has the remains of two buildings a bath house and a dressing chamber. The bath house is fed with water from a channel linked to a nearby spring.[161]

The Impact of the Edwardian Conquest: Following the Norman Conquest of England, the Elwy Basin sporadically came under Norman control but was not finally held until after 1282. The Normans disliked many features of the medieval Welsh church such as hereditary abbots (as at Gwytherin); bishops without cathedrals and dioceses based on secular units of land. All of these were phased out following the 1282 conquest[162]. Further evidence of change brought about by Norman influence was the re-dedication of churches to St. Mary as occurred at Llanfair Talhaearn, Llannefydd and the chapel at Wigfair. Thus only the sites of Celtic churches survived into late medieval times

---

[160] Francis Jones "The Holy Wells of Wales" Univ. Of Wales Press, Cardiff (1992) p9

[161] RCAHM "Inventory of the Ancient Monuments of Wales and Monmouth shire - Denbighshire" (1914)

[162] A D Carr "Medieval Wales" Macmillan Basingstoke (1995) p49.

CHAPTER 7: MEDIEVAL CHURCHES IN THE LANDSCAPE

The churches of the Elwy and Aled valleys still represent important elements in the landscape of the 21st century although most were either rebuilt in perpendicular style in the late fifteenth and early sixteenth centuries or "restored" in the 19th century thus leaving no surviving examples of an early medieval church other than St. Asaph cathedral. The non-survival of any early churches in the valley may reflect the fact that wood rather than stone was used in their construction.. Most of the stone churches in the valley would have been constructed on the sites of early medieval wooden predecessors during the 12th century. It has been claimed that with the exception of Presteigne; the fabric of any stone church in Wales built prior to c1100 has yet to be discovered[163]

GWYTHERIN: Church and Churchyard: The church at Gwytherin is the first one encountered moving downstream from the river's source on Mynydd Hiraethog. The single chamber church is sited on a small promontory above the Afon Cledwen with steep drops to the south east and north. It has been suggested that the site may be that of an Iron Age promontory hill fort but as yet there is no archaeological evidence to support this. A degraded bank lying between the churchyard entrance and the west wall of the church has been identified as a part of a former rampart.[164]

---

[163] Huw Price "Ecclesiastical Wealth in Early Medieval Wales" in N Edwards and A. Lane (ed) "The Early Church in Wales and the West" Oxbow Monograph 16, Oxford (1992) p22
[164] J.W. Evans "The Early Church in Denbighshire" Trans. Denbs, Hist Soc. Vol 35 (1966) p67

The present building dates from a rebuild of 1869 (see Plate 8). It was recorded as being in a dilapidated state by that time. The site, within a large curvilinear churchyard, is clearly very ancient and was one of some importance in early medieval times.[165]. It is said that two well known North Wales saints came to the monastery to spend their retirement.[166]. These early saints: Gybi and Sannan gave their names to Caer Gybi (Holyhead) and Llansannan.

Plate 8

The former church was originally dedicated to *St Eleri (Elerius)* and recorded in the 1254 Norwich Taxation returns. It was later re-dedicated *St. James*. The structure was described by a 19th century writer as "undistinguished"[167], before being replaced by the present building dedicated to St. Winifred. In 1990, the church was re-opened after eight years disuse following its de-consecration in 1982. At the time of writing (2004), the ancient church once again faces imminent closure.

It is thought that the original church on the site was very early and founded by *St. Elerius (Eleri)* although there may be some link to a

---

[165] N. Edwards and A. Lane (ed) The Early Church in Wales and the West" ibid (1992) p9
[166] D.R. Thomas "The History of the Diocese of St. Asaph" Vol.2 Caxton Press, Oswestry (1911) p313
[167] J. O. Westwood : Archaeologia Cambrensis Vol. 4 (1858) p405

St Gwytherin since the island in the then undrained Somerset marshes that we know today as Glastonbury Tor was once known as the Island of *St. Gwytherin*. Excavations have indicated that a small Celtic monastery or hermitage dating from the late 5th or early 6th century may have been located on the summit of Glastonbury Tor[168]. We know that there were strong links with the West Country in the era of Celtic Christianity following the Roman withdrawal as is evident in the neighbouring parish of Llangernyw where the church is dedicated to a Cornishman.

The churchyard at Gwytherin is partly curvilinear and was unusually large; both considered to be key indicators of an ecclesiastical site of pre Norman date[169]. The curved line of the road to the north of the church may indicate that the churchyard was once even larger with the buildings representing a late encroachment. There is also a trace of a relict bank in front of the present stone wall on the north west side A churchyard extension to the south in Gwytherin is thought to have once housed the "chapel of the grave" containing the remains of St. Winifred, the building survived into the early eighteenth century. The building was known as Capel Penbryn. A geophysical survey of the supposed site of the Capel Penbryn made in 1995 revealed nothing of significance. Sites with unusually large churchyards are similar to early church sites in Ireland but Welsh examples also occur as at Corwen, Llanrhaeadr ym Mochnant and Meifod.

---

[168] P. Rahtz "Glastonbury" English Heritage/Batsford London 1993
[169] C. Thomas "The Early Christian Archaeology of North Britain" OUP London (1971) p50-51

The Stone Row: (see Plate 9)Within the churchyard is a stone row of four stones, one containing an inscription of the late 5th or early 6th century which helps confirm the early foundation of the church. The row runs east - west on the north side of the present church. The westernmost stone contains a Latin inscription running vertically in two lines of capital letters. The inscription reads "VINNEMAGLI FILI SENEMAGLI" = Vinnemagius son of Senemagius - a personal memorial. It has been suggested that the edges of the standing stones have been altered to obliterate Ogham inscriptions but this is considered doubtful. However, the format of the inscription "X son of Y", known as the "filation formula" suggests a possible Irish influence, and may originally be of Roman pagan origin since descent was a major factor in status within a pagan society.[170] The format is found predominantly on stones bordering the Irish Sea.

The reference to the father-son relationship was not considered to be in keeping with St. Matthew's words "Call no man your father upon the earth", an order observed strictly in the Continent but less so on the fringes of Europe represented by Ireland, Brittany, western England and western Wales. St Matthew's statement conflicted with Celtic traditions of revering the father-son relationship and in Ireland and Wales tradition won the day despite being something of a heresy. However, this practice was also prevalent in Celtic Gaul perhaps indicative of cultural and religious links during the 5th century British migrations. These links have been exemplified by reference to an

---

[170] L. Alcock "Arthur's Britain" Pelican, Harmondsworth (1973) p 241

inscription from Louannec on the coast north of Lannion in Brittany with a similar vertical inscription in two lines reading "DISIDERI FILI BODGNOUS"[171]

Plate 9

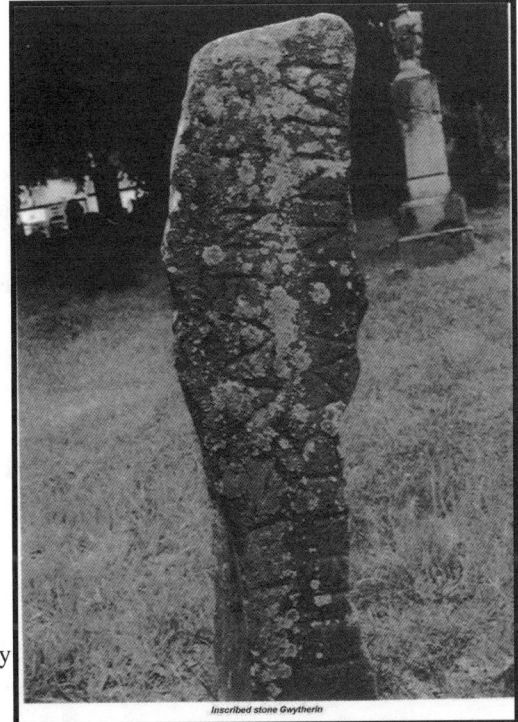

Such inscriptions may also reflect the reluctance of some Celtic churches to adopt Roman church traditions. The use of Latin in this 5th or 6th century inscription is also of interest since it shows that Latin learning did not die even in this remote North Wales valley following the departure of the Romans. The significance of the stone row itself is unknown. It has been postulated that it was the monument of a chieftain rather than a clergyman since the patronymic is used[172]. A motive for creating such an inscription has also been put forward, this being that a Welsh chieftain might have been impressed by the way a Roman emperor was able to record his name and title on a milestone and might consider that his own name and lineage should be similarly marked, particularly if the stone recorded his ownership of a particular piece of territory.[173]

---

[171] J. Knight ibid (1992) p50
[172] C.A. Ralegh Radford ibid (1973) p47
[173] Jeremy Knight "The Early Christian Latin Inscriptions of Britain and Gaul : Chronology 1992 p50

The likeness of the line of stones to earlier stone processional ways has also been noted[174]s. If this is the case then one may have subsequently been used as a memorial stone and may also indicate a pre-Christian date for the site. Inscribed memorial stones such as the one in Gwytherin represent: the earliest evidence of early Christianity in Wales. They date from 5th to 7th centuries. The four standing stones have also been used to reinforce the theory that the churchyard is sited on a former promontory hill fort. It has been established on good authority that local Celtic chieftains were often buried within the boundaries of their homesteads.[175] Applying this to Gwytherin, it has been suggested that one of the four standing stones may have marked the grave of the founder of the churchyard and the other three stones may mark the graves of successive generations of this aristocratic family[176], one of whom may have been named "Vinnemagli". If so, the church site may post-date the standing stones.

From the 7th century, crosses largely replace inscribed stones. Outside of Wales, examples of inscribed stones have come mainly from the western side of England notably Cornwall, Devon, Somerset with a very early example from Wroxeter. The earliest examples record simply the names of fathers and sons and may not necessarily be Christian. The earliest certain Christian examples date from the late 5th century and frequently begin with *"Hic iacet"* Inscribed standing stones are rare in North Wales east of the Conwy Valley but plentiful in Gwynedd. The

---

[174] Lloyd Laing "Celtic Britain" ibid p204
[175] Charles Thomas "Britain and Ireland in Early Christian Times AD 400 - 800 Thames and Hudson, London (1971) p48
[176] J.W. Evans "The Early Church in Denbighshire" ibid (1966) p67

Gwytherin and Llangernyw stones may therefore reflect an eastward extension of Gwynedd's influence. Such influences may have emanated from western Irish Sea routes rather than from the east. On stones of Romano-British origin inscriptions tend to be horizontal while Celtic inscriptions are vertical as is the case at Gwytherin. Many early memorial stones also show a southern Irish influence through the Ogham characters, in which letters were notched to form an alphabet on the edge of memorial stones. This form of stone was commonest in south west Wales but their existence is also known in North East Wales. Clocaenog, 13 kms (8 miles) south east of Gwytherin, on the other side of the Denbigh Moors, has an Ogham inscribed stone of the 5th or 6th century.

The Role of Pilgrims: The church at Gwytherin is linked to the cult of St. Winifred (Welsh *Gwenfrewi*). St. Winifred (died c660 AD) was of noble birth and descended from the kings of Powys. She is alleged to have settled on the site following her unfortunate experience at Holywell joining St. Elerius, her mother's cousin, who already resided at Gwytherin. This has been cited as evidence that the monastery here was a "double" establishment housing both men and women.[177] The male monastic establishment was founded by Elerius (died c 670AD) and the female house by his mother Theonia. St Winifred was eventually buried in the churchyard in Gwytherin. Her shrine attracted pilgrims following the route of her alleged journey from Holywell then on to Gwytherin via Bodfari, Henllan, Ffynnon Meirchion (well and possible chapel) and Nantglyn. The 1254 taxation returns assess Nantglyn and Gwytherin as one entity. This may have been for convenience but may also indicate that the two ancient churches were ecclesiastically linked, hence the diversion in the pilgrims' route to Nantglyn. The two were

---

[177] J.W. Evans "The Early Church in Denbighshire" Trans. Denbs, Hist Soc. Vol 35 (1966) p66.

separately assessed in the following taxation return of 1291. There is a local tradition that claims that yew trees were planted at intervals along the pilgrimage route to Gwytherin. From Gwytherin, many pilgrims continued their journey westwards to Bardsey Island. The whole journey from Holywell to Bardsey was over 200 kilometres.

The Removal of St. Winifred's Remains: A reference in a 12th century document, *"Life of Winifred"* written by a prior of the Benedictine Abbey in Shrewsbury records that her remains were transferred almost 500 years later in 1138 to an elaborate new shrine in the medieval abbey of St Peter and St. Paul at Shrewsbury. This action was initially opposed by the local community; their dispute with the monks of Shrewsbury has been recorded in modern television dramatisation of Ellis Peters' novel *"A Morbid Taste for Bones"* since the churchyard was the scene of a murder investigated by the medieval monastic sleuth *"Cadfael"*. The fact that the English Benedictine monastery had the power to transfer the valuable relics tells us that by the early 12th century, the church at Gwytherin no longer enjoyed its former importance at a time when Gwynedd was re-asserting its control of the lands in the Elwy basin. However, there appears to have been a link between the rulers of Gwynedd and the Benedictines of Shrewsbury Abbey who were left a legacy of twenty pieces of silver by Gruffudd ap Cynan in 1137.[178]

The Site of the Former Shrine: The late seventeenth century writer Edward Llwyd describes a *Gwenfrewi chapel* on the south side of the churchyard that is known to have been destroyed in the early 18th century. A report by the rural dean to the Bishop of St. Asaph in 1729 indicates that at that date it was in ruins but stood within the bounds of

---

[178] Roger Turvey "The Welsh Princes 1063 - 1283" Longmans, London (2002) p 184

the churchyard. A glebe terrier of 1749 refers to a piece of ground a quarter of an acre (1.35 ha) on the south side of the church that was traditionally the site of the church of *Gwenfrewi*[179]. This site later lay outside the churchyard and housed the chapel of *Penbryn* but probably lay within the early medieval "llan". Such multiple use of churchyards is not uncommon in Wales where several such "*Capel y Bedd*" (Chapels of the Grave) are known such as those at Caer Gybi; Llaneilan and Clynnog Fawr. Edward Llwyd's *Parochlia* has a drawing of an elaborate wooden casket allegedly made to contain the relics of St Winifred and housed at Gwytherin until the 19th century[180]/ The 4th edition of Samuel Lewis' "Topographical Dictionary" produced in 1850, records that the reliquary was still at the church although it is said to have fallen into disrepair because numerous visitors to the site took pieces of the casket as keepsakes.. From the drawing, scholars have deduced that the casket was of early Christian date. In 1991, a fragment of what is believed to be one end of the casket was found in the presbytery at Holywell.[181]

The "Clas" at Gwytherin: The 1334, Survey of the Honour of Denbigh tells us that the tenants of one third of the land in the village held it immediately from their lord *"and the lord is called their Abbot"* The other two thirds of the land are held from the family/descendants of "*Canon ap Lauwargh*" (Cynan ap Llywarch). Lands around the church were occupied by bond tenants but the remaining tenants of the village were free men who were liable for military service. It is significant that some lands formerly held by "abbots" had been forfeited since the documents

---

[179] J. W. Evans (ibid) (1986) p66

[180] R H Morris (Ed) "Edward Llwyd's Parochlia" reprinted in Archaeologia Cambrensis 1911.

[181] T. Gray Hulse: "A fragment of a reliquary casket from Gwytherin, Denbighshire *"Antiquaries Journal* 72 91-101 (1994).

states that some tenants had held lands from the family of the said Canon who died *"against the peace."* This probably occurred as a result of the Canon participating in Madoc ap Llewelyn's rebellion against Edward I in 1294/95 which was triggered by a heavy tax burden being placed on the conquered lands after 1292. . These references to canons suggest that Gwytherin was at one time a monastic *"clas"* settlement of canons under an abbot, although by the 14th century, the abbot was probably a layman and possibly a descendant of one of the members of the church community.

The lands of the *clas* were held as *"tir gwelyog"* and were hereditary. The hereditary occupants were known as "abbots" (but may not have been clerics) who often sub-let land to under-tenants.[182] The tenants paid a due referred to as *"abbadaeth"* to the abbots who were the progeny of Cynan ap Llywarch. This form of due is also recorded as being paid at Penmon and Aberdaron, both important pre-conquest ecclesiastical centres. The former importance of Gwytherin is also in evidence from the use of the term "canons" which is linked to major ecclesiastical communities though not necessarily monastic ones. The church at Gwytherin was possibly the "mother" church for the medieval commote of Uwch Aled. Leland makes it clear that there was no late medieval monastery or friary in the Elwy valley although he noted *"divers parish churches"* in each of the four commotes that bordered the river.[183]

---

[182] Translated from Latin text in P. Vinogradoff and F. Morgan (ed) London (1914) p187

[183] Lucy Toulmin Smith " Leland's Itinerary in Wales 1536-1539" Bell, London (1906) p93

LLANGERNYW: Church and Churchyard: The next ancient church encountered in the Elwy Valley lies 5.6 kms (3.5 miles) north of Gwytherin in the village of Llangernyw. The church at Llangernyw is dedicated to *St Digain* and like most of the Celtic foundations in the valley sited on a small knoll above the river within a partly curvilinear churchyard. The churchyard was altered by enlargements in 1850 and a long extension to the east in 1884. Parts of the present church date from the thirteenth century[184] but most of what we see today dates from an almost total rebuild in 1881. The church is approached through an attractive lych gate dated 1745, a Grade II listed building. The plan of the church is cruciform; this is unusual in North Wales

Plate 10: St. Digain's Church, Llangernyw

although it would originally have been as single chamber with the transepts added in the late medieval period. The arch-braced roof is thought to be of sixteenth century date while the internal door to the late nineteenth century vestry dates from the fifteenth century. The font is of late medieval perpendicular design. None of the windows are original. The west end of the church housed a gallery until 1845.

---

[184] CPAT "Eastern Conwy Churches Survey : St Digain's Church, Llangernyw, Welshpool (1997)

The Cornish Connection: St. Digain lived in the 5th century and was reputedly the son of a Cornish chieftain with the Roman name of Constantine but known in Celtic as *Custennin*. "*Cernyw*" is the Celtic (and modern Welsh) name for Cornwall. Digain's brother Meirchion ap Custennin was King of Cernyw. Both were descended directly from the post Roman Kings of Dumnonia. A reference to Digain in Llwyd's "Parochlia in the late 17th century gives him the additional title "*Vrenhin*" - king. This reinforces the importance of the Western seaboard route in influencing the monastic development in this part of Wales. A former township in the neighbouring parish of Gwytherin was known as Cornwal It is also significant that the core of the churchyard itself appears to have had a curvilinear plan, typical of ancient church sites from early Christian times.

St. Digain's Well: St. Digain's well, marked on the OS Map as Ffynnon Digain (GR 870685) lies about 1.3 kms NNW of Llangernyw church on the lower slopes of a steep hill. This may provide evidence that the saint resided here, the site of St. Digain's hermitage cell. There are other examples of hermitages being located some distance away from the monastic centre or church. At Penmon, Anglesey, the hermitage of St. Seiriol was located at the foot of a cliff some distance away from the monastic church.[185] Hermitages such as these may have played the role of a personal retreat for the monks, away from the communal activity around the church

---

[185] Mick Aston "Monasteries in the Landscape" Temple, Stroud (2000) p37

The Early Christian Pillar Stones: Like Gwytherin, Llangernyw churchyard contains early Christian inscribed pillar stones. In Llangernyw, the two stones are inscribed with crosses and are thought to date from the 9th or 10th century[186] AD although Nash-Williams ascribes an earlier date of 7th-9th centuries[187]. Earlier cross marked stones such as these at Llangernyw can be matched in the Paris area were some have been found in situ over 7th and 8th century graves which lends support to Nash Williams' chronology.[188] The stones (see Plate 11) both lie close to the south transept of the church. They may be early headstones. A further inscribed stone has been unearthed in the parish in a field sloping down to the Elwy at *Bryngwylan* (GR 697889) about 3kms north east of the village. However, it is incomplete and contains only the letters "*VERE*" Close to the inscribed stones on the south side of the church lie two large stones deeply embedded into the ground. They may well be the remains of a megalith although what remains is too fragmentary to be clearly identified as such. **Plate 11**

The Ancient Yew: (Plate 12) In the churchyard stands a large yew tree its trunk

---

[186] Helen Burnham "Clwyd & Powys" Cadw/HMSO London (1995) p 94
[187] V.E. Nash Williams "The Early Christian Monuments of Wales" Cardiff (1950)
[188] J Knight "The Early Christian Latin Inscriptions of Britain and Gaul : Chronology and Context In Edwards and Lane (ed) ibid 1992 p50

Ancient yew tree Llangernyw

now dissected by time into several separate sections. The tree caused a stir of excitement in the mid 1990s when researchers discovered that, in their opinion, the tree was at least 4000 years old, possibly the earliest living thing in Wales. This brought interested dendrologists from across the world to this sleepy village. The existence of this tree is of some historical significance since yews were traditionally planted in sacred places which means, if the dating is correct, that this churchyard may have played a religious role long before the time of Christ. However, a recent study is more circumspect about the age of this tree and places it at around 1500 years old, perhaps dating from the first Christian occupancy of the site.[189] Yews were possibly deliberately planted in churchyards as markers, to provide shelter for the dead and symbolism of everlasting life at a site.[190] The worship of trees in Celtic Christian communities has some documentary credibility since a 7th century canon of St. Cummin proscribed the worship of trees and wells.[191]

---

[189] R Bevan-Jones "The Ancient Yew" Windgather Press, Macclesfield (2002) p49
[190] R. Bevan-Jones "The Ancient Yew" Windgather Press, Macclesfield (2002) p33
[191] Francis Jones "The Holy Wells of Wales" Univ. Of Wales Press, Cardiff (1992) p22

Monastic Links ?: A piece of documentary evidence hints that the church at Llangernyw may have had a monastic past, or alternatively, links as a daughter church to a monastic church at Llanelwy. The church is not mentioned in the 1254 taxation returns but is linked with the churches of Faenol and Tremeirchion in the 1291 returns. The evidence is in the form of 13th and 14th century references to an episcopal officer known as *"sygynnab"* being present at both Llangernyw and Llanelwy. The official acted as a bailiff to the bishop and represented him in court The name is derived from the Latin *"secundas abbas"* presumably the prior of a monastic foundation.[192] The house of *Hafodunos*, also in the parish, is according to local tradition, thought to have had monastic connections.

LLANFAIR TALHAEARN: Church and Churchyard: The Church of St Mary and St. Talhaearn at Llanfair Talhaearn, almost 9 kms (5.5 miles) downstream from Llangernyw is set on a steep hill above the river safe from floods. The village may take its name from St Aelhaearn, a follower of St Bueno to whom chapels have been dedicated in the Clwyd Valley. The church was partially re-dedicated to St Mary in post Norman times. It was first mentioned in a taxation document of 1254 as "Llanaber" church although the churchyard is polygonal in shape, there is a hint of curvilinearity on its south side

Plate 13

---

[192] J.W. Evans "The Early Church in Denbighshire" Trans. Denbs, Hist Soc. Vol 35 (1966) p72

which suggests an early medieval date. The curvilinear nature of the churchyard is more obvious in the mid nineteenth century tithe map but the original churchyard was extended in 1870. The present building, is double-naved and dates from around 1600. The lower wall of the north side nave may, however, be of medieval origin.[193]. As with most North Wales rural churches, it was "restored" in Victorian times (1839 & 1876), although it is thought that parts of the roof timbers may be of medieval date [194] The influence of the Wynne family is very apparent in the church with funerary memorials to members of the family dating from 1692 to 1842.

WIGFAIR: St. Mary's Chapel: (Plate III) Some 10 kms (6.25 miles) downstream of Llanfair Talhaearn on the left bank of the Elwy as it emerges from its limestone gorge section, is a ruined medieval chapel that is located within the ancient township of Wigfair. The building served as a chapel of ease for the cathedral at St Asaph until it ceased to be used in the seventeenth century. Such chapels were used to provide a place of worship for rural populations living some distance away from the parish church, in this case the cathedral in St. Asaph was almost 8 km (5 miles) away. Such chapels offered only a mass but no baptism or burials. Unlike many other chapels of ease, Wigfair chapel did not evolve into a parish church although one was built to serve the area in 1865, long after the chapel had become ruinous. The ruins are still very evocative and rather overgrown and indicate that the chapel was built

---

[193] CPAT "Eastern Conwy Churches Survey : St Mary Llanfair Talhaearn Welshpool (1997)
[194] Edward Hubbard: "The Buildings of Wales: Clwyd" Penguin Harmondsworth. P 209

possibly as early as the thirteenth century with some major rebuilding during the fifteenth century.[195] The fifteenth century extension to the chapel may well reflect the wealth created by gifts from pilgrims visiting the adjacent holy well. Certainly money derived from this source was used to enhance the fabric of other churches in North Wales, notably St. Winifred's in Holywell, Llanrhaeadr in the Vale of Clwyd and Llanddwyn on Anglesey[196]. The present ruins are T shaped in plan. The original medieval chapel forming the horizontal of the T with the vertical being represented by the new wing in the fifteenth century. Today, water from the well basin still flows through the interior of the chapel.

Ffynnon Fair: A popular destination of pilgrims in late medieval times when well cults enjoyed some popularity, the well is dedicated to Mary and known as *"Ffynnon Fair"* (Mary's well or spring) It is set within a fifteenth century polygonal stone basin to the north west of the chapel and formerly had a stone canopy[197]. The eight pointed star shape of the stone basin is similar in design to that at the well of St. Winifred at Holywell. The fifteenth century well canopy like the extension to the building may well reflect the wealth derived from gifts from pilgrims visiting the well site. On one side of the well a stone bath has been added, it has been suggested that this was a nineteenth century addition, a time when there was renewed interest in holy wells.[198] The name of the township "Wigfair" is

---

[195] Helen Burnham "A Guide to Ancient & Historic Wales - Clwyd and Powys" Cadw/HMSO (1995) p 180

[196] Francis Jones "The Holy Wells of Wales" Univ. Of Wales Press, Cardiff (1992) p50

[197] Samuel Lewis "A Topographical Dictionary of Wales" 1849

[198] H Burnham (1995) ibid p181 edition.

translated as "Mary's retreat" and thus the chapel and well may have a long history since the township was mentioned in the Survey of 1334.

The use of the well, and indeed all such holy wells, was suppressed along with pilgrimages in the Reformation of the 1540s which brought about the abandonment of many chapels of ease throughout the country[199]. This particular chapel appears to have survived as a place of worship for a further hundred years. There is also some evidence that the pilgrimages to the site continued for at least seventy years after the Reformation, a rhyming calendar dated to 15th August (1609) contains the entry :

"Gwyl fair gyntaf o'r cynhaeaf, y sbort a gair yn Ffynnon Fair" which tells us that there were sport and word(s) at Ffynnon Fair on the first feast of Mary in Harvesttime (The feast of the Assumption). [200]

The site was fenced in during the 1840s and a garden constructed around the chapel in the Ruskinite tradition from which rockeries and some bamboo plantings still survive. The chapel and well stand on privately owned land but are well worth seeking permission to visit. The present day ruins are very romantic and would still have delighted Ruskin. In fact, the ruins inspired one of Britain's most eminent "Romantic" poets, Felicia Hemans, to compose a

---

[199] PEH Hair "The Chapel in the English Landscape" The Local Historian, Vol.21 No.1 (1991) pp 4-10.
[200] D R Thomas "The History of the Diocese of St Asaph" Vil. 1, Caxton Press, Oswestry (1908) p395

poem about the site in the 1820s. The poem was entitled *"Our Lady's Well"*. The opening verse of the poem celebrates the attractive setting of the well within its ruined chapel[201]:

> *"Fount of the woods! thow art hid no more*
> *From heaven's clear eye, as in time of yore.*
> *For the roof hath sunk from thy mossy walls,*
> *And the sun's free glance on thy slumber falls;*
> *And the dim tree-shadows across thee pass,*
> *As the boughs are swayed oe'r thy silvery glass;*
> *And the reddening leaves to thy breast are blown,*
> *When the autumn wind hath a stormy tone;*
> *And thy bubbles rise to the flahing rain -*
> *Bright fount ! thou art nature's own again !*

The township of Wigfair has formed part of the parish of Cefn Meiriadog since its creation from the ancient parish of Llanelwy in 1865. The name Meiriadog relates to a Celtic monk who possibly had a hermitage somewhere in this area, probably close to the River Elwy. Meiriadog moved from the area to Cornwall before founding a chapel with a

---

[201] From "Our Lady's Well" : "Poems" - Felicia Hemans, The Co-operative Publication Society, New York (1914) p 319

holy well at Pluvigner in southern Brittany[202]. We do not know whether these foundations were modelled on the well and chapel at Wigfair but the links with Cornwall and Brittany reinforce the links with other Brythonic Celtic lands along the Western Seaboard that were noted further upstream in the Elwy Valley.

St. ASAPH: Cathedral and Parish Church: Some 8 kms (5 miles) after leaving the limestone gorge, the Elwy reaches the cathedral city of St. Asaph (Llanelwy). The Elwy valley's only urban centre lies on a hill of boulder clay left when the Irish Sea ice sheet melted here some 14000 years ago. A 19th century topographer described the city's location as follows:

Plate 14

"The view of the city from many points around it, is particularly striking, its elevated position on an eminence near the termination of the Vale of Clwyd , crowned on its summit with the Cathedral, and having the parish church at its base, makes it a conspicuous object from every point of view."[203]

Monastic Beginnings: The Cathedral probably has its origins in the late 6th century but here, as in the foundations of early

---
[202] Dewi Roberts "The Old Villages of Denbighshire and Flintshire" Carreg Gwalch Publishers, Llanrwst 1999 p 19
[203] William Davis "A Handbook of the Vale of Clwyd" (1856)

monasteries elsewhere in North Wales, it is necessary to be cautious since the evidence for the earliest church in the city is based on legend and tradition rather than on hard archaeological evidence or any written evidence dating from before the twelfth century. . In "The Life of St. Kentigern", a book written by Jocelyn, a monk from Furness Abbey, around 1180, it is stated that St' Kentigern, the bishop of Strathclyde, was forced to flee his bishopric owing to a rise in anti-Christian sentiment. He settled in the lower Elwy Valley where he founded a church and large monastery at Llanelwy between the years 560 and 573 AD. We do not know whether the church and monastery shared the same site or whether they were on the site of the present day cathedral. It is possible that, as occurred elsewhere in Wales, St. Kentigern made use of the ready made site of the former Roman settlement of Varae which was probably located somewhere on, or very near to, the site of the present day city. As yet, no archaeological evidence of the exact site of either Varae or the monastery has been forthcoming.

In 573, St. Kentigern returned to Glasgow leaving one of his monks, St. Asaph, as abbot of the monastery. St. Asaph died in 596AD but his name lives on in that of the Cathedral and town. St. Asaph's name is also evident in place names in the surrounding areas of North Wales such as Llanasa (Asa's enclosure) GR 107815; Pantasaph (Asa's hollow) GR 161760; Ffynnon Asa (Asa's well) and Onen Asaph (Asa's ash tree) GR 082752, located on the line of the Roman road heading eastwards some 5 kms from St. Asaph. These place names, some of which are up to 13 kms (8 miles) away to the east in Flintshire, support the view that in the late 6th century the monastic "clas" at Llanelwy had expanded to take on the role of a "mother church" serving a much wider community. . The settlement, and presumably its church, survived the Anglo Saxon settlement for Llanelwy is recorded, if only briefly, in the

Domesday Book of 1086 as being held by the Norman Robert of Rhuddlan from Earl Hugh of Chester.[204] It has been suggested that the Church owned lands in the area that fell outside Robert of Rhuddlan's control and that the low population, small amount of arable land and the church at Llanelwy with its attendant hamlet went unrecorded in Domesday Book[205]

The Cathedral The town became a see in 1141 with a Norman known as "Gilbert" as its first bishop. A new cathedral church was built in 1152 on the present site (GR 039743) by Bishop Geoffrey of Monmouth. Whether this previous church was on this site is unknown. The new church was modest in proportion for Giraldus Cambrensis described it as *"a poverty stricken little cathedral"* on the occasion of his visit in 1188. A rebuild was carried out between 1235 and 1240 but the newly refurbished cathedral was accidentally burned down by English troops supporting the Edwardian conquest of Wales in 1282. The troops concerned were promptly excommunicated by Bishop Anian who fell out of favour with Edward I since he had previously refused to excommunicate Welsh rebels. The bishop was forced to flee the diocese and the amount paid for rebuilding by the Exchequer was a paltry £100. Anian returned to his see to supervise the rebuilding of the Cathedral in 1284 and his presence is still evident in the building since his carved effigy can be seen in the aisle of the south nave. Further rebuilding took place in 1381 but much of the work was undine by Welsh soldiery in Owain Glyndwr's rebellion who burned the building in 1402. The major rebuild that followed was not was carried out until 1490 when the square central tower was built to which

---

[204] Philip Morgan (ed) "Domesday Book Vol. 26, Cheshire" Philimore, Chichester (1978) 269a
[205] Glanville R. J. Jones "Medieval Settlement" in Manley et al (ibid) 1991 p 192

battlements were added in 1714.[206]   Also dating from the 15th century rebuild are the finely carved wooden canopied stalls by the high altar now unique in Wales. The impressive pillars and arches of the nave survived the fire and are of 14th century date. The traveller, Jinny Jenks attended a service in the cathedral in 1772 and describes her impressions of the occasion:

"A fine soft-toned organ, extremely well played and they have good voices, particularly a remarkable fine counter-tenor and a very good bass, and they chanted an anthem most delightfully before the sermon"

Miss Jenks was particularly impressed by the bishop who gave the blessing noting that he was *"a very handsome man with a pleasing countenance"* In contrast; she describes the bishop's wife as *"plain"*. Her comments also give an insight into the social milieu of a cathedral service in that period. She concludes that

"it is a pretty sight to see the common people after the service, range themselves in each of the back aisles (as they come in great numbers when the bishop is down) while the gentry make a gay figure down the middle one, and being most genteel families that live at a distance, there is as much chatting as with us"[207]

The Cathedral was "restored" by Sir Gilbert Scott during the period 1867-1875.

---

[206] S. Heath and P. Row "Our Homeland Cathedrals"; Homeland, London (undated) p191
[207] "A Tour in North Wales by Jinny Jenks, 1772" Nat. Library of Wales MS 27753B p 50

St. Kentigern's and St. Asaph Parish Church: A short distance to the west of the Cathedral at the bottom of the High Street, stands St. Asaph's other medieval church double naved parish church dedicated to St. Kentigern and St. Asaph. (GR 040744). The building dates from the 13th century and has magnificent hammer beamed roofs in both aisles of which the south aisle is the older. The double aisled style was a popular way of extending a church in late medieval times and became almost a fashion in the rebuildings of the late 15th and early 16th centuries in the Vale of Clwyd.[208] Other examples in the Elwy basin include Llannefydd, Llansannan and Llanfair Talhaearn parish churches. The church was restored in 1872. The churchyard is curvilinear which may indicate that the site may be very early and possibly that of the original monastic establishment.

Plate 15

---

[208] Edward Hubbard "The Buildings of Wales : Clwyd" (1986) p31

Within the river basin of the Elwy lie three other ancient church sites. Two of these are set in the valleys of tributary streams. These are the church of St. Sadwrn at Henllan on the Afon Meirchion, (Plate 16) and the church of St. Sannan at Llansannan on the River Aled.(Plate 17) In an upland area between these two tributary streams stands the ancient "llan" of Llannefydd with its church dedicated to St. Nefydd and St. Mary the Virgin (Plate 18).

HENLLAN: Church and Churchyard: St. Sadwrn's Church at Henllan (GR 022681) presumably began its life as the cell of St. Sadwrn who was born in Brittany around 485.AD. The name "Henllan" "means old enclosure which indicates an early date of establishment of a Christian cemetery on the site. The churchyard, despite its potentially ancient origins, is not curvilinear but quadrilateral in shape and overlooks the Afon Meirchion.

Plate 16

The medieval church which consisted of a nave and chancel was replaced by a new building in 1806 although a 14th century vestry door and the late medieval east window were retained from the earlier building. The same is true of portions of the lower walls that may date from the fifteenth century or even earlier.[209]. The church was subsequently restored in 1844 and 1879 when the porch was added and a gallery removed. Within the church, only a trefoiled piscina remains from the fittings of the medieval church. Outside the porch is the 2m high octagonal remains of the shaft of a preaching cross that once stood outside the gate of the churchyard and the bowl of the medieval font now set on a modern plinth.

The unusual feature in this church is its detached tower reminiscent of medieval churches in Italy. This stands on a rocky knoll some distance to the east of the church and is of 15th century date. Local tradition states that the detached tower was placed above the church in order for the sound of the bells to carry further. As in Llangernyw, the holy well associated linked with the founder of the church is remote from the site of the church itself. Edward Llwyd recorded that the well of St. Sadwrn was located in the grounds of the house known as Foxhall[210] about a kilometre south east of the church. The site of this ancient well appears to now be lost.

LLANSANNAN: Church and Churchyard: The church of St. Sannan in Llansannan is built high on a river terrace above the Aled River (see Plate 25) and is thought to have begun its existence as the cell of St. Sannan an

---

[209] CPAT "Denbighshire Churches Survey" Welshpool (1997)

[210] R H Morris (ed) "Edward Llwyd's Parochlia" reprinted in Archaeologia Cambrensis Supplement (911)

Irish-born priest and contemporary of St David. The churchyard is partly curvilinear which may support early use of the site as a graveyard.

Plate 17: St. Sannan's Church, Llansannan

The Norwich Taxation documents of 1254 represent the first historical reference to this double-naved church but the oldest surviving elements may date to the fifteenth century. The medieval church was recorded as being in a dilapidated state in 1731 thus it was largely rebuilt in 1778 and "restored" further in 1879 when the gallery was removed. One recent survey has claimed that no medieval architectural features have survived the eighteenth and nineteenth century restorations.[211]

LLANNEFYDD: Church and Churchyard: The parish of Llannefydd extends to the River Elwy

---

[211] CPAT " Eastern Conwy Churches Survey : St Sannan, Llansannan" Welshpool (1997)

which marks its northern boundary. The church of St. Nefydd and St. Mary the Virgin (see Plate 18) lies in the village of Llannefydd about 2 kms (1.25 miles) south west of the river on an ancient route linking the Clwyd and Conwy valleys. The present day church, which has been described by a leading Welsh historian as the most attractive double-naved church in North East Wales,[212] is of the perpendicular style popular in church rebuildings of the late 15th and early 16th centuries. Thus the church may be representative of the many churches re-built in Wales after the end of the Wars of the Roses in 1485. Inside the church there are clues to its much older origins, the font is dated 1668 and a stone circular-headed cross slab thought to date from the early 14th century.[213] There is also a late 14th century effigy of Edward ab Iorweth. The church was whitewashed inside and out in the early nineteenth century as where most churches in the valley. The double western bellcote was rebuilt during a restoration in 1859.

Plate 18

---

[212] John Davies "The Making of Wales" Cadw/Sutton, Stroud (1996) p63

[213] Edward Hubbard : "The Buildings of Wales :Clwyd" Penguin Harmondsworth p200

In 1909, the interior of the church was re-structures with the removal of the gallery and box pews. The pulpit was also moved to its present location at that time.[214]

Plate 19 Remains of preaching cross, Llannefydd Churchyard

The church is thought to have been originally the cell of St. Nefydd and thus of 5th or 6th century origin but is not mentioned in any documentation until the Lincoln Taxation assessment of 1291. The church is described in the document as *a* chapel subject to the cathedral at St Asaph: *'Ecclesia de Laundid est Capella Cathedral'*" However, the raised churchyard is curvilinear on its north-east side which possibly indicates that this churchyard was originally curvilinear and therefore probably an ancient one. There is some field name evidence that the church once stood to the south west of its present site outside the churchyard for there is a field known as "*Pant yr hen eglwys*" (hollow of the old church) at this point. In 1966, the church roof was in need of repair in 1966 and, in keeping with the disregard for our architectural heritage that typified that decade, it was suggested that the church be demolished. Fortunately, common sense prevailed and the roof was repaired in 1972.

Cross shaft Llannefydd

---

[214] Gwyn Foulkes Jones "A History of the Church of St. Nefydd and St. Mary Llannefydd" (1995)

A Monastic Past ?: There is also a very tenuous indication that perhaps the original hermitage of St. Nefydd was, or had links to, a monastic *"clas"* settlement. The sole indication of this is in the name of one of the parish's ancient townships known as *"Tir yr abad"* which translates as "land of the abbot" One authority has claimed that Llannefydd was once a "mother" church in the area.[215] However, the lack of parish status in 1291 would bring this into question. *Tir yr abad Isaf* was also known as *Llannefydd uwch mynydd* and now forms the parish of Pentre Foelas. However, until 1729, it was part of the parish of Llannefydd. This area of upland grazing once formed part of the estates of the monks of Aberconwy. Neither this township nor the village itself is recorded in the 1334 Survey of the Honour of Denbigh. It has been shown that elsewhere in Wales there were some federations of monastic houses. These formed scattered communities which were subject to the abbot of the "mother" house[216]. However, it seems possible that in the case of Llannefydd, the mother church would have been that of the monks of Aberconwy or more likely the cathedral at St. Asaph of which the village church was a chapel.

In the Elwy valley, as elsewhere in Wales, our knowledge of early churches has been impaired by the actions of late 19th century "restorers" who made major structural changes or even completely demolished medieval church structures. Only rarely has it been possible to excavate church sites in order to investigate earlier structures on the site.

---

[215] D.R. Thomas "The History of the Diocese of St. Asaph" Vol.1 Caxton Press, Oswestry 1908)
[216] W Davies "The Myth of the Celtic Church" in N Edwards and A. Lane (ed) ibid (1992) p15

CHAPTER 8: THE MEDIEVAL POLITICAL LANDSCAPE

Post Roman Political Structures: Following the departure of Roman forces, Wales in the 5th century could be described as being made up of a number of petty, nominally Christian, states almost permanently at war with one another. Yet, the period AD 400 - 600 has been described by an eminent Welsh historian as *"wholly central to the history of Wales"* a period that saw the transformation of the language of the Brythonic Celts into what was to emerge as Welsh.[217] At the apex of Welsh society were successful British warlords who established successful tribal dynasties.[218] The establishment of these dynasties was to some extent related to their success in repelling attacks by the Irish. The Elwy Valley would perhaps have been threatened by Irish attacks from c429AD but there is no evidence to date of Irish settlement in the valley.

A recent research paper has explored the social context of the tribal groups who inhabited Wales in the immediate pre and post-Roman eras. The author claimed that in tribal societies, the landscape was an expression of the economic process of exchange rather than one of production. Thus tribal leaders in these early societies controlled people, not land. The role of the chieftains was to control and regulate the processes of exchange through the tribal centres such as the fort at *Mynydd y Gaer* that would be the focus of their authority. The emergence of larger

---

[217] John Davies "A History of Wales" Penguin, London (1993) p45
[218] N. Higham "Rome, Britain and the Anglo Saxons" Sealy, London (1992) p87

kingdoms in Wales by the eleventh or twelfth centuries was to change this since the new ruling classes diverted their ambitions to the control of territory through cantrefi, commotes and townships, rather than people.[219]

Political Structures in North Wales: A strong relationship has been noted between the areas ruled by the larger early medieval Welsh kingdoms and those inhabited by tribal groups in the pre Roman Iron Age.[220] The lands of the Elwy basin would have been in lands probably occupied by the Deceangli tribe although the western and south western areas may have been occupied by the Ordovices tribes. The lands of the latter were to emerge as the nucleus of the powerful kingdom of Gwynedd. The Elwy river itself was the boundary between two *"cantrefs"* in early medieval times and it is possible that both these cantrefs of Rhufoniog and Rhos were themselves petty kingdoms for a time following the Roman withdrawal. The lesser dynasties that controlled these cantrefs may have lasted until the 1120s under the control of Gwynedd to whom they had turned for protection and later would have been subsumed into the patrimony of Gwynedd.[221]

A Possible Role fir Mynydd y Gaer Hill Fort: The stratum of Welsh society immediately below the warrior king was made up of the king's bodyguard, *"comitatus"*. Contemporary documents indicate that this layer of lesser

---

[219] Rhys Jones "Institutions in Medieval Wales - the change from a tribal landscape to a landscape of the state." Conference Report of the Society for Landscape Studies. (1996)
[220] M. Green and R Howell "Celtic Wales" University of Wales Press, Cardiff. (2000) p87
[221] Roger Turvey "The Welsh Princes 1063 - 1283" Longmans, London (2002) p 22

aristocracy was frequently led by a person related to the warrior king, either a son or nephew.[222] There is place name evidence of early medieval occupation of the hillfort at *Mynydd y Gaer*. Early documents refer to the fort as "*Din Gadfael*" (Cadfael's fort), the ancient township in which the fort is situated also bears that name. Cadfael was thought by Ellis Davies to be synonymous with Catguallaun (Cadwallon), son of the early seventh century king of Gwynedd (Cadfan) and a descendant of the chieftain Cunedda[223]. However, Cadwallon was a major political figure on a national scale killed in a battle with the English in 634,[224] and it looks unlikely that he would have lived in such a remote location as *Mynydd y Gaer*. If, on the other hand, Davies was right, it may indicate post Roman occupation but there are no traces of hut circles and until a scientific excavation of the site is carried out, the answer to the question will remain within the realms of speculation. If the fort was occupied in this period, its occupant was perhaps one of the king's bodyguards holding estates in the Elwy valley.

The Re-occupation of North Wales Hill Forts: There is, however, evidence of post Roman occupation of hilforts from this area of North East Wales such as nearby *Dinorben,* where, in post Roman times a kinship group dwelt under the auspices of a clan chief. Excavations have revealed that *Dinorben* had a large round hut occupied in the 3rd and 4th century AD, this was superseded by an aisled house at the end of the 4th century. It has been suggested that the aisled dwelling is possibly the result of the clan chief choosing to live within a secure area of the hillfort

---

[222]/ Alcock "Arthur's Britain" Pelican, Harmondsworth (1973) p 324

[223] Canon Ellis Davies "Prehistoric and Roman Remains of Denbighshire" (1929)

[224] John Davies " A History of Wales" Penguin, London (1993) p63

following the Roman withdrawal. Possible parallel developments in *Castle Dore* in Cornwall and *Tidbury Rings*, Hampshire have been identified[225]. Hill forts close to the coast at *Bryn Euryn* and *Deganwy* were also occupied in the post Roman period probably to protect the population from the Irish raids of the 5th and 6th centuries. Throughout North Wales, many hill forts were still in use in the 6th century AD, they were used as sites of rulers' households in the troubled times of the post Roman period until relative stability allowed the use of a more favourable lowland site from the 7th century after which most hilltop sites were abandoned until the advent of Anglo-Norman invasions of the 11th and 12th centuries.

The Role of Cunedda: The situation was complicated further by invasions of the North Wales coastal lands by outsiders. According to *Historia Brittonum*, a 9th century compilation of historical data, Cunedda, and his sons are thought to have led an invasion of North Wales. It is not known whether the invaders were Christian but they are thought to have arrived from Scotland by sea in the early 5th century. Cunedda's home territory is believed to have been that of the *Votadini*, from around the shores of the Firth of Forth near Edinburgh[226]. The raison d'etre for the invasions assumed to be to protect North Wales from Irish invaders in the post Roman period, a task apparently carried out successfully. It is possible that Cunedda's men actually arrived during the Roman occupation having

---

[225] S Applebaum : "The Pre Roman Heritage" in HPR Finberg (ed) The Agrarian History of England & Wales , Vol1 (ii) AD43 - 1042; CUP (1972)

[226] M. Green and R Howell "Celtic Wales" University of Wales Press, Cardiff. (2000) p79

been invited in as mercenaries in the second half of the 4th century by Magnus Maximus, the commander of the Roman army in Britain and a future contender for the imperial throne of Rome.[227]

By the time the monk Gildas was writing *De Excidio Brittaniae ("Concerning the Fall of Britain")*, around 530-540 AD, the writer was able to identify the emergence of five major kingdoms in Britain From this, it is likely that the Elwy valley fell under the control of one of these emergent kingdoms, Gwynedd, ruled by Maelgwn (born c480), a great grandson of Cunedda, whose citadel was located at *Deganwy*[228] just 14 kms (8.75 miles) North West of the Elwy valley.

There are numerous churches in North Wales dedicated to the saintly descendants of Cunedda. Dedications include those to *Einion, Meirion, Frenhin, Seiriol, Eurgain and Edern*. In addition many North Wales royal houses later claimed descent from Cunedda in fact the sub-kingdom of Rhufoniog takes its name from the son of Cunedda who was given these lands: "*Rhwfon*" born around 426 AD. A northern chieftain associated with the Cunedda incursion, *Coel Godebog* is said to have sired numerous saints after whom further dedications ensued throughout North Wales. These include *Deiniol, Collen* and the Elwy valley's *Asaph*. Professor Emrys Bowen claimed that the points of entry of northern settlers influenced the setting up of early Christian dioceses. Those that entered via the Menai Straits and

---

[227] Leslie Alcock "Arthur's Britain" Penguin, Harmondsworth (1973) p 98
[228] Leslie Alcock "Arthur's Britain" Pelican, Harmondsworth. (1973) p121

Conwy estuary created the Bangor diocese while those that entered via the Clwyd and Dee estuaries created the St Asaph diocese[229].

The Rise of Gwynedd: During the second half of the 9th century, the Elwy Valley still lay within the kingdom of Gwynedd which controlled both the kingdoms of Powys and Ceredigion with the king Rhodri Mawr (d.877) ruling most of Wales. By exploiting the internal divisions among the Welsh during the early10th century, Anglo Saxons were able to extend their influence to the Clwyd valley at Rhuddlan, the site of Wales' only known burh "*Cledemutha*" founded in 921 by Edward the Elder. It has been suggested that this burh was built with the acquiescence of Gwynedd as a protection against the Viking raids that plagued the area from the ninth to eleventh centuries[230]. *Cledemutha* failed as a settlement around the mid 10th century at a time that the power of Gwynedd was once more being extended westwards into north east Wales by Rhodri Mawr's grandson, Hywel Dda (c920-950), who consolidated these gains and extended the kingdom by marriage to the heiress of Dyfed from 942. After Hywel's death Welsh inheritance traditions of dividing lands between the sons again split the kingdom. A persuasive case has been made to support the claim that after Hywel's death, Gwynedd fell under the control of Irish Sea Vikings during the late tenth and early eleventh centuries[231] although there is no evidence of their presence in the Elwy river basin.

---

[229] Emrys Bowen "The Settlements of the Celtic Saints in Wales" Univ. Of Wales Press, Cardiff (1954) p72
[230] Nancy Edwards "The Dark Ages" in Manley et al (ibid) (1991) p139
[231] Wendy Davies "Patterns of Power in Early Wales" Clarendon Press Oxford (1990) pp56-60

Gruffudd ap Llewelyn of Gwynedd (1039-1064) re-united much of Wales between 1055 and 1064. His defeat and death at the hands of the forces of Harold Godwinson, the future king of England, in 1063 led to fragmentation of Wales making it a disunited region at the time of the Norman Conquest and vulnerable to attacks by the newly established marcher lords. The Normans were thus able to make initial headway into North Wales and held most of the coastal strip through castles at Rhuddlan and Deganwy. They do not appear to have had a secure hold on the Elwy Valley until the Edwardian Conquest of Wales was completed in 1282. However, modern historical opinion is that there was no real desire for the Anglo Saxons, Normans and Anglo Normans to conquer Wales until 1282 since the rulers of England were content with a Wales that was subservient rather than annexed.[232] By 1118, Rhos and Rhufoniog were recovered by Gwynedd and for a time, in the late twelfth century, Gwynedd under Owain Gwynedd (1137-1170) extended to the banks of the Dee itself.

Perfeddwlad: The area to the east of the Conwy and west of the Dee which, of course included the whole of the Elwy river basin, was known as *"Perfeddwlad"* - the "middle" country. The *"Perfeddwlad"* lay between the ancient kingdoms of Powys and Gwynedd and later between the Anglo Saxon settlements of Cheshire and north Shropshire and the Welsh heartland of Gwynedd. Between 1081 and 1282, there were no less than 23 royal military expeditions into Wales. There seems little doubt that the lands in the Elwy valley changed hands on a number of occasions and that life here from the fifth to the thirteenth centuries was often turbulent.

---

[232] Roger Turvey "The Welsh Princes 1063 - 1283" Longmans, London (2002) p 65

Political Units in Medieval Wales: Cantrefi; Commotes; Maenolau; Townships: The political unit of land at the heart of early medieval administration of lands in Wales was the *"Cantref"*, a concept possibly copied from the Saxons[233], made up hypothetically of 100 townships and sub-divided into two *"commotes"*. In turn, the commote *(cwmwd)* was made up of 12 *"maenolau"* together with two other township units reserved for use by the king. Originally the commotes *(cymydau)* were political and dynastic in their roles but by the 13th century as kingdoms grew in complexity, the commote, containing a nominal 50 townships, had become the basic unit of administration for lands within Wales[234]. The *"Maenol"* (*"Maenor"* in South Wales) was a smaller administrative unit, an area made up of four townships. The system of *cantrefs* and *commotes* appears to have evolved from the eighth and ninth centuries as a means of governing territory.

Natural frontiers such as the course of rivers or the ridges that formed their watersheds always played a significant part in the history of medieval Wales[235]. The *"Perfeddwlad"* was made up of lands in several *cantrefi*. The cantref of *Rhos* lay between the Elwy and Conwy giving the Elwy importance as an important territorial boundary marker (see Fig.4). *Tegeingl,* a derivation of the Celtic tribal name *"Deceangli"*, lay between the lower Clwyd and the Dee; to the south of the Elwy lay *Rhufoniog*. Each cantref usually contained two commotes. Within the Elwy river basin

---

[233] Gwyn A Williams "When was Wales?" Black Raven Press London (1985) p 48
[234] Roger Turvey "The Welsh Princes 1063 - 1283" Longmans, London (2002) p26
[235] A. D. Carr "Medieval Wales" Macmillan, Basingstoke. (1995) p27

lay two cantrefs, the cantref of *Rhos* was made up of the commotes of *Isdulas* and *Uwchdulas* and the cantref of *Rhufoniog* unusually was made up of three commotes: *Uwchaled*; *Isaled* and *Ceinmeirch*.

The "capital" of a commote was known as a *"maerdref"*, a royal village or township that functioned as the centre of local government[236] from which local taxation and services could be organised. It has also been argued that "mother churches" had large parishes that were sometimes coterminous with the secular boundaries of cantrefs or commotes[237]. If this was the case in the Elwy valley, did the possible *"clas"* at Gwytherin serve pastoral needs of the commote of Uwchaled?

Local Administrative Structures: On an even more local scale, the lord's court or *"llys"* formed the basis of administration of services and collection of payments in kind within a township or group of townships that made up an estate. A *llys* originally denoted an enclosure but later came to refer to the group of buildings within that enclosure.[238] Local lords or their representatives visited their *llysoedd* (plural) to collect their dues which had been assembled there. The royal court was also peripatetic and moved through the maerdrefi collecting taxes. The

---

[236] Glanville R.J. Jones "Some medieval rural settlements in North Wales" Transactions of the. Institute of British Geographers Vol.19 (1953) p 51

[237] N. Edwards and A. Lane (ed) "The Early Church in Wales and the West" Oxnow Monograph 16, Oxford (1992) p3

[238] I.H. Adams "Agrarian Landscape Terms - A Glossary for Historical Geography" Inst. Of British Geographers Special Publication London (1976) p 96

administration of land through the *llysoedd* and *maerdrefi* appears to have been breaking down by the 13th century by which time many services had been commuted to cash payments[239].

"Llysoedd" in the Elwy Basin: There are *several "llys"* place names within the Elwy river basin of which two may represent the former locations of *"llysoedd"*. In Llanfair Talhaearn parish is a riverside farm known as *Henllys*: "old court" (GR 908696) although in this case the "old" should be translated as "former" in most cases. *Henllys* is possibly a moated site[240], drawing water from the Elwy to flood the moat. The moats in sites such as this were not militarily significant and at best could hold off marauders and wild animals. Moats also provided food through fish and wildfowl and may have also carried some social status, impressing other landowners. Could *Henllys* be the predecessor of Garthewin, lying just one kilometre to the north east on a flood free site, as the local *llys*? Garthewin was a township by 1334 and later the home of one of the leading families of local gentry, The Welsh antiquary, Thomas Pennant stated that *Henllys* was once the seat of one *"Hedd Molwynog"* a descendant of the 9th century Welsh prince Rhodri Mawr (Roderic the Great). *Molwynog* is said to have been the chief of one of the 15 tribes of North Wales and a contemporary and supporter of David, son of Owain Gwynedd (1137-1170) which would place

---

[239] Longley D. "The Royal Courts of the Welsh Princes in Gwynedd Ad400 - 1283" in N. Edwards (ibid) (1997)
[240] Jack Spurgeon in Manley et al (1991) p 172

Fig. 4

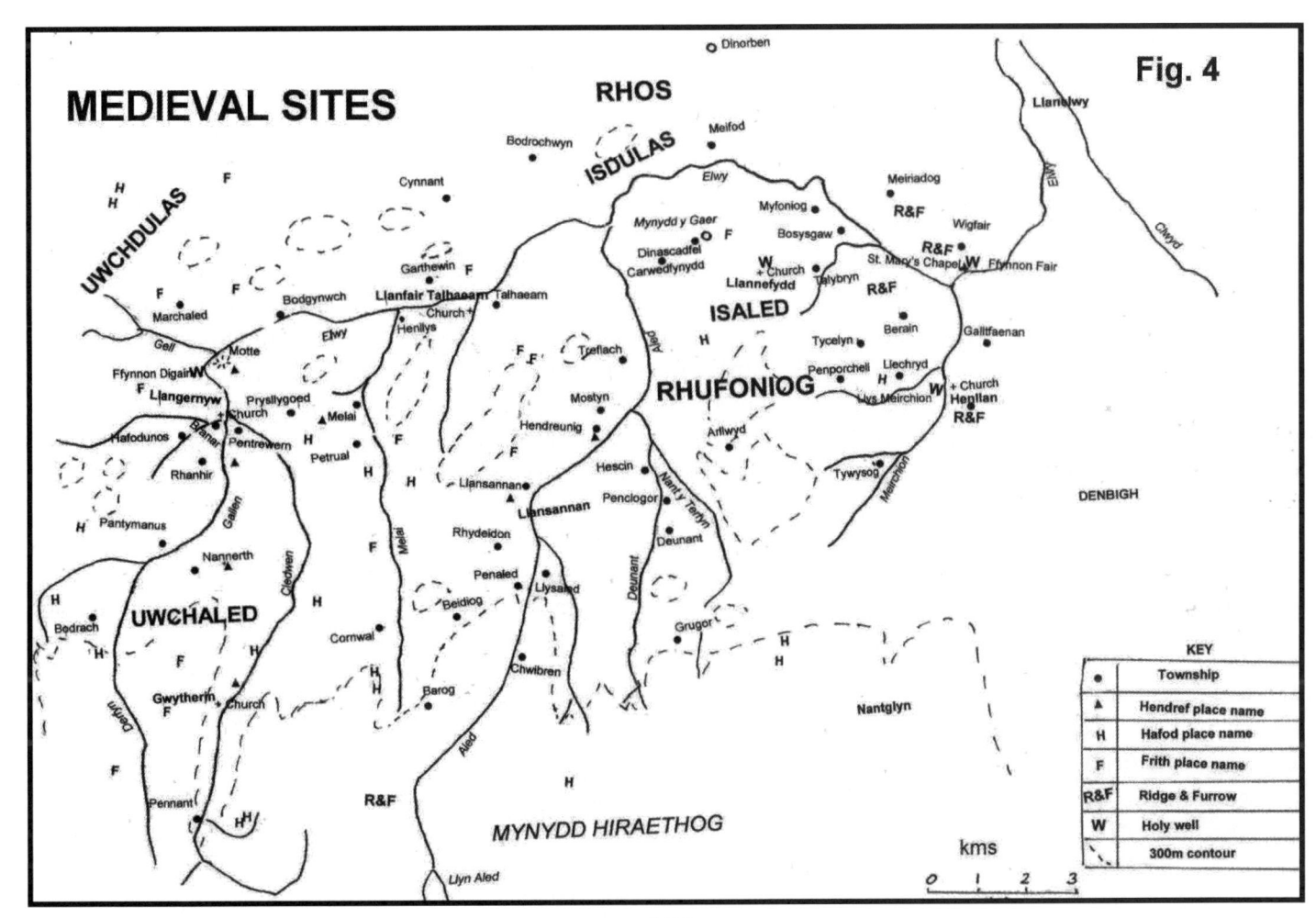

MEDIEVAL SITES

Regions labelled: UWCHDULAS, RHOS, ISDULAS, ISALED, RHUFONIOG, UWCHALED, DENBIGH, MYNYDD HIRAETHOG

Rivers labelled: Elwy, Clwyd, Aled, Meirchion, Nant y Teryn, Deunant, Melai, Cledwen, Gallen, Brân, Gell, Dulyn

Townships and sites: Dinorben, Llanelwy, Bodrochwyn, Meifod, Meiriadog, Cynnant, Myfoniog, Wigfair, Mynydd y Gaer, Bosysgaw, St. Mary's Chapel, Ffynnon Fair, Dinascadfel, Carwedfynydd, Llannefydd, Talybryn, Gartewin, Llanfair Talhaearn, Talhaearn, Marchaled, Bodgynwch, Henilys, Treflach, Tycelyn, Berain, Galltfaenan, Ffynnon Digair, Motte, Penporcheli, Llechryd, Langernyw, Church, Pryslygoed, Melai, Mostyn, Arllwyd, Llys Meirchion, Henllan, Hafodunos, Pentrewern, Petrual, Hendreunig, Rhanhir, Hescin, Tywysog, Pantymanus, Llansannan, Penclogor, Nannerth, Rhydeidon, Deunant, Bedrach, Penaled, Llysaled, Cornwal, Beidiog, Grugor, Gwytherin, Church, Barog, Chwibren, Nantglyn, Pennant, Llyn Aled

KEY

●	Township
▲	Hendref place name
H	Hafod place name
F	Frith place name
R&F	Ridge & Furrow
W	Holy well
⌇	300m contour

kms 0 1 2 3

his residence here in the early 13th century.[241] This would be in keeping with the dating of most of Wales' 140 known moated sites to the period 1200 - 1325.[242]

A second important early medieval *"llys"* can also be identified near Henllan on the banks of the Afon Meirchion, a tributary of the Elwy. The *llys* itself is known as "*Llys Meirchion*" (GR 019682). Thomas Pennant identified this *llys* as the seat of one Meredith ap Meirchion, lord of the commote of Isdulas. The *llys* itself lies in the commote of Isaled. At the time of Pennant's visit (1790) the chapel of the medieval *llys* was in use as a farmhouse. Pennant observed that "some very extensive foundations show its former importance"[243] The farm was not listed as a township in the 1334 Survey of the Lordship of Denbigh and it would seem had lost its role as a *"llys"* by that time. Today's castellated buildings on the site date mainly from 19th century re-building.[244]

The Llangernyw Motte: The Norman Conquest of the lands around the River Elwy was a protracted affair and not fully completed until the Edwardian Conquest of Wales in 1282 when the lands lying within the Elwy Basin were granted to Hugh de Lacy, Earl of Lincoln as part of the newly created marcher lordship of Denbigh or Rhufoniog.

---

[241] Thomas Pennant "A Tour of Wales 1770 " (Vol II)Bridge Books, Wrexham (1991) p 56
[242] John Davies "The Making of Wales" Cadw/Suttin, Stroud (1996) p49
[243] Thomas Pennant (ibid) p 53
[244] Edward Hubbard : "The Buildings of Wales :Clwyd" Penguin Harmondsworth p 179

Only one motte site has been identified in the Elwy valley as a relict landscape feature dating from the troubled period 1066-1282

Medieval motte near Llangernyw

Plate 20

This is therefore possibly one of the 242 mottes built in Wales in the period 1066 - 1200.[245] The motte is small with a 7 metre high mound surrounded by a 2 metre deep ditch.[246] (see Plate 20) There is no bailey although this may lie under the farmyard of the farm standing adjacent to the motte.

Most mottes in Wales represent efforts in the late eleventh century to consolidate the initial Norman territorial gains. The area changed hands on a number of occasions but there is just the single

---

[245] J. Spurgeon "Mottes & Moated Sites" in Manley et al (1991) p 157
[246] Conwy Sites and Monument Record PRN105504

small motte in the valley located about 1.5 kms north of the village of Llangernyw (GR 874688). In the absence of archaeological evidence, it is impossible to date this defensive feature. It may date from the initial eleventh century surge of Norman successes in a Wales when Rhufoniog cantref was annexed by the Norman earls of Chester. There is some similarity in construction to the mottes at Pulford and Dodleston west of Chester built soon after the Conquest.

The Domesday Survey of 1087 says little about the Elwy valley which was not covered other than the settlement of Llanelwy, the ecclesiastical settlement lying close to the river's confluence with the River Clwyd. William I gave Chester to Hugh d'Avranches in 1070 and Hugh's cousin Robert of Rhuddlan was in turn given the motte and bailey at Rhuddlan with a brief to contain the Welsh. Robert unilaterally it seems, decided to extend his sphere of influence and crossed the Clwyd to establish a castle at Deganwy, formerly a Welsh llys in the cantref of Rhos. After capturing Gruffudd ap Cynan, king of Gwynedd, in 1081, Robert assumed control of Gwynedd.

The question arises: was the motte at Llangernyw built to protect these new gains? Robert was killed by raiders supporting Gruffudd ap Cynan, King of Gwynedd, at the foot of the Great Orme in 1093. Gwynedd was free again soon afterwards following an uprising in 1094 when the Normans were pushed back to the east of the Conwy. William II made unsuccessful attempts to regain control in 1095 and 1097. It can be speculated that this could be a raison d'etre for the Llangernyw motte since the eastern border of Gwynedd was, until, 1118, the Conwy Valley and the tiny motte stands some 10 kms east of the Conwy frontier.

There is good documentary evidence that mottes continued to be constructed in Wales until the 13th century[247]. The 12th and early 13th centuries were a time of constant pressure on the lands of Perfeddwlad with the Welsh themselves under Llewelyn the Great (1194-1240), grandson of Owain Gwynedd, building mottes to consolidate control. It could be argued that the Llangernyw motte date might be such a Welsh motte of which there are other examples in North Wales such as *Tomen y Rhodwydd* at Llandegla which was built in 1149 by Llewelyn's grandfather. Welsh motte sites were often chosen for their strategic location as at *Bryn y Castell* in the Conwy valley which guarded the ford *Cafn Gronant* close to the present bridge at Tal y Cafn or the motte at Corwen built by Owain Gwynedd in 1165 to protect access to Snowdonia along the Dee valley. The motte at Llangernyw can also claim a strategic location since it protected a ford over the Elwy 200 metres away known as *Rhyd Pentre*. .

Thus the Llangernyw motte may have been built as a stronghold protecting access to the Conwy valley from the east. However, there is a documentary clue that the motte may well be English and date from this same period of conflict. Welsh chroniclers recorded that King John attacked Perfeddwlad in 1210 forcing the Welsh to flee *"with their chattels"* to Eryri (Snowdonia). In order to consolidate his control of Gwynedd, the king *"built castles therein"*……and then *"went across the River Conwy towards the mountains of Eryri"*. Llewelyn was forced to concede defeat and was obliged to grant the lands of Perfeddwlad to the king *"forever"*[248] "Forever" was something of an understatement since the Welsh regained control of Perfeddwlad in 1212. Thus the occupation of the motte

---

[247] Neil Johnstone "An Investigation into the Location of the Royal Courts of Thirteenth century Gwynedd" in N. Edwards (ed) ibid (1997)
[248] Thomas Jones "Brut y Tywysogion" or the "Chronicle of the Princes" Univ. Of Wales Press, Cardiff (1952) p85

may have been short-lived and may help explain the absence of any contemporary medieval references to its existence.

Finally, there is one further possibility that the motte dates from the final phase of the conquest of 1282 for it is known that in September 1282, that Edward I and his supporter, the Earl of Lincoln made Llangernyw their headquarters in part of a strategy to isolate the Welsh garrison of Denbigh by encircling it.[249] Thus the motte may have been built as part of this campaign. However, it is also possible that Edward I occupied or re-fortified an earlier motte on the site.

Motte Sites and Maerdrefi: One authority has noted that in Gwynedd there is a correlation between the sites of mottes and the locations of *maerdrefi* and that Norman castles were placed deliberately in Welsh centres of administration, hence their links to *maerdrefi*..[250] It has also been argued that this association may also reflect Welsh lords' efforts to defend their *llysoedd*.[251] In neighbouring Caernarfonshire, the Royal Commission noted that there was a pattern of one motte to each commote[252] while a strong relationship has been noted between Norman

---

[249] L.F. Salzman "Edward I" Constable, London (1968) p71

[250] Longley D. "The Royal Courts of the Welsh Princes in Gwynedd AD 400 - 1283" in N. Edwards (ed) ibid (1997)

[251] Neil Johnstone "An Investigation into the Location of the Royal Courts of Thirteenth Century Gwynedd" in N. Edwards (ed) ibid (1997) p61

[252] Royal Commission on Ancient and Historical Monuments in Wales (1964)

mottes and commotal centres in the former county of Meirioneth.[253] The sites of North Wales mottes at Deganwy, Rhuddlan, Denbigh, Bala and Caernarfon correspond to the sites of 13th century maerdrefi. This also suggests that the *maerdrefi* were functioning during the 11th century when these mottes were constructed.[254].This continued use of *maerdrefi* by Norman conquerors suggests that they wished to assume control of existing arrangements for collecting local dues.

The question arises as to whether the Llangernyw motte was located on the site of a lost *maerdref*. This is most unlikely, the motte is undocumented although we know that there were links between the village of Llangernyw and the Diocese of St. Asaph which may have been a major landowner in the village which is not mentioned in the 1334 survey of the Honour of Denbigh. Llangernyw and its townships may therefore have been omitted from the survey because the lands here lay outside of the Honour of Denbigh. One clue to the function of the motte lies in the name of the township in which its stands : "*Marchaled*" The name may well be Norman meaning Aled frontier, perhaps indicating that the motte was located to protect the lands of the commotes of Isaled and Uwchaled presumable from attacks from the west.

Under the Treaty of Aberconwy in 1277, when Llewelyn the Last ceded Perfeddwlad to the Crown, the cantref of Rhos, to the north of the Elwy was seized by the King and Rhufoniog, to the south of the Elwy was given to

---

[253] Neil Johnstone "An Investigation into the Location of the Royal Courts of Thirteenth century Gwynedd" in N. Edwards (ed) ibid (1997)
[254] GRJ Jones "Medieval settlement" in Manley et al ibid (1991)

Llewelyn's brother Dafydd. The Survey of 1334, drawn up to inform the Lord of Denbigh about the state and worth of his newly acquired lands covers most of the Elwy river basin and gives a picture of a society and settlement pattern in transition following the final conquest of the area by the English. Nevertheless, it is clear that in 1334, Welsh traditions of landholding and service were still very much in use throughout the valley. [255]

---

[255] P. Vinogradoff and F. Morgan (ed) "A Survey of the Honour of Denbigh 1334" London (1914)

CHAPTER 9: THE EVOLUTION OF RURAL SETTLEMENT AND AGRICULTURE IN THE MEDIEVAL PERIOD

The fifth and sixth centuries saw deterioration in climate which must have been evident at the time of the Roman departure from Britain. To what extent this deterioration in conditions contributed to the demise of Rome through a reduction in crop yields is a matter of debate. Certainly, studies of cores from present day glaciers indicate a cooling of conditions in northern Europe from c250 to c 450 AD.[256] This climatic deterioration may have contributed to some retreat of permanent settlement from the most inhospitable uplands surrounding the Elwy valley in this period. However, since the dominant form of land utilisation in these uplands was probably transhumance, little may have changed.

Traditions of Mixed Farming: Modern research has shown that the former description of the inhabitants of upland Britain as "footloose Welsh cowboys"[257] was an over simplification and that a much more diverse economy prevailed with a coherent and symbiotic relationship between the valley lowlands and the uplands above the valleys. The overall economy of the Elwy basin in the centuries following the fall of Rome would have changed little from what had gone on before the arrival of Roman forces, namely a mixed farming regime with perhaps some cottage

---

[256] N. Higham "Rome, Britain and the Anglo Saxons" Sealy, London (1992) pp79-80.
[257] S. Piggott "Native Economies" in J. A. Richmond (ed) "Roman and Native in North Britain" Edinburgh (1958) p 25

industries such as leather production and small scale mining of local lead and copper ores. There would have been little trade and no money economy after the turn of the fifth century.

Recent research has also exploded the myth that Welsh hill farming was solely dependent on pastoral activities since the production of arable food crops was always important on favoured sites.[258] This is supported by contemporary evidence for Giraldus Cambrensis; writing in the late twelfth century describes the importance of oats for which land was ploughed three times a year. He noted that the whole population (of Wales) lived almost entirely on oats and the produce of their herds: milk, cheese and butter.[259] Nevertheless, pastoralism was of major importance to local agriculture throughout the medieval period.

Seasonal Movement of People and Animals: Seasonal transhumance was pracrised and in 1334, the waste of Mynydd Hiraethog was used by tenants of all five commotes that made up the Lordship of Denbigh as a source of summer grazing.[260] In the bond hamlet of *Penporchell* in Llannefydd parish bondmen held land 19 kms (12 miles) to the south in the uplands of Mynydd Hiraethog reaching an altitude of 460m (1500 feet). These lands were in the

---

[258] Robert J Silvester "Medieval Upland Cultivation on the Berwyns in North Wales" Landscape History Vol.22 (2000) p47

[259] Lewis Thorpe (translator) "Gerald of Wales : The Journey through Wales/ The Description of Wales" Penguin, Harmondsworth (1988 edition) p233

[260] P. Vinogradoff and F. Morgan (ed) "A Survey of the Honour of Denbigh 1334" London (1914) p 96

township of *Trebrys*.[261] The summer grazing lands were occupied from the traditional moving day: May Day *(Calan Mai)* with All Saints Day *(Calan Gaeaf)* being the traditional day of return to the valley. The departure of the herds to the upland pastures freed the lower land for the production of oats and hay.

The earliest documentary evidence of seasonal occupance of Mynydd Hiraethog dates from the early fourteenth century when several *hafodydd* are mentioned in the 1334 Survey. We also know that by the later twelfth century, extensive properties on the western sides of Mynydd Hiraethog in the cantrefi of Rhufoniog and Rhos were in the hands of the Cistercian monks of Aberconwy who were likely to have exploited these upland pastures for sheep ranching.

"Hafod" Place Names: An insight into the nature of temporary summer occupance of the highest lands in the Elwy river basin may be gained from evidence elsewhere in Wales. The place name *"Hafod"* was often given to the summer residence of the pastoralists. In a study of transhumance in the Black Mountains, it was noted that the majority of summer dwellings in the uplands lay between altitudes of 250 and 350m OD. The majority of the structures were made of dry stone walling, were 10 - 30 m in length and usually contained two compartments. The second compartment or adjacent outbuildings would have been used as a dairy where cows and goats could be

---

[261] G. R. J. Jones The Distribution of Bond Settlements in North West Wales" Welsh History Review Vol.2 (1964). p26

milked and butter and cheese manufactured. The oldest buildings date from the later medieval period, perhaps reflecting the climatic amelioration during the climatic optimum between 1000 and 1300 AD.[262]

A study of Denbighshire *hafod* place names concurs with the above findings in that most *hafodydd* place names occur at around a median altitude of 300 metres.[263] In the Elwy river basin most *hafodydd* place names occur in the more mountainous south west of the basin in the tithe parishes of Llangernyw, Llansannan and Gwytherin (see Fig. 4) on the northern fringes of Mynydd Hiraethog at a slightly lower mean altitude of 256m. In most cases, small enclosures surround the site of the *hafod*. These may represent small milking closes or pens for ewes or calves since both butter and cheese were produced in the *hafodydd*.

"Hendre" Place Names: The winters were spent in the permanently settled home farms often in hamlets in sheltered locations at lower altitudes (at a mean altitude of 205 metres in Elwy basin) frequently bearing the name *"Hendref"* often shortened to *"tref"* which in time became synonymous with a township rather than an individual farm. These were much more substantial structures than the summer dwellings often with a strong cruck frame[264]. It

---

[262] A Ward "Transhumance and Settlement on the Welsh Uplands" in N. Edwards (ed) "Landscape and Settlement in Medieval Wales" Oxbow; Oxford 1997
[263] E Davies "Hendre and Hafod in Denbighshire" Trans. Denbs. Hist. Soc. Vol 26 (1977) p57
[264] E Davies "Hendre and Hafod in Denbighshire" Trans. Denbs. Hist. Soc. Vol 26 (1977) p49

has been suggested that in Cornwall, an area with strong cultural links with North Wales, that the distribution of *tref* place names is an indicator of where the more substantial families lived by the eleventh century.[265]

Arable Sharelands: In the fields around these home farms (known as *tir priod* - clan land) crops were grown to provide bread grains. In some cases, these arable fields were scattered open fields known as "sharelands" (*tir gwasgar*) divided into strips known as quillets (Welsh *lleiniau*). A typical holding of arable land in the early fourteenth century has been estimated to have been between five and ten acres (2 - 4.04 ha) made up of parcels of land in several open field sharelands. A strong case has been made to suggest that communities worked these lands co-operatively sharing ploughs, oxen and labour[266].

Ridge and Furrow in the Landscape: At times, suitable land in the uplands above the valley floors was also brought into cultivation. In North West Wales, land at an altitude of up to 305m (1000 feet) was brought into arable use when the need arose[267]. Recently published research has identified former arable land lying at an altitude of

---

[265] Charles Thomas "Christians, Chapels, Churches and Charters – or "Proto-parochial provisions for the Pious in a Peninsular" (Land's End) Landscape History Vol.11 (1989) p24

[266] GRJ Jones "Field Systems of North Wales" in Baker & Butlin (ed) " Studies of Field Systems of the British Isles" CUP Cambridge (1973) p449

[267] GRJ Jones "Field Systems of North Wales" in Baker & Butlin (ed) " Studies of Field Systems of the British Isles" CUP Cambridge (1973) pp 431-437.

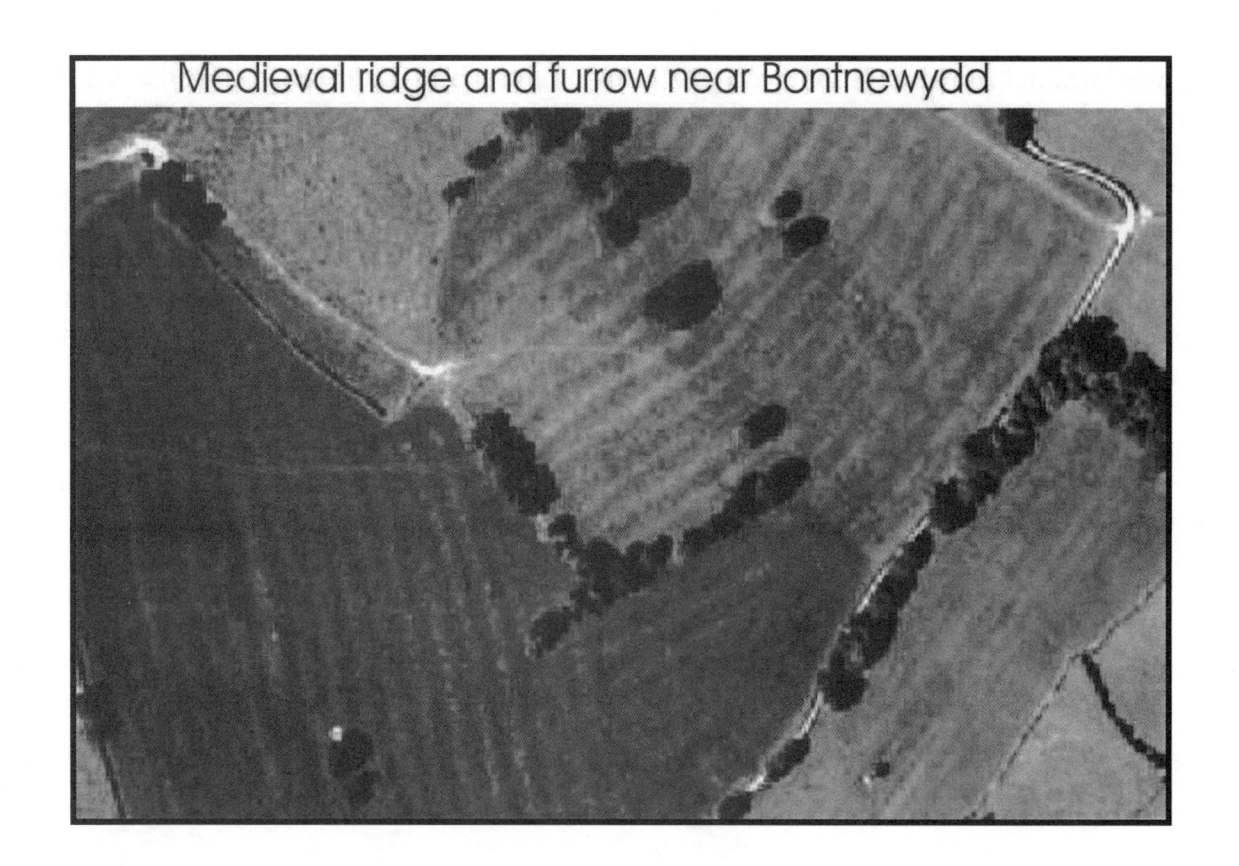

Plate 21

Medieval ridge and furrow near Bontnewydd

around 350m. in Cwm Pennant in the river Dee basin some 27 kms south west of Gwytherin.[268] Aerial photography has identified several sites in the Elwy basin where "ridge and furrow" representing former arable strips are in evidence. As in the case of Cwm Pennant described above, one example alongside the abandoned homestead of *Waen Isaf Las*, is located at an altitude of 380m on a south east facing slope above the upper Aled valley on Bryn Poeth, Mynydd Hiraethog.[269] (GR 905599).

Other examples of ridge and furrow identified from aerial photographs lie at a lower altitude on the Carboniferous limestone rocks in the eastern end of the valley where the soils would have been more easily worked and were more productive. These sites can be seen in Fig. 4 and lie mostly in Cefn Meiriadog parish where the sites were identified from a study of aerial photographs taken in the 1940s[270]. Further sites have been identified in Henllan village and close to the north bank of the Elwy in Bontnewydd. The author has also identified ridge and furrow from recent aerial photographs on the Carboniferous limestone plateau in Llannefydd parish (see Plate 21) 0.75 kms north east of *Berain* (GR 013713). The existence of the majority of ridge and furrow sites from the air in the east of the river basin may reflect the thin nature of the limestone soils and should not be taken as evidence of the absence of arable sharelands elsewhere in the river basin since it is likely that other sites have been ploughed out since medieval times.

---

[268] R. J. Silvester "Medieval Upland Cultivation on the Berwyns in North Wales" Landscape History Vol.22 (2000) p50
[269] W G Owen & R J Silvester "The Mynydd Hiraethog Survey, Clwyd" (64) CPAT, Welshpool (1993) p5
[270] CPAT SMR 34043/4 and 34047/8

Place Name Evidence of Former Arable Lands: Place name evidence does however provide a clue to the location of other arable sharelands in the valley. The place name *"Rhanhir"* translates as shareland and has survived in three locations in the river basin. *Rhan Hir Farm* lies 05 kms south of Llangernyw village (GR 875670) while a further *Rhan Hir* place name is recorded on the first edition OS map at an altitude of 370m on Mynydd Hiraethog (GR 696370) 2 kms south west of Bylchau. Like the ridge and furrow at *Waen Isaf Las*, just 6 kms to the west on Mynydd Hiraethog, the sharelands here may have been established to serve the needs of an expanding population at a time of relatively favourable climatic conditions, possibly in the thirteenth century. The township of Tywysog in Henllan parish (GR 003667) was once also known by the name *Rhan Hir*. The township of Tywysog was described in the 1334 Survey of the Honour of Denbigh and thus the alternative name refers to former arable sharelands in the area now occupied by Tywysog Farm. Documents of the medieval period make it clear that both grain and bread held an important place in the rural Welsh economy.[271] In the Elwy valley, the importance of local grain production is reflected in the large number of water powered corn mills in the river basin (see Chapter 13)

Waste Lands: Areas around each homestead or hamlet were areas described as waste or *"Tir cytir"* which was of vital economic importance to the resources of the community as a source of grazing land and fuel.[272] John Leland, writing in the late 1530s gives us an insight into conditions in the upland fringes of the Elwy river basin at the very end of the medieval period. Leland described the landscape of Uwchaled as *"the worst part of Denbighland and the*

---

[271] L. Alcock "Arthur's Britain" Pelican, Harmondsworth (1973) p315

[272] C. Thomas "A Cultural-Economical Model of Agrarian Cultivation in Upland Wales" Landscape History Vol. 14 (1992) p38

most barren" [273] It was made up of boggy, rocky moorland to cold to grow corn although in some places some oats and rye could be cultivated. It is also clear from entries in the 1334 Survey that oats constituted the main crop in the area. The traditional English manorial system with its clearly defined collective practices and services had clearly not developed to any extent in the Elwy valley by the early 14th century but was in place in an embryonic form in the more favoured agricultural lands to the north of the valley on the limestone ridge at Dinorben and around the castle town of Denbigh.[274]

The Role of Bondmen: The key players in the mixed farming economy in early medieval Wales were bondmen, so called because they were bound to their lord by strict rules of service and who were also bound to provide the lord with food gifts at various times of the year. The tilling of the soil around the home settlement or township was the responsibility of bondmen who themselves cropped small crofts close to their hamlets. Below the bondmen were slaves, not thought to make up a large proportion of the later medieval Welsh population [275] but part of an active market in slaves throughout Wales in the ninth century.[276] There is evidence that in early medieval times, the majority of the population of Wales were of unfree status but from around 1100, many bondmen were gaining their freedom creating two strands within the lower echelons of Welsh rural society, bondmen and freemen.

---

[273] Lucy Toulmin Smith " Leland's Itinerary in Wales 1536-1539" Bell, London (1906) p95
[274] P. Vinogradoff and F. Morgan "A Survey of the Honour of Denbigh 1334" (1914) Introduction p. xv
[275] L. Alcock "Arthur's Britain" Pelican, Harmondsworth (1973) p 325
[276] Gwyn A Williams "When was Wales?" Black Raven Press, London (19865) p 49

Kinship Lands *"Gwelyau"*: Many *gwelyau*, the kinship lands occupied by freemen, grew out of long established bond settlements as individuals gradually acquired "free" status. These settlements of a kinship group usually practised mixed pastoral and arable farming and were based upon a *"Hendref"* the original core settlement *(gwely)* of their free ancestor. A typical *priodor* (member of a *gwely*) had about three to four hectares (7.5 - 10 acres) of land around the homestead plus grazing rights and access to woodland and waste where new lands could be cleared for his sons to inherit. The number of stock kept on each farmstead was relatively limited. Each *"priodor"* (clan member) perhaps owned two oxen, three cows, six sheep, a pig and a few hens[277].

A Prehistoric Origin for the Bond System?: The *Book of Iorweth*, written in Welsh and compiled around 1240, describes how a group of bond settlements was attached to a lord's court within the arrangement known as a *maenol* or *maenor*[278] It is claimed that in medieval times two out of every three vills and hamlets in North West Wales were at least partially bonded. In some cases, the bondmen themselves had under-tenants.[279] A controversial, but nevertheless plausible theory, is that the relationship between a lord and his bondmen may have its origins in the Iron Age when bond settlements may have provided the labour resources to build hillforts. Caesar noted that in Celtic Gaul the common people were treated as slaves and burdened by debt through tribute. The lord's *llysoedd* in

---

[277] John Davies "A History of Wales" Penguin, London (1993) p189
[278] John Davies "A History of Wales" Penguin, London (1993) p 91
[279] G. R. J. Jones The Distribution of Bond Settlements in North West Wales" Welsh Hist. Review Vol.2 (1964). p26

Gwynedd, for instance, contained buildings erected for the lord by local bondmen. Thus it is argued that this form of service may provide a possible explanation for a social structure that could provide the vast amounts of labour required to construct hillforts such as Old Oswestry or Maiden Castle. At Cadbury Castle where in post Roman times (between 450 and 600 AD) 1200m of timber-reinforced stone walling was added to the defences - a massive civil engineering undertaking given the technology of the time.[280]

Ancient Federal Estates: This interaction between a lord and his bond tenants had an impact upon the territorial organisation and emergent settlement pattern throughout rural Wales. Welsh law books of the twelfth and thirteenth centuries, together with medieval surveys record the existence of what have been called "ancient federal estates". Such estates included not only the lord's *"llys"* (court) but also surrounding hamlets and farms. The tenants of the farms and hamlets, either bondsmen or freemen, paid rents in kind or offered services in return for their land. Significantly the services were diverse and included the tillage of the demesne, construction and repair of the *llys* and maintenance of distant encampments used in transhumance.[281]

If the above social arrangements had their origins in the Iron Age, then it must be the case that despite ongoing political changes, the society of the Elwy river basin remained stable and conservative for centuries. Such conditions were not common to Wales; recent research has indicated that a stable society with its institutional origins in the

---

[280] G, R.J. Jones The Distribution of Bond Settlements in North West Wales" Welsh History Review Vol.2 (1964)...

[281] GRJ Jones "Earliest Settlers in Britain" Geographical Magazine Vol XLII No 5 February (1970)

Iron Age may have existed in neighbouring North West England.[282] They are also recorded in late twelfth century Durham where there were federal estates called "shires" Services performed by tenants in Durham bore British names. This possibly infers that such arrangements pre-date the Anglo Saxon settlement. The hunting lodges of the Bishop of Durham were erected by the bondmen of Aucklandshire. (a similar service to transhumance camp construction in Wales).This implies that federal estates had survived into the late medieval period from pre Saxon times. It is also possible that the Romano British labour force on such estates may also have been retained by their new Anglo Saxon owners. Thus it was the estate, rather than a pattern of settlement, that survived the Anglo Saxon invasion[283]

"Llys", "Llan" and "Dinas": In terms of the implications for rural settlement in Wales, federal estates represent a mechanism for the integration of upland and lowland agriculture. A lord's multiple estate contained three elements, a *"llys",* the lord's court or *caput*; a *"llan",* an enclosure (graveyard) surrounding a church and a hilltop refuge known as a *"dinas".* The lands of the estate included meadows, arable land and upland pastures. The lower areas contained the *llys* of the local lord that provided the secular focus of the estate.[284] We can speculate on whether such a tripartite arrangement existed in the Elwy valley with the hillfort at *Mynydd y Gaer* forming part of a former federal estate. If the fort served as a refuge for the estate, the *"llan"* of the estate is represented by the site of the

---

[282] K J Matthews "The Iron Age of North West England" Journal of the Chester Archaeological Society Vol. 76 (2001-02) p 34
[283] GRJ Jones "The Earliest Settlers in Britain" Geographical Magazine Vol XLII No 5 February (1970)
[284] Gwyn A Williams "When was Wales?" Black Raven Press, London (1985) p 48

church at Llannefydd, less than 2 kms (1 mile) to the south east. The site of the lord's *"llys"* is more problematical but the ancient site of Llys Meirchion lies just 3 kms (under two miles) further to the south east. On the other hand it may be argued that the *Mynydd y Gaer* hillfort was linked to the llan at Llanfair Talhaearn with the lord's *llys* at Henllys, the *"llan"* with its church in Llanfair Talhaearn since all three sites lie within a 6 kilometre area. Of course, the hillfort may have served the needs of two early medieval estates based on *Henllys* and *Llys Meirchion*.

The existence of such ancient federal estates may account in part for the existence of many hill forts on the flanks of the fertile Vale of Clwyd. These estates provided stability in both pre and post Roman Wales. The labour for constructing and maintaining hillforts may have come from bond settlements within a *maenol*. Many hillforts in the region adjacent to the Elwy valley such as *Parc y Meirch*, *Castell Cawr* and *Pen y Corddyn* lie adjacent to bond settlements. *Parc y Meirch* hillfort lies close to *Dinorben Farm*, the site of a fourteenth century *"llys"* of the lord of the commote of the cantref of Rhos : Isdulas. The hill fort and later *"llys"* site may represent centres of an ancient large estate in use throughout medieval times. Further west, at *Tre'r Ceiri*, the settlement below the hillfort was Llanaelhaearn that was occupied between the fifth and seventh centuries from which time several inscribed stones in the churchyard have survived.

Post 1282 Changes: Place name evidence is helpful in reconstructing such former landscapes but the documentation of many Welsh place names is quite late. Apart from a few names, documentation begins in the twelfth century. In

North Wales, many church and parish names are not in evidence before 1200.[285] Clearer written evidence on the distribution of settlement in this part of North Wales comes from surveys made following the Edwardian conquest of Gwynedd in 1282. In the following year, Edward changed the status of the lands of the *cantrefi* of Rhos and Rhufoniog that lay on either bank of the Elwy River and were part of an area known as *Gwynedd Is Conwy* that was formerly under the control of Llewelyn ap Gruffudd, the prince of Gwynedd. This was done by placing both *cantrefi* within a new marcher lordship, that of Denbigh which was given to the de Lacy family, the Earls of Lincoln. A case has been made that suggests that the creation of a marcher lordship such as Denbigh made little difference to the local people since the new English overlords merely took over the reigns from their Welsh predecessors.[286] The 1344 Survey of the Honour of Denbigh was made to inform the new overlords of the nature of their newly acquired lands. The survey covers most of the river basin and describes several "vills", tracts of land containing habitations (not necessarily nucleated), arable, pasture and usually woodland.

The situation has been confused by Giraldus Cambrensis, writing at the close of the twelfth century indicated that typically the Welsh did not occupy either towns nor villages but led a solitary life in the woods living in temporary huts of wattle[287]. Giraldus' evidence is contradictory since he records that during Henry II's disastrous expedition of

---

[285] Tomos Roberts "Welsh Ecclesiastical Place Names and Archaeology" in N. Edwards and A. Lane (ed) "The Early Church in Wales and the West" Oxnow Monograph 16, Oxford (1992) p41
[286] A. D. Carr "Medieval Wales" Macmillan, Basingstoke. (1995) p 47
[287] Lewis Thorpe (translator) "Gerald of Wales : The Journey through Wales/ The Description of Wales" Penguin, Harmondsworth (1988 edition) p252

1165, the English army moving towards the Berwyns destroyed several Welsh churches with their villages and churchyards. Thus it appears that in some cases, churches were the focus of rural settlement in parts of North Wales, perhaps this was the case at Gwytherin where such development probably pre-dates the English Conquest. Furthermore, surveys record the existence of a quite dense range of medieval "vills" in the Elwy valley during the late twelfth century.

Bond Settlements: Bond settlements had a land tenure system known in the as *Tir Cyfrif* or "reckoned" land. Typical settlement types under this system were known as *"trefgardd"* which were usually nucleated hamlets set between the river and upland pastures as at Llanfair Talhaearn, Llannefydd, Llangernyw, Llansannan and Gwytherin.[288] Sometimes bond settlements took the form of dispersed settlements of around nine dwellings housing a co-operative group of tenant bondmen [289] or *"taeogion"*. The lands of bondmen (villeins) could not be passed on to heirs since it was considered that bondmen were without pedigree Their arable land was divided equally per capita between the bondmen and lay in open fields adjacent to the hamlets separated from each other by "skirts" (turf balks) .In some cases the lands of bondmen lay in small crofts.[290] Despite often onerous services to the king or overlord, the bondmen often occupied the best agricultural land including those of the *"maerdref"* in order to ensure

---

[288] D. Longley "Medieval Settlement and Landscape Change on Anglesey" Landscape[e History Vol.23 (2001) p44
[289] GRJ Jones : "Medieval Rural Settlements in North Wales" Transactions of the Institute of British Geographers Vol. 19 (1953) p 51
[290] P Vinogradoff and F Morgan : (ed) "A Survey of the Honour of Denbigh 1334" London (1914) p li

that the lord's food services and rents could be delivered.[291] The area of open arable field around a bond hamlet was usually greater than that in the arable sharelands of free communities.[292]

The Impact of Inheritance Customs: The kinship lands of freemen were known as *"tir gwelyog"*. In *tir gwelyog*, the land could be passed on to heirs and divided equally between sons each having his own *"gwely"* (homestead). The holder of clan land was known as a *priodor*. The inheritance system known as *"Cyfran"*, was dimilar to the English "gavelkind", a Celtic tradition that enjoyed resurgence in post Roman times. In townships where one kinship group had sole control over the land, the primary unit of settlement was known as the *"hendref"* the original home place of the kinship group. Thus in such circumstances, the *"gwelyau"* of the heirs of the lands of the *"hendref"* grew as a result of the apportionment of arable land around the original homestead.[293] This often found expression in dispersed settlement with holdings scattered about in the land of the members of the kinship group resulting in a number of long narrow parcels. To conserve the best arable land, homesteads were often located around the edges of the arable sharelands This gave rise to a distinctive pattern of rural settlement in the form of a girdle of dispersed dwellings of either bondmen or freemen (or a mixture of both) around a central arable core.[294] This may have been the case at Llannefydd.

---

[291] L. Alcock "Arthur's Britain" Pelican, Harmondsworth (1973) p325
[292] GRJ Jones "Field Systems of North Wales" in Baker & Butlin (ed) " Studies of Field Systems of the British Isles" CUP Cambridge (1973) p438
[293] F.V. Emery "Wales" in "The World's Landscapes" ed. J.M. Houston Longman, London (1969) p52
[294] GRJ Jones : "Post Roman Wales" in HPR Finberg (ed) The Agrarian History of England & Wales , Vol1 (ii) AD43 - 1042; CUP 1972 p331

Plate I : Elwy at Llanfair Talhaearn   (After watercolour by M O Jones)

II Aled Headwaters

Rhaeadr-y-bedd

The Aled Gorge

PLATE III : St, Mary's Chapel and holy well, Wigfair

St. Mary's Chapel Ruins

St. Mary's Well

IV : Garthewin House (from a watercolour by M.O.Jones)

Plate V : The Elwy at Bontnewydd (from a watercolour by M.O.Jones)

Plate VI   Gwytherib stone row   Henllan bell tower

Plate VII: Cledwen Headwaters

South of Gwytherin

Cledwen at Pennant

Plate VIII: Afon Aled at Bryn-rhyd-yr-arian

Permanent Arable Land: *"Tir Corddlan"*: A further form of ancient tenure mentioned in the medieval is *"Tir Corddlan"* known also as "nucleal land". Under this system of tenure arable land was shared by dividing it into strips or quillets. These lands were known as "gardens" *(gerddi)* and were matured annually. The *gerddi* were cultivated permanently and thus equate to the Scottish "infield" The infield was made up of small arable strips that could be amalgamated to fit pre-existing small Celtic fields. The holders of this land were cottagers, possibly descended from slaves. In older settlements, particularly those that were once *"clas"* communities these lands surrounded an area termed the *"mynwent"* - synonymous with a graveyard. The permanently tilled arable land thus encircled the churchyard. It is possible that Gwytherin was once an example of this form of tenure since it was a former *clas* community and even today one of the oldest cottages in the village lying at the edge of the curvilinear churchyard in known as "Ty'n yr Ardd" (House in the garden).

Farmhouses and Inheritance Laws: The style of farmhouse buildings was also influenced by the pattern of inheritance through a system known as the "unit" system of building where two or more separate dwellings were built for the families of different sons on the same site. Later extensions often make such dwellings difficult to identify in the present day but examples are known in Llannefydd at *Plas Harri, Plas Uchaf* and *Berain*. In Henllan, examples include *Plas Chambres* and *Plas Heaton Farm*.[295]

---

[295] E. Hubbard "The Buildings of Wales :Clwyd" Penguin Harmondsworth p 51

Lanes and Footpaths in the Landscape: According to early Welsh law books every house ought to have two footpaths, one to the church and one to the watering place. This may account for the proliferation of lanes and paths on both sides of the Elwy valley, particularly in the parish of Llannefydd where several lanes and public footpaths converge upon the church (see Fig.17).

Sites of Church and *Llys*: Churches were not always sited close to the lord's hall *(llys)* in the early medieval period; the nearest mother church served the llys. This was the case at both Llangernyw and Llanfair Talhaearn. The same was true even at the more important *"maerdrefi"* in North Wales as at Deganwy were the *llys* may have been served by the church of Eglwys yn Rhos and the royal palace at Aberffraw on Anglesey served by the ancient Eglwys Ail in Llangadwaladr. At Trefiw in the Conwy Valley, the Welsh prince Llewelyn ap Iorweth built a church close to his *llys* because he found it inconvenient to travel to Llanrychwyn church some 1.7 kms to the south of his hall.[296]

Townships and Their Boundaries: In theory, every Welsh commote contained 50 "vills" or townships which have been described as "the base building block of secular administration"[297] so forming the basic unit of settlement and

---

[296] N. Johnstone "An Investigation into the Location of the Royal Courts of Thirteenth century Gwynedd" in Edwards N. (ed.)ibid (1997) p62
[297] A.J.L. Winchester "Dividing Lines in a Moorland Landscape - Territorial Boundaries in Upland England" Landscape Vol. 1, No 2, (Oct. 2000) p25

taxation, although in reality, an individual may have farmed land in more than one township[298]. A township would have been made up of one or more hamlets and a string of scattered farms. The boundaries between individual medieval townships in the area are obscure although there are two streams in the south of the Elwy basin running north from Mynydd Hiraethog that bear the name *"terfyn"* meaning a boundary which suggests that watercourses may have acted as boundaries for townships in some cases. The first such stream *"Afon Derfyn"* possibly marked the eastern boundary of the ancient township of *Bodrach* in Llangernyw parish while the other stream, *"Nant y Terfyn,"* a tributary of the Aled in Llansannan parish, may have been the western boundary of the township of *Arllwyd*. Both streams are marked on Fig. 1. These ancient township boundaries possibly have much earlier origins.

Research on the North Yorkshire Moors showed that prehistoric boundaries between Bronze Age estates were based upon features in the natural landscape such as watercourses, on hill tops along the watershed between river basins, the upland boundaries were marked by tumuli (round barrows).[299]. Other research has claimed continuity of use of Iron Age burial places as boundaries in medieval Wessex[300]. Thus township boundaries may, at least in part, have originated as boundaries in pre-Roman times. The same may therefore be true in the Elwy river basin where barrow chains survive close to medieval parish boundaries. (See Fig.2) A link has been identified in Northern England

---

[298] F.V. Emery "Wales" in "The World's Landscapes" ed. J.M. Houston Longman, London (1969) p51
[299] D.A. Spratt "Prehistoric Boundaries on the north Yorkshire Moors" in GW Barker (ed) "Prehistoric Communities in Northern England" University of Sheffield (1981) pp87-103
[300] D J Bonney : "Early Boundaries in Wessex" in P J Fowler (ed) "Archaeology and the Landscape" Baker (1072) p169

between the boundaries of medieval townships and those of landholdings[301]. Significantly, many of the townships in the Elwy basin that are described in the 1334 Survey of the Honour of Denbigh survive as large farms in the present day landscape. (See Fig. 4)

The First Parishes: Following the conquest of 1282, the process of establishing parishes as units of ecclesiastical administration was completed in the decades following 1300[302]. However, it is possible that some of the present parishes may date from the twelfth century, a period of rapid population growth. It has been shown that in Gwynedd, of which the Elwy basin formed a part, the drawing up of parishes was largely complete by the end of the reign of Owain Gwynedd (d1170)[303]. The creation of the Diocese of St. Asaph (1143) also falls within this period and the creation of parishes would have been essential to organise the payment of tithes. There is also documentary evidence to support this conclusion since parish churches were recorded for Llanfair Talhaearn, Llansannan and Gwytherin in 1254 [304] and Llangernyw in 1291, indicating that these parishes were in place before the conquest of Wales was completed in 1282. It is possible (but unproven) that all four may have their origins as monastic establishments. Two other village churches in the eastern side of the basin at Llannefydd and Henllan held the status of chapels of ease for St. Asaph cathedral in the thirteenth century but went on to gain parish status possibly in the century after the

---

[301] Angus Winchester "Discovering Parish Boundaries" Shire Publications, Princes Risborough (2000) p 25
[302] John Davies "A History of Wales" Penguin, London (1993) p174
[303] C A Gresham "Medieval parish and township boundaries in Gwynedd" Bulletin of the Board of Celtic Studies (1987) p146
[304] D. Pratt: "St. Asaph Diocese, 1254" Trans. Denbs. Historical Society Vol.42 (1993)

Fig.5 PARISH BOUNDARIES : RHOS DEANERY

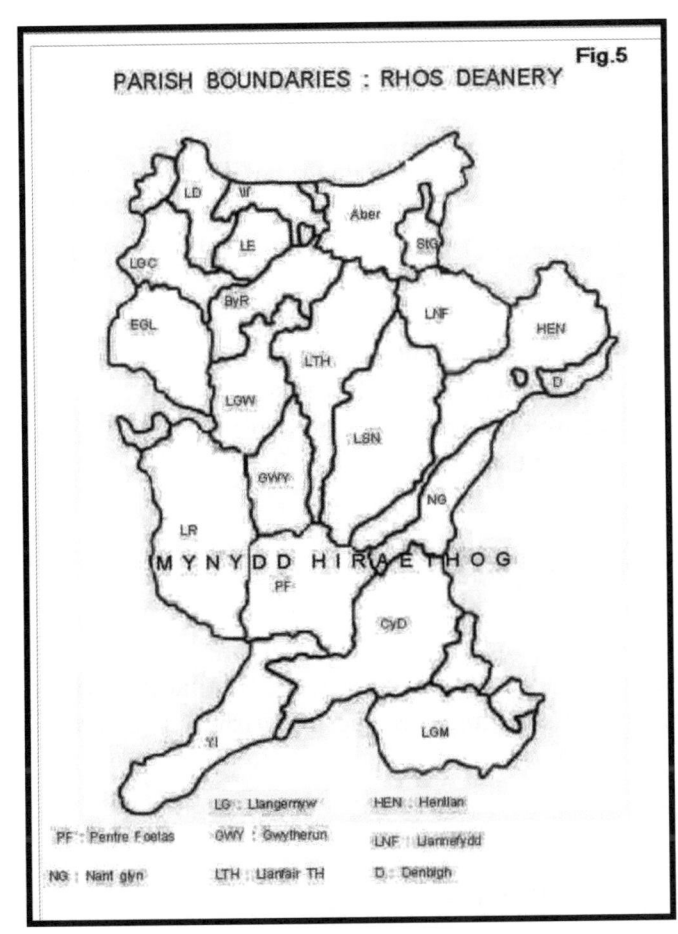

PF : Pentre Foelas   LG : Llangernyw   HEN : Henllan
NG : Nant glyn   GWY : Gwytherun   LNF : Llannefydd
                      LTH : Llanfair TH   D : Denbigh

1282 conquest. The parish initially had a purely religious function and did not achieve any real significance in 77secular administration until the Poor Law function developed during the Tudor period.

Parish Boundaries: The Royal Injunctions of Elizabeth I (1559) ordered the perambulation of parish boundaries at Rogation tide. In post-Reformation Britain this was generally Ascension Day. However, the practice may have much earlier roots for the pagan rite known as *Robiglia* took the form of processions through the cornfields to pray for the survival of the crop from attacks of mildew. The Christian version involved asking God to bless the parish and its crops and livestock. The custom was widely used across Europe and reached England around 800AD. Denbigh Corporation records describe the exact route of the perambulation of the town boundaries which include the boundaries with the Elwy basin parishes of Henllan and Llannefydd. The western boundary of the town follows the course of the Afon Meirchion for much of its length. The route reached a well known as *Ffynnon Meirchion*, the source of this tributary of the Elwy. This well is one of three along the town boundary. The well of *Ffynnon Meirchion* is said to have once had its own chapel[305] and may have had a link with the medieval pilgrims' route from Holywell to Gwytherin.

The importance of parish boundaries to local communities is illustrated with the way that they are marked in the landscape. To some extent, as in the case of township boundaries, they followed natural features such as streams, ridges and springs but in some cases included the sites of Bronze Age tumuli or cairns. The boundary between Llanfair Talhaearn and Llansannan is marked by the round barrow of *Boncyn Cynfir Cleirach* as it crosses open moorland.

Elsewhere, elaborate systems of standing stones have been erected as boundary markers on open moorland. The southern boundary of the former Gwytherin parish high on the northern slopes of Mynydd Hiraethog is marked by a series of marker stones set at 400m intervals. These survive to the present day marking the boundary between Gwytherin and the former parish of *Tir yr Abad -Isaf* (Lower land of the abbot) now Pentre Foelas. Similar lines of stones between 50 and 100m apart act as boundaries between Llanfair Talhaearn and Gwytherin parishes. They are

---

[305] D.R. Thomas "The History of the Diocese of St. Asaph" Vol.2 Caxton Press, Oswestry (1911) p32

thought to date from the early nineteenth or late eighteenth centuries.[306] Elsewhere, substantial banks and ditches survive as markers of moorland parish boundaries such as that between Llansannan and Henllan on Mynydd Hiraethog. These structures also reflect the importance of common upland grazing to the communities of the lower valleys. The shape of parish boundaries reflects this. As can be seen from the accompanying map (Fig. 5), the boundaries of Llansannan, Llanfair Talhaearn and Henllan parishes extend south westwards into the uplands of Mynydd Hiraethog to include common pastures.

Townships and Parishes: The township *(tref)* formed the basic unit of administration and tax collection within a Welsh commote *(cwmwd)*. In free townships *(trefi)* the family occupying the hendref would have provided the common component within the unit. In bond townships, the community would have been the common link.[307] Thus, as in parts of northern England the township would have been occupied by some farming families who frequently worked their lands co-operatively.

In the large parishes of the Elwy river basin, several townships (also referred to as vills in some late medieval documents) made up a parish. Llanfair Talhaearn had twelve townships; Llangernyw had nine, Llannefydd ten and Llansannan thirteen reflecting the fact that a large area of land was required in this part of North Wales to support a

---

[306] CPAT Project 761 "Historic Landscape Characterisation : Mynydd Hiraethog - Ffrith uchaf, Llangernyw HLCA 1100"" Welshpool (2001)
[307] D. Longley "Medieval Settlement and Landscape Change in Anglesey" Landscape History Vol. 23 (2001) p43

single church. This contrasts with western parts of Gwynedd where generally a single township boundary fitted neatly into those of the parishes in which they were located and any diversion from this is indicative of later changes to parish boundaries.[308]

An interesting factor in the make up of parishes in the Elwy valley is that two of them contain townships lying on either side of the Elwy which marked the frontier between the ancient *cantrefi* of Rhos and Rhufoniog. Thus, in the case the two parishes concerned: Llanfair Talhaearn and Llangernyw, the drawing up of parish boundaries by the Diocese of St. Asaph ignored the ancient political lines of the cantrefi and settled on contiguity. *Cantrefi* lost further significance after the 1282 conquest, but townships continued to be the basis of landholding in Wales until the later seventeenth century.[309]

A Typical Township in the Elwy Basin: Typical of many of the townships in the Elwy valley is that of *Carwedfynydd* in Llannefydd parish. A farm bearing the name of the township still stands (GR 961 714) about 2 kms WNW of Llannefydd village. The township is thought to have once been part of the estate of *Marchweithian*, a lord of the commote of Is Aled (in which the township is located) and a member of the royal clan of Gwynedd. The original township was mentioned in the 1334 Survey of the Lordship of Denbigh and was made up of three farms. These were *Vron*, the main farm of the township that changed its name to *Tan y Gyrt* in the late eighteenth century,

---

[308] N. Johnstone ibid (1997) p61

[309] A Gresham "Medieval Parish and Township Boundaries in Gwynedd" Bulletin of the Board of Celtic Studies Vol. 34 (1987) pp 146-147

Plas Harri and *Tyddyn* (formerly called *Ty'n y pwll*) The farms of the township had access to grazing lands on friddau on the adjacent hills of Fron Fawr and Mynydd y Gyrt.[310] The township's arable sharelands would have been located around the township's home farm: *Vron*. Thus the lands of the township were devoted to a mixed farming economy making full use of the townships varying types of land.

"Ffrith" Lands: In upland areas such as those that surround the Elwy valley, townships, like rural parishes, were larger in area and although the narrow valley bottoms allowed some arable production to take place, pastoral pursuits dominated the farming economy. On upland pastures, several townships often shared common grazing rights. On the lower slopes, large enclosed pastures lying between the heavily tilled sharelands and the moorland grazing lands known as *"ffriddoedd"* were created and were heavily grazed. These lands can be identified from the many place names in the Elwy river system bearing the name *"ffrith"*. (See Fig. 4) Most of these place-names occur at altitudes between 200 - 400m (c600 - 1200 feet).

The "Tyddyn": Small scattered farms with perhaps only around 10 acres (4.94 ha) of land and known as *"tyddynod"* (homesteads) were established to house the heirs to a *gwely* and came to dominate the settlement pattern in the upland margins by the end of the 13th century. As population pressure increased in the 12th and 13th centuries, many former *"hafodydd"*, seasonally occupied farms on the summer pastures, became permanently occupied. The upland pastures were therefore vital for the economic survival of such farms.

---

[310] W.A. Morris "The Morris Family of Carwedfynydd" Trans. Denbs. Hist. Soc. Vol.19 (1970) p133

The *Book of Iorweth* (c1240) through its details of units of tax assessment gives an idealised structure for rural Welsh society. It is stated that four Welsh acres (1,440 square yards) known as *(erwau)* made up a homestead *(tyddyn)* and that four homesteads *(tyddynod)* made up a shareland *(rhanhir)*. The use of multiples of four continued in that four sharelands made up a holding *(gafael)* and four holdings made up a township *(tref)* Four townships *(trefi)* made up a *maenol* described above which in turn was related to the larger administrative units of the commote and Cantref.[311]

The situation in practice was not as straight forward as the *Book of Iorweth* would lead us to suppose. In the Elwy river basin, upland townships had their grazing lands parcelled off from the waste with each kinship group *(gwely)* enjoying grazing rights over an area known as a *"gafael"* (holding).[312] In 1334, this system was particularly evident in Uwch Aled commote where tradition died hard. A *gafael* was not always located within a single township. In 1334, the *gafael* of a man known as *"Audouni Goch"* not only included the whole of the township of Llwyn in the Clwyd valley south east of Denbigh but also a share of lands in four other distant townships including

---

[311] G.R.J. Jones ""Field Systems of North Wales" in ARH Baker & RA Butlin (eds) "Studies of Field Systems in the British Isles" CUP Cambridge (1973) p431.
[312] GRJ Jones "Field Systems of North Wales" in Baker & Butlin (ed) " Studies of Field Systems of the British Isles" CUP Cambridge (1973) pp441-442.

35 acres (14.2 ha) in the upland township of *Treflech* in the Elwy river basin two kilometres south east of Llanfair Talhaearn and over 14 kilometres (9 miles) from the home township.[313]

By the end of the fourteenth century, the effects of the Black Death, a changing labour market and deterioration in climatic conditions would all combine to change the systems of agriculture and rural settlement that had been evolving for centuries

---

[313] P. Vinogradoff and F. Morgan (ed) "A Survey of the Honour of Denbigh 1334" London (1914) pp 33-37

CHAPTER 10: THE LATE MIDDLE AGES: UPHEAVAL AND CHANGE IN THE LANDSCAPE

In the late medieval period, following the Edwardian conquest of 1282, legal and institutional changes were leading to the steady disappearance of the traditional Welsh systems of land tenure throughout North Wales. The 1334 Survey of the Honour of Denbigh, which related to most of the lands of the Elwy basin, indicated that about 10,000 acres (4167 ha) were occupied by English families at that date[314]

The Black Death: The latter half of the fourteenth century was a period of crisis in Western Europe and Wales was no exception to this development. Much historical argument has been generated as to the extent to which the bubonic plague contributed to social and economic upheavals in the second half of the fourteenth century. It is difficult to say what the effect of the Black Death, which probably reached the area by the early summer of 1349, was, on the population of the Elwy basin. It is known that the impact of the plague was worse in urban and flatter parts of the country. Thus, the people of the upland areas surrounding the rivers Elwy and Aled may have suffered a little less. Nevertheless, a conservative estimate would be that at least a quarter of the population may have been killed by the plague which returned again to haunt the population in 1361 and 1369. In the neighbouring Lordship of Ruthin, the plague was first reported in the town of Ruthin itself in June 1349 and 139 deaths were recorded in the

---

[314] A D Carr "Medieval Wales" Macmillan, Basingstoke (1995) p 95

following two weeks.[315] In Ruthin, lordship stewards reported that they were unable to collect a third of the rents due to the lord owing to the impact of the plague while in Nan Conwy commote a little to the west of the upper Elwy valley, two thirds of the population died as a result of the plague[316]. It is likely that in the Elwy basin, as elsewhere in rural Wales, it was the bondmen class who suffered the highest rates of mortality. One factor in this may have been that many of them lived in close proximity to one another in nucleated settlements. In Deganwy, just 14 kilometres to the North West, the bondmen were almost wiped out by the plague.

Other Causes of Economic Distress in the Fourteenth Century: However, the onset of economic decline preceded the onset of the Black Death and the area probably did not escape the impact of climatic deterioration in the fourteenth century with serious harvest failures in 1315-17 and the onslaught of serious cattle diseases in 1315, 1348 and 1363 that must have had a devastating impact on the local pastoral economy leading to depopulation. The depopulation was symptomatic of social upheaval that found expression in popular protest and rebellion throughout Western Europe. The Peasants' Revolt in late fourteenth century England had no impact in Wales but serious upheavals followed in 1400 in the form of the Glyndwr rebellion in Wales. The pre-plague Survey of the Honour of Denbigh gives us a picture of a landscape of hamlets and isolated farms subject to strict customs and dues. It is also clear that many of the food services formerly paid by the inhabitants to their lord had been converted into cash

---

[315] A D Carr (ibid) p 100
[316] Huw Pryce "Medieval Experiences, Wales 1000 - 1415" in G E Jones & D Smith (ed) "The People of Wales" Gomer, Llandysul (1999) p35

equivalents which, together with high taxation, must have placed a tremendous financial burden on those who survived the 1349 bubonic plague. However, it should be also borne in mind that both the economy and the population of Wales were in decline even before 1349.

Migration of Bondmen: In the Elwy river basin in 1334, there were many "mixed" hamlets made up of free and bond tenants. We know that in the late fourteenth and early fifteenth centuries many of North Wales' bondmen *(taeogion)* fled their hamlets[317], often re-settling across the English border as freemen in Cheshire where there was a severe labour shortage[318]. As a result many bond hamlets became deserted.[319] This also reflects a rising tax burden after the 1282 conquest since taxes were collected from a township area rather than from individuals thus the rising tax burden would be the same regardless of the number of persons inhabiting a particular township[320]. Consequently, the general shortage of tenants in the aftermath of the Black Death[321] and opportunities for bondmen *(taeogion)* to acquire their own land to rent without onerous customs and dues had great social significance.

---

[317] John Davies "A History of Wales" Penguin, London (1993) p 208

[318] E. D. Evans "The Crown Lordships of Denbighshire" Trans. Denbs. Hist. Soc. Vol. 50 (2000) p25.

[319] N. Johnstone ibid (1997)

[320] John Davies "A History of Wales" Penguin, London (1993) p168

[321] W.G. Hoskins "The Making of the English Landscape" Hodder & Stoughton, London (1955) p92

Changes in Landholding The former arable land held by bondmen was of relatively high quality and it has been noted that their lands were avidly acquired by the lesser gentry eager to extend their estates.[322] Thus, by the end of the medieval period, freeholders far outnumbered bond tenants. It must be remembered, however, that the system of administration of land through the *llys* and *maerdref* was also breaking down even by the 13th century with many services having been commuted to cash payments.[323]

Climatic Deterioration: "The Little Ice Age": In the highland areas of England, the Black Death and a deteriorating climate associated with the period known as the "Little Ice Age" (1350-1750 AD) led to a retreat of settlement from the more marginal lands on the upper hill slopes.[324] This followed a period of warmer and agriculturally more productive climatic conditions between about 1100 and 1300. The contribution to climatic change in the "Little Ice Age" to the retreat of settlement from marginal lands has been recently questioned since pollen analysis indicates that on the northern Cheviots, cereal production continued through this period.[325] Such a scenario may be relevant in the higher sections of the Elwy valley on the northern and western slopes of Mynydd

---

[322] D Longley "Medieval Settlement and Landscape Change on Anglesey" Landscape History Vol23 (2001) p45

[323] Longley D. "The Royal Courts of the Welsh Princes in Gwynedd Ad400 - 1283" in N. Edwards (ed) ibid (1997)

[324] W.G. Hoskins ibid (1955) p 92

[325] Richard Tipping "Climatic Variability and "Marginal" Settlement in Upland British Landscapes a Re-evaluation" Landscapes Vol.3 No.2 (2002) p13

Hiraethog where colonisation continued in the Little Ice Age period, albeit in scattered hill farms probably concentrating on sheep farming.

Changes in the Pattern of Human Settlement: Nevertheless, there can be little doubt that economic and social upheavals were having an impact on the nature of upland settlement. It has been claimed that by 1360, some of the bond townships occupied by *taeogion* (villeins) were already virtually uninhabited[326]. By the end of the Middle Ages the process was almost complete and very few bond hamlets or girdle settlements around the arable sharelands were left.[327] This conclusion has some documentary support since John Leland, writing c 1540, gives an indication that perhaps no villages or even hamlets survived the social upheavals of the late 14th century following the Black Death for he states that in the commotes around the Elwy valley, people did not live *"vicatim"* (in villages or hamlets) but *"sparsim"* (in dispersed settlement).[328]

Early Estate Building: Gavelkind (*Cyfran* in Welsh) too was in decline by the early 14th century partly because under Welsh law, the land was inherited in equal portions by all male heirs and by that time was leading to uneconomic divisions of land around a *hendref* into tiny parcels. This breakdown supported the beginnings of estate

---

[326] John Davies "A History of Wales" Penguin, London (1993) p189

[327] GRJ Jones "Field Systems of North Wales" in Baker & Butlin (ed) " Studies of Field Systems of the British Isles" CUP Cambridge (1973) p460

[328] Lucy Toulmin Smith " Leland's Itinerary in Wales 1536-1539" Bell, London (1906) p93

building as the small strips and parcels were consolidated into larger fields thus bringing about a major transformation of the rural landscape of the Elwy valley where there is little evidence of the former field system in the present day landscape. This development was encouraged by a fluid land market after the Black Death, the Glyndwr revolt and the dissolution of monasteries. There is also some evidence that in North Wales, the English conquerors retained the use of ancient Welsh land laws for their own convenience. Under the *gwely* system, the land of a man who died without heirs escheated to his lord so extending the amount of land available for sale to build an estate or consolidate the lands of another expanding farm.

The Decline of the *Gwely* System and the Land Market: The *gwely* system was in decline by the early fourteenth century but persisted until around 1450. A key factor in its final demise was the use of a Welsh mortgage or *"tir priod"*. As a result of the sub division of *gwely* land into holdings of uneconomic proportions and the burden of taxation, there was an increasing need for a *priodor* to raise cash. Under the still extant Welsh land laws, he was forbidden to sell his share of the *gwely* land in order to free himself from these burdens. Hence the emergence of the Welsh mortgage, a device that enabled cash to be raised against the security of the land.[329] The attraction to the lender was that after the mortgage had been renewed for sixteen years, the ownership of the land was transferred into the hands of the mortgagee. Once the lands had been freed from the hold of the *gwely,* the mortgagee could sell the land to neighbours eager to consolidate them into their farms or to those wanting to extend their estates. Wealth

---

[329] A D Carr "Medieval Wales" Macmillan, Basingstoke (1995) p92

and power became reflected in the amount of land held by an individual and thus primogeniture replaced gavelkind on the larger estates to support the build up of power of the local "gentry".[330]

It is significant that the economically oppressed *priodorion* (clansmen), including, no doubt, many from the Elwy river basin, formed the backbone of the supporters for Owain Glyndwr in the final acts of military defiance and rebellion against English rule in the decade following 1400. As a result of the uprising, the Lordship of Denbigh, which included the lands of the Elwy valley, had no income for years owing to the devastation caused by the rebels.[331]

The Acts of Union of 1536 - 1543 brought about the full incorporation of Wales into the English state together with a formal end to Welsh inheritance laws and the creation of a regulated land market.

---

[330] F.V. Emery "Wales" in "The World's Landscapes" ed. J.M. Houston Longman, London (1969) p55
[331] John Davies "A History of Wales" Penguin, London (1993) p212

CHAPTER 11: THE MAKING OF THE PRESENT DAY LANDSCAPE RURAL SETTLEMENT AND AGRICULTURAL CHANGE AFTER 1500

Enclosure and the Landscape: The present settlement pattern and landscape of this part of North Wales has its origins in the Late Middle Ages with the decay of ancient traditions of inheritance, land holding and farming practices such as transhumance which led to a consolidation of land in distinct farmsteads[332] In terms of the landscape, estate building led to the enclosure of former arable sharelands, small crofts in the lower, sheltered sections of the valley once held by bondmen, and the scattered parcels of the old *gwely* lands and *ffidd* pastureland on the lower slopes It has been recognised that between 1530 and 1620, the population of parishes in upland Wales increased by up to four times more rapidly than those of lowland Wales so reversing the trend of outward migration from these areas that was evident in the later fourteenth century.[333] These upland areas had been used for summer grazing for sheep flocks by freeholders and tenants for centuries but the practice of transhumance had all but disappeared by the turn of the eighteenth century.[334] This enclosure was, to some extent, initially fuelled by rampart inflation during the sixteenth century with the price of wool trebling between 1500 and 1550.

B [332] Charles W J Withers "Conceptions of Cultural Landscape Change in Upland North Wales : A Case Study of Llanbedr y Cennin and Caerhun parishes c1560-c1891" Landscape History Vol. 17 (1995) p35
[333] John Davies "The Making of Wales" Cadw/Sutton Stroud (1996) p80
[334] Richard Moore-Colyer "Welsh Cattle Drovers" Landmark, Ashbourne (2002) p30

The Re-settlement of Mynydd *y Gaer*: The re-settlement of the uplands is typified by the experience on a hillside in Llannefydd parish. By the late nineteenth century the summit of the hill topped by the Iron Age ramparts of *Mynydd y Gaer* was dotted with small farmhouses each with three of four small enclosed fields adjacent to them. (See Fig. 3) One of the farms with its three small fields (*Pant-yr-ogof*) stood entirely within the ramparts of the fort. Another hilltop farm, *Pen-y-ffrith* "top of the ffrith" was probably so named because it stood in former common grazing lands lying higher up the hillside than the better quality pastures of the ffrith. By the late nineteenth century, these small farms were mostly occupied by agricultural labourers indicating that they were no longer viable as individual farms.

Landscape Change in the Upper Cledwen Valley: The fundamental landscape change that accompanied this early piecemeal enclosure was the replacement of hitherto open arable sharelands, meadows, summer pastures and *ffidd* lands with compact hedged or walled units.[335] Lower down the valleys there was some rationalisation in the number of *tyddynod* as new farms for rent were established within the areas newly enclosed by the gentry.[336] In the upper Cledwen valley to the south of Gwytherin, the valley assumes a U-shaped cross-section probably due to widening and deepening of the valley by ice flowing from Mynydd Hiraethog during the last Ice Age. On the lower slopes and floor of this steep sided valley, new farms were being established from at least the seventeenth century. (See Fig. 6)

---

[335] GRJ Jones "Field Systems of North Wales" in Baker & Butlin (ed) " Studies of Field Systems of the British Isles" CUP Cambridge (1973) p 455

[336] F.V. Emery "Wales" in "The World's Landscapes" ed. J.M. Houston Longman, London (1969) p55

Fig. 6: Pennant and the Upper Cledwen Valley

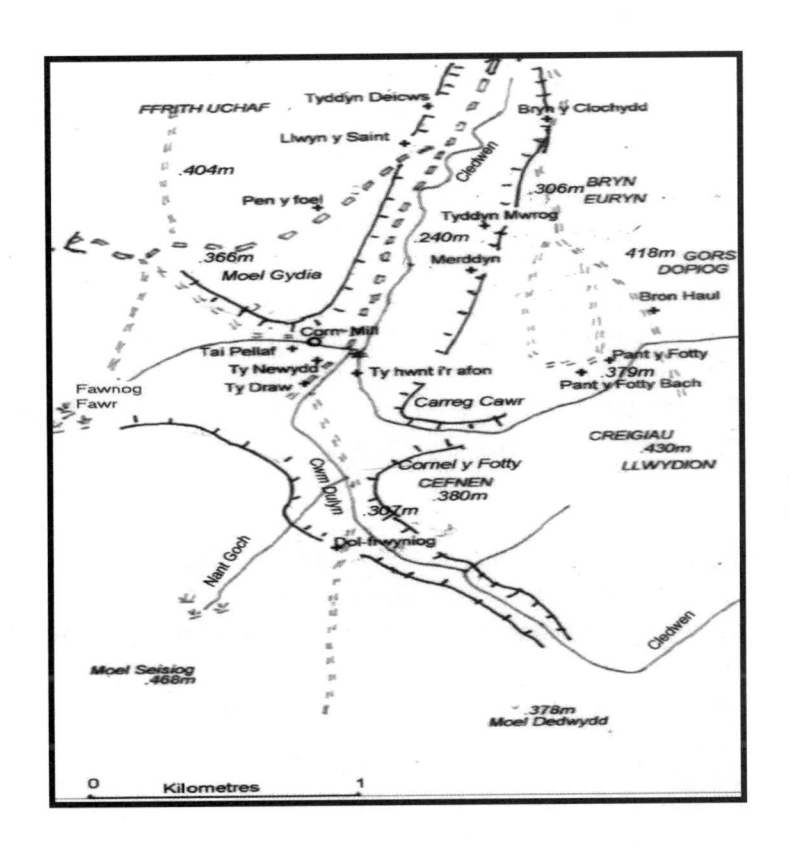

The parish records for Gwytherin refer to families living in these farms from dates in the late seventeenth century although details of addresses are lacking in many of the early parish records and so their initial occupation may pre-date these dates by over a century.[337] The earlier farms established were *Llwyn Saint* (by 1684); *Dolfadryn* (1689); *Bryn Clochydd* (1719); *Merddyn (*1735) and *Ty Newydd* in Pennant (1714).

The Upper Margins of Settlement: Ffrith- Uchaf: Associated with some of these valley floor farms, is a further example of landscape change at the upper margin of settlement in the area lying above the western side of the valley. This area (see Fig. 7) has been identified in what has been termed the "key historic landscape" of *Ffrith-Uchaf*, an area of just over three square kilometres in extent overlooking the valley of the Afon Cledwen (upper Elwy). In this area, the farms of the lower valley extended their land by enclosing the area of upland grazing known as *Ffrith-Uchaf* (GR 865605). This may have been a result of rising wool prices in the sixteenth and early seventeenth centuries.

On the western edge of the ffrith at an altitude of between 300 - 400 m. above sea level farms were established by 1700 which had enclosed adjacent land on Ffrith Uchaf. These were the farms of Pen *y Foel* (GR 869603) that was in occupation by 1685, *Llwyn Saint* (by 1684) and *Tyddyn Deicws* (by 1685). On the northern fringes of Ffrith Uchaf, a similar development occurred with farms peripheral to the ffrith enclosing small fields. The farms were established generally later than those on the south eastern fringes possibly under the stimulation of rising prices

---

[337]Clwyd Family History Society "Gwytherin Parish Registers 1667 - 1812" Vols. 1 & 2 Ruthin (1996)

during the French Wars (1793 - 1815). These farms included the appropriately named *Ty'n y Ffrith* (house in the ffrith) established by 1806, *Nant yr Henfaes* (by 1790), *Graig Bach* (by 1806) and *Pen y Fron* 1812-1841). These farms were relatively small, in 1881, *Nant yr Henfaes* was of 60 acres (24.3 ha) in size, not large given the quality of the land, *Bwlch y Gwynt* (31 acres or 12.5 hectares) and *Graig Bach* farmed 26 acres (10.5 ha) *Ty'n y Ffrith* had no land and was occupied by an 85 year old pauper. Two farms appear to have been established in the northern part of the ffrith itself. These were *Pen y Graig* (established by 1698) and *Bwlch y Gwynt* built after 1812. New fields were enclosed in piecemeal fashion from the ffrith lands with a large bank and ditch which is still identifiable. This upper limit of farming is clearly shown on the 1842 tithe map for Gwytherin. Parts of these early field boundaries have been abandoned with the retreat of farming from the moorlands in more recent times. The 1879 Ordnance Survey map shows that the process of abandonment was already underway with several fields on *Ffrith Uchaf* having reverted to rough pasture. In 1881, *Pen y Graig* was listed as unoccupied. It appears to have been subsequently occupied but today once again lies empty and is currently being used for storage. Today's upper limits of farming are instead marked in places by post and wire fences at a lower altitude.[338] This landscape area is easily accessible via the mountain road that runs from Gwytherin to Nebo and Pentre Foelas and by footpaths leading from Pandy Tudur and Gwytherin. One of these footpaths follows the ridge top for some distance and may have been part of an important north-south track way in the past. Possible users would have been summer herders, peat diggers and drovers.

---

[338] CPAT Project 761 "Historic Landscape Characterisation : Mynydd Hiraethog - Frith uchaf, Llangernyw HLCA 1100"" Welshpool (2001)

There is, to date, no archaeological evidence to support the tempting speculation that this ridge-top route is of prehistoric origin. The track descends into the upper Cledwen valley at Pennant before once again heading southwards over the moors avoiding the extensive peat bog of *Fawnog Fawr*.

The Re-Use of *Hafodydd*: Rising demand for Welsh wool saw some former summer homesteads (*hafodydd*) becoming permanently occupied as transhumance fell into decline[339]. This is reflected in a change in the use of *hafod* place names which, from the sixteenth century onwards refer to actual locations rather than areas of waste[340]. During this period of high prices there was an expansion of rural settlement on to the higher waste lands such as that known as *Hafod Elwy* (GR 939562) at an altitude of 400m that was settled permanently in that period. There is a

---

[339] John Davies "A History of Wales" Penguin, London (1993) p259
[340] E. Davies "Hendre and Hafod in Denbighshire" Trans. Denbs. Hist. Soc. Vol26 (1977) p57

documentary reference to enclosed *ffriddoedd* at *Hafod Elwy* dated 1537[341]. *Hafod Elwy* lies 2 kms south east of Llyn Aled in lands drained by the headwaters of the Alwen although part of the estate lands lay on the watershed with the Elwy system. The name may indicate that the area once supplied summer grazing for animals from farms in the Elwy Valley to the north. At the time of the Survey of the Honour of Denbigh in 1334, the estate was described as comprising 650 acres (263 ha) of waste capable of providing grazing for 180 animals. Some newly established upland farms such as *Hafod Dafydd* (GR 941600) in Llansannan parish, located on Mynydd Hiraethog at an altitude of 412 m, were almost exclusively involved in sheep production. A recent study has noted a similar expansion of farming into nearby upland areas above the Conwy valley at the end of the fifteenth and through the sixteenth century.[342] In this area, enclosure associated with early estate building appears to have affected former upland grazing lands at altitudes of up to 400m less than 12 kilometres (7.5 miles) to the west of the upper Elwy valley on the western side of the Conwy valley has been dated to the sixteenth century.[343]

Islands of Upland Settlement: The Conwy valley enclosures are at a similar height and appearance to islands of settlement on the high moors located around the farms of *Pant y Fotty* (GR 884593) ("hollow of the summer house") and the adjacent *Pant y Fotty Bach* (GR 883593) at a height of 379m. above the upper Cledwen valley in Gwytherin

---

[341] See CPAT Project 761 "Historic Landscape Characterisation - Mynydd Hiraethog" Welshpool, (2001)

[342] Delia Hooke " Place Names and Vegetation History as a key to understanding Settlement in the Conwy Valley" in Edwards N. "Landscape and Settlement in Medieval Wales" Oxbow Oxford 1997

[343] C W J Withers "Conceptions of Cultural Landscape Change in Upland North Wales c 1560 - 1891" Landscape History Vol, 17 (1995) p41

tithe parish. (See Figs. 6 and 8) Their names suggest that these enclosures probably had their origins as medieval summer dwellings with the small enclosures close to the farms representing holding pens for milking or the rearing of calves. Recent analysis of aerial photographs of these upland areas has shown the existence of ridge and furrow within later enclosed fields in the same area at *Waen Isaf Las* (GR 905599) in the upper Aled valley. The ridge and furrow represents evidence of at least temporary cultivation during the medieval period[344]. (See Fig 9 for location). This provides additional evidence for the occupation of these moorlands in the period preceding the climatic deterioration that took place from the late fourteenth century. Although the names of many of these upland farms do not appear in print until the nineteenth century, it is tempting to view the earliest permanent occupation of these sites as a sixteenth century expansion of permanent settlement in the uplands in response to rising wool prices. The process of piecemeal enclosure on the moorland continued into the eighteenth and nineteenth centuries for islands of settlement with similar enclosures around an isolated farm known as *Ty'n y Llyn* (GR914577). This lies 3.5 kms to the east in Llansannan parish at a height of 380m on the north side of Llyn Aled. This farm, lying along the southern rim of the Elwy river basin on Mynydd Hiraethog, is of eighteenth or nineteenth century origin.[345]

The size of tenanted farms on Welsh estates in the late seventeenth and eighteenth centuries ranged from ten to sixty acres (4-25 ha).[346] Much of the moorland in the north of the Elwy river basin was never enclosed on a large scale above an altitude of around 300m.

---

[344] CPAT SMR 105359
[345] CPAT Project 761 "Historic Landscape Characterisation : Mynydd Hiraethog" Welshpool, (2001)
[346] Geraint H Jenkins "The Foundations of Modern Wales 1642-1780" OUP Oxford (1993) p113.

Fig. 8 PANT-Y-FOTTY
Pen bryn y clochydd

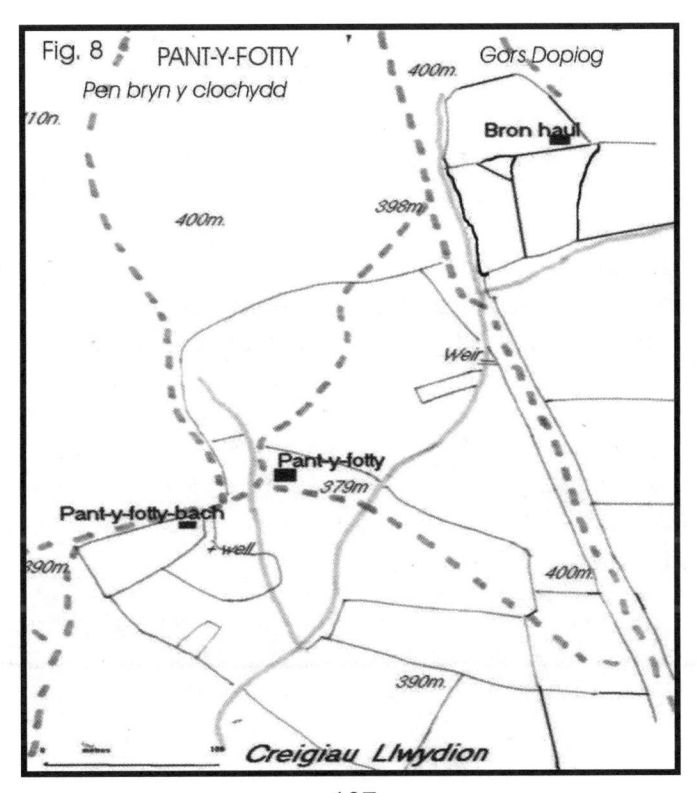

410m.
400m.
Gors Dopiog
Bron haul
398m.
Weir
Pant-y-fotty
379m.
Pant-y-fotty-bach
well
390m.
400m.
390m.
Creigiau Llwydion

Fig. 9

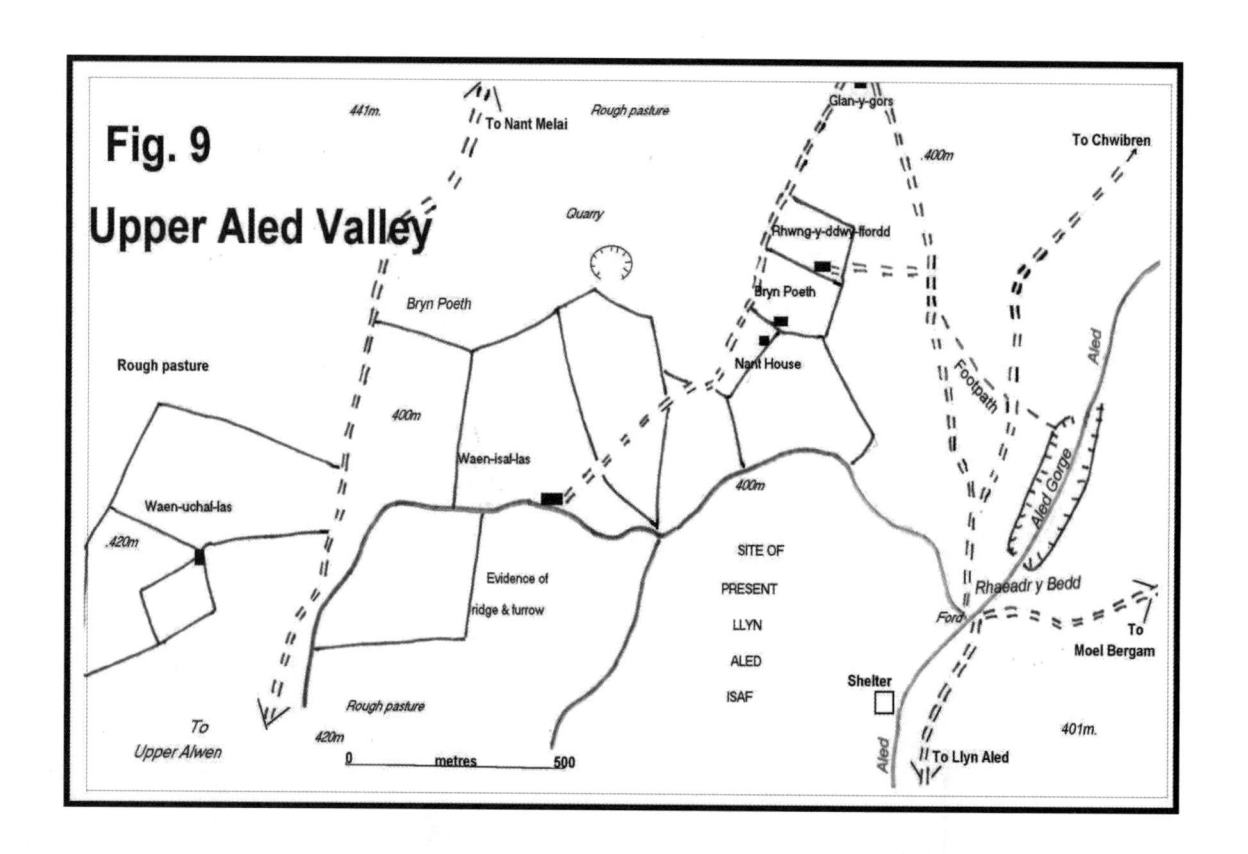

Upper Aled Valley

Today's soils in the area are no longer suitable for arable cultivation and show the impact of heavy annual rainfall (around 1366 mm)[347] and are either waterlogged or have had their mineral bases removed by rainwater constantly percolating through them to produce infertile soils known as podzols or gleys. These soils support moorland vegetation with blanket bogs and peat formations in the damper hollows. There is some grassland mainly covered with *Nardus Strictus* grasses that provide grazing land of poor or moderate value. Whether or not settlement of the area was continuous from medieval times until the sixteenth century is not known but the sixteenth century expansion of settlement on the northern side of Mynydd Hiraethog should perhaps be seen as a re-occupation rather than as colonisation.[348]

The Retreat of Settlement from the Uplands: Pollen analysis from lands on the west side of the Conwy valley, only 12 kms west of the upper Elwy valley) indicates that some parts of the upland pastures were cultivated for cereals in the period of high prices during the Napoleonic Wars. As with the highest pastures lying on the fringes of Mynydd Hiraethog in the headwaters of the Elwy and its tributaries, such landscapes have degenerated into open moorland with peaty ill drained valleys. However, a field survey of these moorlands to the west of the Conwy valley

---

[347] Environment Agency figure for Llyn Aled Isaf.
[348] For a discussion of field evidence see CPAT Project 761 "Historic Landscape Characterisation : Mynydd Hiraethog" Welshpool (2001) pp42-3

indicates quite widespread settlement of the area in the past through old field walls and rectangular long house foundations.[349]

The Mynydd Hiraethog Survey and aerial photographic analysis of the area suggest that a more intensive occupation of the upland margins was also true on the northern and western slopes of Mynydd Hiraethog. The survey identified thirty eight habitation sites in the survey area which was made up of a 1.5 kilometre wide strip running for 11 kms north south across Mynydd Hiraethog[350]. Of the farms in the northern half of the survey which falls within the boundaries of the Elwy river basin, over half the farms had been abandoned. It is not known exactly when these former farmsteads met their demise but it seems that many of them were deserted in the years between 1816 and 1900. Nineteenth century newspaper reports indicate that many small hill farms did not have the capital to invest in increased grain (or wool) production during the boom years of the Napoleonic Wars and succumbed to the high prices, higher rents and heavier taxation of the boom years, many such farms were absorbed by larger neighbours.[351]

On the upper slopes of the northern rim of Mynydd Hiraethog the landscape of well-established enclosed fields of the lower slopes gives way to one where the moorland vegetation has been cleared in places around small farmsteads many of which have been abandoned in the last 150 years. The 1879/1880 large scale Ordnance Survey

---

[349] Delia Hooke " Place Names and Vegetation History as a key to understanding Settlement in the Conwy Valley" in Edwards N. "Landscape and Settlement in Medieval Wales" Oxbow Oxford(1997)
[350] W G Owen & R J Silvester "The Mynydd Hiraethog Survey, Clwyd" (64) CPAT, Welshpool 1993 pp 5-6
[351] A.H. Dodd "The Industrial Revolution in North Wales" Bridge, Wrexham (1990) p45

maps and the contemporary Census of 1881 give an insight into the extent of settlement in the area of land around the headwaters of the River Aled and to the north of Llyn Aled towards the close of the nineteenth century when agricultural depression exacerbated by unfair tithe demands was hitting the farming communities of this area sufficiently hard to provoke serious rioting at Llannefydd and Llansannan[352]. Life was never easy for those who chose to live on these high moors, one family living on the estate of *Hafod Elwy* high on Mynydd Hiraethog was described in the early nineteenth century as living with a wooden box as a table and stones for seats.[353]

Plate 22 Ruins of Glan-y-gors

Abandoned Farmhouses: These former farmsteads lie mainly in the shallow valleys of upland streams in islands of enclosed and improved land which, like the farm buildings themselves are slowly changing as the forces of nature gradually increase the dereliction of the farmhouses and byres and natural moorland vegetation re-colonises the small enclosures around each farm. This sort of North Wales landscape can be seen in the ruins of *Glan-y-gors* farmhouse (see Plates 22 & 23) in Llansannan parish and is encapsulated in two lines of a poem by R S Thomas:

---

[352] Tim Jones "Rioting in North East Wales 1536 - 1918!" Bridge Books, Wrexham (1997) pp 56- 74
[353] CPAT Project 761 "Historic Landscape Characterisation - Mynydd Hiraethog" Welshpool, (2001) p43

*"There are holes in the roofs that are thatched with sunlight,
And the fields are reverting to the bare moor"*[354]

In some cases, the only clue to the location of a former farmstead is a stand of sycamore, ash or hawthorn trees that once served as a windbreak (see Plate 23). The abandoned farmsteads remain in varied states of preservation. Some lie beneath vegetation and are identifiable only as building platforms or as foundations of long stone huts measuring up to 9m. in length by 5m in width. Platforms were areas of flat land on which a building was erected cut into the slope of an upland river valley. Earth was removed from the slope and re-deposited lower down the slope to create a flat surface. The buildings erected on the platform were built with whatever was to have: stone quarried from the hillside near the house, turfs, locally cut timber and earth and clay mixed with straw and manure. Reeds were often used as thatch.[355] Some early dwellings, perhaps of late medieval date, were abandoned as a result of the switch to sheep production in the sixteenth century but were re-utilised as sheep folds or as shelters for shepherds.

Plate 23 : Windbreak : Glan-y-gors

---

[354] R S Thomas *"The Welsh Hill Country"* from R Garlick & R Mathias "Anglo-Welsh Poetry 1480 - 1980" Poetry Wales Press, Bridgend (1984) p 178

[355] Kate Roberts : "Local Farmsteads and Forgotten Hamlets" Heritage in Wales Issue 25 Cadw (2003) p16

Figure 9 illustrates a typical example of this landscape. The map shows a group of farmsteads lying on the south east facing slopes of Bryn Poeth forming a former island of settlement, close to the headwaters of the Aled River just to the north of Llyn Aled itself at altitudes between 360 and 390 metres. The valley sides provided shelter and the stream a plentiful water supply. Today, all these farmsteads are abandoned and illustrate the retreat of settlement from these hills over the last 150 years. *Waen Isaf Las* (GR 906600) is a pointer to active depopulation taking place in the second half of the nineteenth century. Today no remains of this farmstead are visible on the ground; presumably its stone has been used elsewhere. The house was of the *ty hir* type with a linear arrangement with the living accommodation at one end and outbuildings at the other. The buildings of the farm and its enclosed fields are shown clearly on the map of 1881 indicating that the site was at least considered habitable at that time. This is supported by the 1881 Census return lists the building as unoccupied suggesting that its vacation may have been relatively recent[356].

The nearby farmstead of *Waen Uchaf Las* (GR 901599) is also shown on the 1881 map but is not recorded on the 1881 Census at all suggesting that abandonment had taken place some time before and that possibly the Census enumerators did not consider the house to be habitable. Today, the ruins of the foundations of the house are still apparent and show that it was three roomed. Behind the house is a small stone quarry face from which some of the materials to build the house would have been obtained. Most of the pre nineteenth century dwellings were single storey. Documentary evidence suggests that the roofs some were thatched with rushes over heather underthatch, the

---

[356] PRO RG11 Piece 5533 Folio 87

roof ridge was made up of sods. Nineteenth century farmsteads in the area were generally of two storeys with a slate roof.[357]

A little to the north east lay the single storey farmstead (GR 912604) known as *Rhwng-ddwy -ffordd* (translated as "between two roads") another *"ty hir"* dating perhaps from the mid nineteenth century as a moorland encroachment[358]. The house was occupied at the time of the 1881 Census by Richard Edwards aged 50 who was born in Llansannan parish. The Census entries put a human face on the ruined house. Richard, a widower, shared the house with his ten year old son, and a "servant", Catherine Thomas aged 35 an un-married mother from Cerrig y Druidion who lived there with her twelve year old daughter, Margaret. The entry is poignant in that it also reminds us of the difficulties facing un-married mothers at a time when illegitimacy, although very common, was considered socially abhorrent. The Census also gives a clue as to why this farm of just 15 acres (6 ha) was still occupied as others around it were being abandoned. Richard's occupation is listed as gamekeeper and farmer. He presumably worked on the grouse moors that were being established at this time. Nearby stood two other farmhouses that are now derelict, these are known as *Bryn Poeth*, a former three roomed house with pigsty adjacent (GR 911603) and *Nant House*. The former had been abandoned before 1880 but *Nant House* was still occupied by an agricultural

---

[357] CPAT Project 761 "Historic Landscape Characterisation - Mynydd Hiraethog" Welshpool, (2001) p43

[358] CPAT : "Historic Landscape Characterisation - Mynydd Hiraethog: *Creigiau Llwydion* HLCA 1102" Welshpool (2001)

labourer, John Foulkes (54) at the time of the 1881 Census. The latter farmhouse appears to have been occupied until well into the twentieth century since its roof is still apparent as is an extension made from concrete blocks.[359]

It is difficult to assign a date of origin to this group of mountain farms. They may have originally been "*hafodydd*" serving as seasonal bases for herdsmen. Their sheltered locations close to free running water and the existence of surrounding regular enclosures tend to support this mode of origin. Their conversion to permanent occupation is more problematical since they were very small in terms of farm size and hardly likely to be viable in times of lower prices. This, together with the fact that the land on which they are located is still subject to rights of common suggests that at least some of the sites may have been occupied by squatters in the post medieval period, possible the eighteenth century, once transhumance had fallen out of use. These farms failed because they were small (less than 20 acres or 8.1 hectares) and were located at a relatively high altitude. One nearby farm at this altitude did survive the nineteenth century depression this being *Ty'n Llyn*, the site of the present day Llyn Aled Sailing Club's headquarters. The farm was more substantial in terms of available land with the farmer, Hugh Owens, farming 80 acres (32.4 ha) in 1881.

Squatter Settlement: The process of enclosure of waste land in North Wales had two facets, on the one hand there were, as we have just seen, estate building landlords purchasing and enclosing open pastures to extend their estates and on the other hand squatters occupying a corner of the waste with a cottage and garden. The squatters based their

---

[359] CPAT SMR 105430 & 105431

occupation on a long standing tradition (not backed up by law) that if a cottage could be built in a day and a night, then it was legally tenable. Such cottages were known as *"caban un nos"* Each squatter's house occupied a roughly circular enclosure delineated traditionally as the distance the squatter could throw an axe in various directions from the newly erected house[360]. It has been suggested that many North Wales landlords tolerated this practice since it helped keep the squatters off the Poor Rate.[361] Only those squatters who had held their land for twenty years before an Enclosure Act were allowed to remain in situ. Others were evicted or invited to buy their land back. In the Henllan Enclosure Act, twenty two poor cottagers were allocated a cottage on the waste each built at a cost of £450.[362] By the mid nineteenth century many of the circular enclosures carved out by squatters had disappeared engulfed within the rectangular enclosures that were created by the Enclosure Acts.

The Attack on the Commons: The process of enclosure did not occur without opposition from the local population, a violent riot broke out in Denbigh in 1563 over the appropriation of common lands. A considerable amount of common land remained in the uplands above the Elwy and its tributaries. In fact, the enclosure of commons in the area was not completed until after 1800. The area at the mouth of the Elwy was enclosed in 1808/9' and the upper Elwy Valley around 1840[363]. The motive for the purchase of upland grazing lands during the eighteenth and

---

[360] GRJ Jones "Field Systems of North Wales" in Baker & Butlin (ed) " Studies of Field Systems of the British Isles" CUP Cambridge (1973) p478
[361] A.H. Dodd ibid (1990) p 59
[362] A.H.Dodd p 80)
[363] .(Dodd p62)

nineteenth centuries was, in some cases, agricultural improvement and the desire to raise income during the years of high prices that coincided with the Napoleonic Wars. Even today in the north western part of Mynydd Hiraethog, farmers living on farms on lower slopes to the north of the area still hold rights of common on parts of Mynydd Hiraethog owned today by the Crown Estate Commissioners and Welsh Water.[364]

Sheep Farming and the Upland Landscape: The development of sheep farming from late medieval times to the present day has left its mark on the landscape. The grazing of the boggy slopes around the headwaters of the streams that feed the Elwy and Aled Rivers has left a number of relict features. These include temporary habitation sites or shelters, sheepfolds and sheep-dipping strictures close to small streams. An example of such a shelter is located on Figure 9. These structures of earth or stone often include the walls of abandoned homesteads re-utilised to provide sheep shelters. The sheepfolds of the uplands vary in both date and shape from single enclosures to more elaborate structures with several pens. Similarly windbreaks vary from a simple bank to more complex L or Z - shaped structures giving protection from winds blowing from several directions. Such relict features may be found along the courses of Nant Bach and Nant y Foel, small streams draining into the river Aled a few hundred metres to the north of Llyn Aled.

Agricultural Improvement and the Nineteenth Century Landscape: The Sandbach family of *Hafodunos* estate in Llangernyw were instrumental in transforming the landscape of their estates by supporting both enclosure and agricultural improvements on their 4300 acres (1740 ha) from the late 1830s.

---

[364]WG Owen & R J Silvester "The Mynydd Hiraethog Survey, Clwyd" (64) CPAT Welshpool (1993) p 2

Plate 24 Improved Pastures – Upper Cledwen Valley

In 1895, Colonel Sanbach of *Hafodunos* gave evidence to the Royal Commission claiming that his family had transformed their lands around Llangernyw from "*a howling wilderness into a fertile and productive district*"[365] Samuel Sandbach, the colonel's grandfather, had been the chairman of the Parliamentary Enclosure Board that dealt with the enclosure of the upper Elwy valley in 1838. Among the improvements brought about on the Sandbach estates were the conversion of common pasture to arable land producing oats, barley and turnips; the rebuilding of farmhouses; the draining of wetlands; the

View across Upper Cledwen Valley from Ddol-frwynog

---

[365] R.H. Teague & R.L. Brown: "Griffith Jones' Pious Minister - The Reverend John Kenrick, Vicar of Llangernyw 1730 - 1755" Trans. Denbs. Hist. Soc. Vol. 49 (2000) p18

planting of 300 acres (121.4 ha) of trees and the removal of old banks and hedges and the creation of new field boundaries. There can be no doubt that the Sandbach family brought about significant changes to the landscape of the upper Elwy valley during the nineteenth centuries.

Enclosed lands might be "improved" in order to produce grain, raise the output of beef, mutton and wool or yield valuable timber. However, the costs of improving the quality of grazing land were high for local farmers who, without the vast wealth of the Sandbach family, often existed at subsistence level. Nevertheless, there is evidence of some attempt to use lime as a means of reducing soil acidity, this was certainly the case on the Sandbach lands[366]. The Sanbach family also promoted selective breeding of stock and the use of imported guano as a feriliser.

Crops grown: On more favoured lower slopes and valley bottoms, oats, rye, barley and hay were grown as an important source of winter feed for stock and as a staple part of the human diet. Attempts were made to grow oats on some parts of Mynydd Hiraethog although Walter Davies, writing at the turn of the nineteenth century noted that such crops frequently never ripened. During the 1830s, another, more unusual, crop was grown for fodder this being furze remnants of which can still be seen growing wild on the steeper slopes. The furze was crushed and bruised by machine (sometimes water powered) and fed as a supplement to hay and straw[367]. Small numbers of pigs and poultry would have been kept on the farms themselves, mainly for the sustenance of the family of the tenant farmers who

---

[366] R.H. Teague & R.L. Brown: "Griffith Jones' Pious Minister - The Reverend John Kenrick, Vicar of Llangernyw 1730 - 1755" Trans. Denbs. Hist. Soc. Vol. 49 (2000) p19
[367] Richard Moore-Colyer "Welsh Cattle Drovers" Landmark, Ashbourne (2002) p35.

rented the estate lands of the lesser gentry of the valley. Some of the highest pastures were left unfenced with the sheep walks left for joint use by the several proprietors.

Lack of Farming Capital in the Nineteenth Century: An early nineteenth century observer commented that the greatest obstacle facing agricultural improvement on the farms of North Wales was "want of capital"[368]. The high legal, surveying and fencing costs of enclosure were too high for some smaller farmers who sold their land to larger neighbours or did not renew their leases. By the mid eighteenth century, typical farm sizes ranged from 30 to 100 acres. (12-40 ha)[369] On the Sandbach estates around Llangernyw some smaller farms were abandoned and their lands consolidated into larger more economically viable holdings. In some cases, new tenants were recruited from Scotland to farm these larger farms. One such family, the Roxburghs, farmed over 700 acres (283 ha) in the 1860s. The consolidation of holdings and the enclosure movements of the nineteenth century had a fundamental impact on the landscape. Field boundaries had previously been influenced by the edges of the former open arable land with quillets and the small parcels of land created through the inheritance process of *cyfran* (gavelkind). This gave a landscape of irregular shaped fields. Where nineteenth century improvements were carried out, the old field boundaries disappeared to be replaced with larger fields with ruler straight edges.[370]

---

[368] Walter Davies "General View of the Agriculture and Domestic Economy of North Wales" London, (1810) p460
[369] Geraint H Jenkins "The Foundations of Modern Wales 1642-1780" OUP Oxford (1993) p283
[370] D Longley Medieval Settlement and Landscape Change on Anglesey" Landscape History Vol.23 (2001) p46

The Droving Trade: The high costs of improving grazing land and maintaining a stock of breeding animals meant that most Welsh hill farmers concentrated on the production of store cattle in the enclosed fields close to the valley floors[371]. The export of beef from North Wales to the growing London market through the droving trade developed from the late fifteenth century when cattle from Anglesey were walked to English markets[372]. We know for certain that West Denbighshire played a part in supplying cattle to the droving trade to England[373] from the sixteenth to eighteenth centuries. The leather industry of Northampton was another destination of drovers from North Wales. The trade expanded rapidly in the eighteenth century when there was a buoyant demand for Welsh store cattle for fattening on the rich pastures of the English Midlands, Essex and East Anglia. A Denbighshire Quarter Sessions record of 1754[374] records the imprisonment of a Llansannan drover, Thomas Williams at Ruthin Gaol for an unpaid debt. The Rolls record Williams' assets including money owed to him by others. This gives a good insight into the complex financial dealings of Welsh drovers since he lent money as well a carrying out his droving activities. Williams had financial dealings with a Coleshill (Warwickshire) butcher, an Essex landowner and a farmer at *Cas Gan Ditw*, Llandegla, and a local focus of droving routes. In addition there were local contacts in Grugor, Pentre Foelas, Groes and a blacksmit from Ysbytty Ifan.[375] The extensive local contacts suggest that cattle were procured locally before making their way to Essex via Llandegla and Warwickshire. Welsh drovers were termed the "*Spanish*

---

[371] Richard Moore-Colyer "Welsh Cattle Drovers" Landmark, Ashbourne (2002) p18
[372] Richard Moore-Colyer "Welsh Cattle Drovers" Landmark, Ashbourne (2002) p59
[373] A.H. Dodd "The Industrial Revolution in North Wales" Bridge, Wrexham (1990) p8
[374] DRO QSD/SR/185/49
[375] Bryn Ellis "Some Interesting Items from the Quarter Sessions Rolls" Clwyd Historian No. 45, Autumn 2000 p. 13

fleet of Wales" by the Bishop of Bangor in the mid seventeenth century since they not only provided currency in the local economy but in some cases acted as bankers, messengers, and investors. They also provided isolated communities such as those in the Elwy valley with news and gossip from the outside world[376].

The drovers must have been an impressive sight with between 100 and 400 cattle being tended by 4-8 men and their dogs. They made slow progress through the countryside covering only 15 - 20 miles (24 - 32 kms) per day travelling mainly on hilltop tracks often dating from prehistoric times.[377] The trade not only brought wealth to the owners of estates in North Wales but also gave birth to many taverns and smithies along routes taken by the drovers. Much research is still required on the North Wales droving trade but a clue to one of their routes lies in the name of a small house on the north side of the Elwy valley in Llangernyw parish. The house named "*Dafarn Bara Ceirch*" lies close to the isolated intersection of two mountain lanes at a height of just over 290 metres (GR 897712). The name translates as "Oat -bread Tavern" perhaps indicating the simple fare on offer to the passing drovers.

The Elwy basin was therefore crossed by drovers and Llangernyw was, according to local tradition, a stopping place for the droving trade. The village had five annual fairs; it was at such fairs that drovers acquired many of their animals. Llangernyw parish records include a letter from the Vicar to the Bishop of St. Asaph dated April 1750 in which it is claimed that upwards of 2000 "horned beasts" had been for sale in the village's March Fair. It is also the

---

[376] Geraint H Jenkins "The Foundations of Modern Wales 1642-1780" OUP Oxford (1993) p113.
[377] Richard Moore-Colyer "Welsh Cattle Drovers" Landmark, Ashbourne (2002) p87

case that in some cases, drovers in North Wales travelled from farm to farm and bought animals directly from farmers[378].

The Local Droving Trade 1850 -1900: The long distance droving trade gradually died out with the spread of the railway network in the middle decades of the nineteenth century but some local droving survived with cattle being driven the relatively short distance to local fairs and railway yards[379]. The 1881 Census possibly identifies one such local drover living in Llangernyw at *Mill Cottage* two miles to the south of the village (GR 876665). The man concerned, William Lloyd (54) had been born in Caernarfonshire and was described as a *"cattle dealer employing two men."* There is also evidence that some long distance droving of cattle from Denbighshire to Essex still continued into the Railway Age. A recent piece of research has shown that a Bryneglwys drover drove 105 black cattle to Barnet Fair in Middlesex as late as 1865. Unfortunately the drover concerned was financially ruined by the trip since he lost almost all the cattle to cattle plague.[380]

Dairy Produce: Since the Elwy valley was fairly isolated from major urban areas, it is likely that here, as elsewhere in Wales, small amounts of butter were produced for sale in the small markets at Abergele, Llanrwst and Denbigh. An attempt was made to expand the dairy trade in the upper valley in 1916 when a cheese factory was established in

---

[378] Richard Collier "Welsh Cattle Drovers in the Nineteenth Century" NLW Journal; Vol.XVII/4 (1972)
[379] Richard Moore-Colyer "Welsh Cattle Drovers" Landmark, Ashbourne (2002) p118
[380] A. Fletcher "Cattle Plague and Droving, 1865" Clwyd Historian No.47 Autumn 2001 p17

Llangernyw village. Sadly the venture failed in 1922 and the extensive stone buildings now lie abandoned and derelict close to the centre of the village.

Other Farm Products: It is also likely that farms in the valley supplied hides for use by the tanners, glovers and cordwainers of Denbigh who had a flourishing long distance market for their wares in the eighteenth century. There was also a market for local wool to meet the needs of local domestic weaving. In the early sixteenth century, Leland described the lands of Isdulas commote that lie on the north side of the upper Elwy valley as being *"hilly ground, good for goats"* while the uplands of Uwch Aled commote around the headwaters of the Elwy produced *"neat horses and sheep"*[381]. The rise of Abergele as a "bathing place" in the last years of the eighteenth century no doubt added an extra market for local agricultural produce

Grouse Moors: Grouse shooting in the late nineteenth and early twentieth centuries also left its mark on the landscape. On Bryn Mawr, in the neighbouring land drained by the headwaters of the Afon Alwen, the remains of 29 nineteenth century grouse shooting butts still exist.[382] *Tan y Graig* farmhouse was extended to provide accommodation for shooting parties. Although it lies slightly beyond our study area in the neighbouring Alwen river basin, the shooting rights no doubt extended into the Elwy river basin catchment area. The farm, possibly dating from the seventeenth century (date stone of 1647 survives on an outbuilding), was the centre piece of an estate which re-used the medieval name for this part of the moorland *"Hafod Elwy"*. In 1864, It was bought for £4175 by A

---

[381] Lucy Toulmin Smith " Leland's Itinerary in Wales 1536-1539" Bell, London (1906) p95
[382] W G Owen & R J Silvester "The Mynydd Hiraethog Survey, Clwyd" (64) CPAT, Welshpool 1993 pp 5-6

R Cox from Broxton Park in Cheshire from Charles Chester, described as a gentleman formerly of Southport and Waterloo near Liverpool. The house still survives today as a hotel. It could well be that the loss of open grazing land to grouse shooting also contributed to the demise of local farms during the second half of the nineteenth century.

The Development of a "Managed" Landscape in the Uplands: In the last years of the nineteenth century and the early twentieth century, the heather moorland above the northern edge of Mynydd Hiraethog around the headwaters of streams flowing into the Elwy and Aled rivers became a managed landscape. The area lies 3 kms to the north of *Hafod Elwy* on a high point of the watershed between the Aled and Brenig river basins. A key individual in this development was the Liverpool entrepreneur Hudson Kearley who became the first Viscount Devonport, who created a large shooting estate in the area. The most lasting feature of this period is his now derelict shooting box known as *"Gwylfa Hiraethog"* where he housed his shooting parties which until recently dominated the landscape of the high moor. The lodge, known as *"Gwylfa Hiraethog"*, stood at an altitude of 496m (1627 feet) and dates from the early 1890s when Viscount Devonport erected a timber lodge of Norwegian construction on the site. This was later replaced by an imposing stone building still well known as a landmark to those crossing the moors by car from Pentre Foelas to Denbigh[383]. The building stood empty for many years after falling into dis-use in the mid twentieth century. It was known locally as "the haunted house".

---

[383]CPAT Project 761 "Historic Landscape Characterisation - Mynydd Hiraethog" Welshpool, (2001)

A short distance away, also on the Aled/Brenig watershed, stands the *Sportsman's Arms* public house still serving the needs of travellers crossing the moors on Telford's new turnpike road (now the A543). The owner of the nearby Hafod Elwy Estate at the time when the new road was constructed in the 1820s built the Inn at *Bryntrillyn* (meaning hill of 3 lakes). The hill gave its name to the inn until the present name was adopted around 1870 no doubt reflecting the growing popularity of grouse shooting at that time. The inn, at an altitude of 455m., is said to be the highest pub in Wales. Behind the inn lie several elongated and banked rectangular fields enclosed out of the former common presumably to provide grazing for draught animals using the turnpike road.

Little organised grouse shooting now takes place on the high moors although vast expanses of heather moorland still remain. One such area lies to the east of the upper Aled valley and has been designated as the *Moel Bergam Historic Landscape Characterisation area*[384]. This 13.5 square kilometre area ranges from 280 to 490m in altitude and contains the source of the Afon Deunant, one of the larger streams in the Elwy river system. The tranquil and little known glacial lake known as *Llyn y Foel Frech* occupies an area of about 1.75 ha (just over 4 acres) and lies in a glacial hollow above *Llyn Aled Isaf*. (GR 919592)

In the twentieth century, the economy of the area changed yet again through the creation of large reservoirs on the upland plateau close to the watersheds of the rivers Elwy, Aled and Alwen at Aled Isaf(1938) which supplies Rhyl and Prestatyn, Alwen (1912) which supplies Birkenhead and Brenig (1970s) supplying North East Wales. The man-

---

[384]CPAT : "Historic Landscape Characterisation - Mynydd Hiraethog: *Moel Bergam*, HLCA 1102" Welshpool (2001)

made *Aled Isaf reservoirs* is 1.3 kms in length and 200 m. wide The 0.3 square kilometre lake was formed by building a curved dam of concrete blocks at an altitude of 360m. The dam carries the minor road from Llyn Aled to Llansannan across the Afon Aled. Below the dam are the spectacular waterfalls of Rhaeadr y Bedd Upstream, at an altitude of 370m. lies *Llyn Aled*, the largest lake in the Elwy/Aled river basin It a natural lake of glacial origin that forms the source of the Afon Aled. It was enlarged to form a reservoir by the building of a stone and earth dam at its northern end. in 1934. The dam with its stone clad valve tower carries the access road to Llyn Aled Sailing Club.

Plate 25

More widespread use of these upland areas has resulted through recreational pursuits such as sailing, fishing and hill walking bringing in more people from outside the region and changing the traditional locally focused economic base of the area from hill farming to the related roles of leisure and water collection.

CHAPTER 12 - LAND OWNERSHIP AND THE "GREAT RE-BUILDING" FROM 1575.

The Rise of Local Gentry: The break up of traditional structures of *llys, gwely* and *gafael* led to the development of a social structure in post medieval Wales that in many ways paralleled that which pertained in England. The emergence of a gentry class actively building estates has its origins following the late 13th century conquest of Wales, was well underway by 1450 [385] and was being consolidated during the sixteenth century. The expansion of personal fortunes of the local gentry reflected the economic growth, inflation and population expansion in the period from early sixteenth century until the mid seventeenth century. Political developments also supported these changes,: the lands of the Lordship of Denbigh were acquired by the Crown on the accession of Edward IV in 1461 which paved the way for the sale of land to local gentry. This process was taken a step further in the reign of Elizabeth I (1568 - 1603) who actively sold land to raise cash to meet her military expenses[386]. The lands disposed of in this period included those of the Lordship of Denbigh, acquired by Elizabeth's "favourite" Robert Dudley, Earl of Leicester in 1563.

In 1772, a lady traveller from Enfield staying as a guest in the homes of the local gentry voiced the opinion that *"There is no part of Wales in which so many fine seats, for ten miles around St' Asaph"*. This statement is of dubious accuracy but in keeping with the distribution of houses of the gentry shown in Figure 10 which shows a significant

---

[385] John Davies "A History of Wales" Penguin, London (1993) p163
[386] E. D. Evans "The Crown Lordships of Denbighshire" Trans. Denbs. Hist. Soc. Vol. 50 (2000) p29

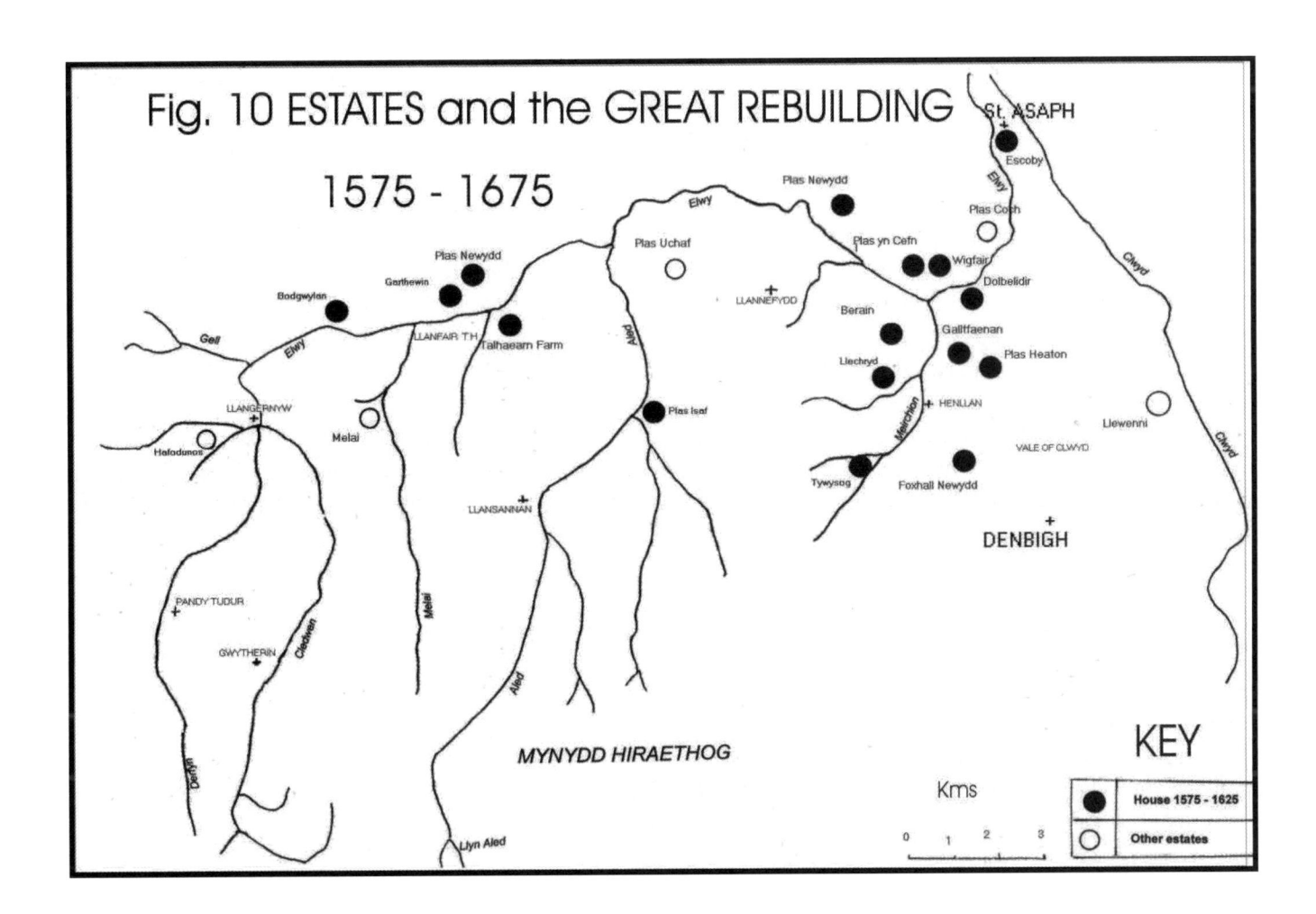

Fig. 10 ESTATES and the GREAT REBUILDING 1575 - 1675

clustering of such houses in the Vale of Clwyd and the lower Elwy river basin. The creation of private estates has been described as *"the vehicle through which authority found expression in the landscape"*.[387] Such estates could therefore be interpreted as symbols of local power, areas reserved for the exclusive use of an elite family group. The gentry class in the Elwy valley was mainly of Welsh princely roots such as the Lloyds and Wynnes and even in the case of the Salisburys of *Galltfaenan* and the neighbouring *Llewenni*, who were of English roots, they were still identifiably Welsh.[388] The Salisburys acquired the *Galltfaenan* estate in sixteenth century when they purchased it from the Ravenscrofts whose main seat was at Bretton, Flintshire.

The Adoption of Anglicised Surnames: In the sixteenth century the estate-centred gentry began the use of anglicised surnames although the general population continued to use patronymics[389]. The process of losing the prefix "ap" from surnames began officially in the early 1530s when the judiciar of the Council of Wales at Ludlow forbid the use of this prefix in an attempt to simplify records.[390] An extreme examplel of the extent that patronymics had evolved by the sixteenth century is revealed in a record of the arrest in Gwytherin parish of Thomas

---

[387] Richard Muir "The New Reading the Landscape" Univ. of Exeter Press. (2000) p119
[388] G.E. Jones ""Modern Wales - A Concise History" CUP Cambridge (1984) pp 6-10
[389] G.E. Jones ""Modern Wales - A Concise History" CUP Cambridge (1984) p 4
[390] Gwyn A Williams "When was Wales?" Black Raven Press, London. (1985) p 118

ap Llewelyn ap Gruffudd ap Tudor and Richard ap Thomas ap Llewelyn ap Gruffudd for the theft of clothes from a house in Dwygyfylchi.[391]

The transition from Welsh to anglicised surnames among the general population can be traced from parish records which indicate that change was slow to spread from the Marches to the Elwy basin. In the Gwytherin parish records for the second half of the seventeenth century Welsh surnames using "ap" are still common but during the succeeding century they were being modified and thus "ap Owen" became merely "Owen"; ap Hugh became "Pugh" or "Hughes" while "David" became "Davies"[392].

The Anglicisation of the Gentry: The adoption of English in lieu of Welsh as the everyday tongue in the homes of the gentry was also a slow process that was not complete until the first half of the eighteenth century. In 1760, Richard Morris, a leading Welsh literary figure and founder member of the influential "Morris Circle" of writers and poets came to the conclusion that the Welsh gentry actually bore malice towards the Welsh language. Thus, by 1780, the ruling landed classes had more or less severed their links with the Welsh culture of their predecessors.[393] In their search for acceptance by their English counterparts, the Welsh gentry also sought to impress upon them that

---

[391] W Ogwen Davies (ed) "Calendars of the Caerns. Quarter Sessions Records" (1956) p68
[392] Clwyd Family History Society "Gwytherin Parish Registers 1667 - 1812" Vols. 1 & 2 Ruthin (1996)
[393] Geraint H Jenkins "The Foundations of Modern Wales 1642-1750" OUP Oxford (1993) p399

people who dwelt on their estates were orderly people, a far cry from the rustic Welshmen lampooned as buffoons in English satirical cartoons of the early years of the eighteenth century. The change in attitude found expression in the romantic landscape paintings of Welsh scenes by late eighteenth artists such as Richard Wilson and the illustrator Moses Griffiths which depicted Welshmen as hardy and upstanding folk.[394] Such paintings encouraged tours into Wales by the English upper classes who felt it was safe to venture into what was previously seen as inhospitable wild territory.

The Role of Genealogy: In general, the Welsh gentry were significantly less prosperous than their English counterparts and placed great emphasis on their genealogies, real or imagined rather than wealth. A number of falsely constructed genealogies were produced in the sixteenth century in the early days of gentrification.[395] The aim of a Welsh genealogy was to trace its ancestry back to one of the early saints or Welsh military heroes of the post Roman period. Families claiming noble descent claimed to be members of either the five "Royal" or fifteen "Noble" tribes of Wales, a practice that had its roots in the late fifteenth century. The Wynne family of *Melai* in Llanfair Talhaearn parish claimed such a pedigree tracing their ancestry to its founder: Marehudd ap Cynan a ninth century descendant of Beli Mawr "King of Britain" The family claimed to be the eighth "Noble" tribe of Wales. The

---

[394] Prys Morgan ""Among our Ancient Mountains" Travellers in Wales and the appreciation of mountainscape in the 18th and 19th centuries" Conference Report of the Society for Landscape History Vol 18 (1996)

[395] Gareth Elwyn Jones "Modern Wales - A Concise History" CUP, Cambridge 2nd Ed. (1994) p30

Wynnes of *Melai* were able to extend their estates following the dissolution of the Cistercian abbey at Maenol in the Conwy valley in 1537. The family acquired the site of the former abbey and the lands around it.[396]

Marriage and Estate Building: In some cases, marriage was used to acquire more land as in the case of the Wynne family of *Melai*. In the late sixteenth century, William Wynne of *Melai* married Mary Clough daughter of landowner Sir Richard Clough and Katherine of Berain. His descendant, Robert Wynne, the son of William Wynne, a Royalist colonel of *Melai*, who married Margaret Price, the heiress to *Garthewin* estate, Llanfair Talhaearn, in the late seventeenth century. The wealth from owning land was derived mainly from rents paid by tenant farmers. By the mid eighteenth century a key feature was the concentration of property within the grasp of a few very rich families leading to the eighteenth century being described as "*the golden age of the Welsh landlord*".[397] The process of acquisition of land and power through a judicious marriage continued into the nineteenth century. A local example was when the large *Galltfaenan* estate passed to the Mainwaring family when Townshend Mainwaring of Marchwiel Hall, near Wrexham, second son of the Reverend Charles Mainwaring of Oteley Park, Staffordshire, married Anna Maria Salisbury, owner of the estate, in 1837. The estate remained in the hands of the Mainwaring family until its sale in 1926.

---

[396] R O F Wynne "The Wynne family of Melai and Garthewin" Transactions of the Denbighshire Historical Society, Vol.5 (1956) p73

[397] Geraint H Jenkins "The Foundations of Modern Wales 1642-1780" OUP Oxford (1993) p261.

Large Estates in the Elwy Basin: Estate-building in Wales reached its apogee in the late nineteenth century when there were twenty estates exceeding 8000 hectares (19,760 acres) in size.[398] In 1873, there were four landowners of estates in the Elwy valley that exceeded 3000 acres (1214 ha) in size: Townshend Mainwaring of *Galltfaenan* 4046 ha (10600 acres); Henry Robertson Sandbach of *Hafodunos* 1877 ha (4640 acres); Brownlow Wynne of *Garthewin* 4094 ha (10,119 acres) and John Lloyd Wynne of *Coed Coch* (just outside the Elwy basin), 4126 ha (10,197 acres). These estates yielded significant incomes to their owners, in 1873, *Garthewin* rental income amounted to £4670 per annum.[399]

Plate 26: Galltfaenan

A good example of estate building with its origins in the late medieval period is provided by the acquisition of lands in the township of Meifod on the north side of the Elwy valley some 6.4 kms (4 miles) north east of Llanfair Talhaearn. Here, lands were being bought up by the Holland family who owned the ancient estate of *Dinorben* just to the north of the area. At the time of the 1334 Survey of the Honour of Denbigh, the township of Meifod was made up of 360 acres

---

[398] John Davies "A History of Wales" Penguin, London (1993) p208
[399] B Ll Jones "The Great Landowners of Wales in 1873" Nat. Library of Wales Journal Vol XIV/3 (1966)

(146 ha) of land and waste. In 1583, Piers Holland of *Dinorben* held an area ten times larger than the average individual holding of land in the township in 1334. His lands consisted of three parcels divided by quickset hedges into closes and fields divided among several tenants. This is indicative of the fact that estate building was frequently accompanied by enclosure. In 1583, one of Holland's parcels of land close to the river Elwy was described as being "very barren arable ground" which required a period of ten-twelve years in fallow after producing crops for two to three years. In the eighteenth century, the Holland's estates were sold to the Hughes family who acquired the title Lord Dinorben. This family owned over 90 per cent of the land in Meifod township by 1840.[400]

"The Great Re-building" in the Elwy Basin: The wealth derived from land and agricultural surpluses found expression in the landscape in the form of newly built residences for the local gentry and larger tenant farmers generally on a fairly modest scale many of which still feature in the landscape of today[401]. There was, however, sufficient activity to indicate that even this relatively remote part of Wales experienced what has been referred to as the "Great Rebuilding" in the English countryside between 1575 and 1625. (See Fig. 10). However, as Figure 10 reveals, the majority of the houses that experienced re-building in this period were located close to the western edge of the more anglicised lower Vale of Clwyd and the English border. The remainder were sited close to routes through the Elwy and Aled river valleys.

---

[400] GRJ Jones "Field Systems of North Wales" in Baker & Butlin (ed) " Studies of Field Systems of the British Isles" CUP Cambridge (1973) pp469-471

[401] Matthew Griffiths "Land, Life and Belief, Wales 1415 - 1642" in G E Jones & D Smith (ed) "The People of Wales" Gomer, Llandysul (1999) p62

Late Medieval Houses: In the Elwy basin, many late medieval houses survived into the Tudor period often bearing the word *"plas"* in their name. The use of this term appears to have developed in the period after the 1282 conquest to signify the home of a gentleman. Several of these houses survive into the present day often concealed beneath later additions to the building.[402]. The majority of these were of similar type to those found further east on the Cheshire and Shropshire borders and were timber-framed and of cruck or box construction. These medieval dwellings were open to the roof through which smoke from an open fire on the floor escaped via a roof vent. They were known as "hall houses". Such houses were typical of Wales north east of a line from Machynlleth to Newport.[403]

Timber - framed Houses: Timber framed houses were commonest on the eastern side of the Elwy basin with the recently-restored house of *Dolbelidir* being typical if this style. To the west they gave way to stone-built houses. Windows ran down each end of the long axis of the hall house. They had wooden mullions except for the houses of the richest individuals which would have had stone mullions. Windows had shutters on the inside. No glass was used in the windows in many cases owing to its high price. In the Elwy river basin, the half-timbered "hall" houses represent the recovery of the Welsh economy in the late fifteenth century.

---

[402] A J Parkinson "Vernacular Architecture" in J Manley et al (ed) "The Archaeology of Clwyd" Clwyd CC., Mold (1991) p294/5
[403] John Davies "The Making of Wales" Cadw/Sutton, Stroud (1996) p62

Sometimes, older late medieval structures were enlarged as at *Berain*, a house that gave its name to one of the medieval townships of Llannefydd. The house stands 2 kms ESE of the village church (GR 008698), and has a late medieval hammer beam roof. However, most of present structure dates from a re-building of the late 16th or early 17th century. The house is the former home of Katherine of Berain (1535 - 1591), an astute woman, reputedly a kinswoman of Queen Elizabeth I, who married four of the leading local gentry in succession. (Salisburys' Cloughs, Wynnes and Thelwalls).

Tudor Adaptations to House Designs: The new buildings of the post 1575 era replaced earlier half timbered houses with stone or brick houses. More typical of the Tudor period was the building of *Plas Newydd*, on a south facing slope about one kilometre north of the Elwy River in Cefn Meiriadog parish (GR 001723). The plan of the house reflects the development from the mid 15th century of open hearths being gradually replaced by fireplaces with chimneys at one end of the building. By 1550, all new houses had internal fireplaces. By dispensing with the need for open fires, it was now possible to add upper floors to a building.[404] In *Plas Newydd*, the upper floor was lit by new dormer windows added in 1583. The similarly named *Plas Newydd* (Plas Newydd is translated as "new hall"), a house in Llanfair Talhaearn parish (GR 927715), 1.5 kilometres to the north of the village alongside the old road that once linked the village with Abergele, shows that the local gentry also paid close attention to the interior of their new properties, the house has a decorated timber partition separating different bays dated 1575.[405] The

---

[404] G.E. Jones ""Modern Wales - A Concise History" CUP Cambridge (1984) p32

[405] Edward Hubbard : "The Buildings of Wales :Clwyd" Penguin Harmondsworth (1986) p47

provision of upper storeys spelt the end of cruck construction since the curved crucks limited headroom on upper floors. By 1600, this form of timber framing had been abandoned.

Similar internal evidence of the "Great Re-building" also survives at *Galltfaenan* in Henllan parish, centre of a large estate held traditionally by the Salisbury family, standing on the south side of the Elwy valley close to its confluence with the Afon Meirchion (GR 027698). The house (see Plate 26) has a "cyclopaean" doorway set in massive upright stones dated to 1601.[406] Across the Elwy valley, the manor house of *Plas yn Cefn*, was begun in 1597 and became the seat of a branch of Wales' most powerful family dynasty, the Williams-Wynns. The present house is mainly early nineteenth century in date but a beam over the main entrance is dated 1611.[407]

On the south eastern limits of the river basin, John Panton, the Recorder of Denbigh built the now ruined *Foxhall Newydd* (GR 029675) in 1608. Another ruined house dating from the Great Re-Building of the sixteenth century was *Dolbelidir (*GR030709) on the south bank of the Elwy. This house was built by one of the valley's eminent literary figures, Henry Salisbury, one of the Salisburys of *Llewenni*, complier of the first English-Welsh grammar text. The house is currently being restored by the Landmark Trust.

---

[406] E. Hubbard (ibid) (1986) p50
[407] Conwy Sites and Monuments Record PRN102139

Rebuilt Farmhouses: Just over two kilometres to the south west of *Foxhall Newydd*, the local Parry family re-built the house at *Tywysog* (GR 003687) in 1575. *Tywysog* was the site of a medieval township in Llannefydd parish. An early seventh century sculptured stone is incorporated into a wall of the house. Other re-built farmhouses in Llannefydd parish are *Llechryd* (GR 010688) dating from the late sixteenth century and *Ty Uchaf* (GR 986720) dating from the following century. These later houses were able to incorporate glass panes in their windows since glass became much more available during the seventeenth century.

The Wynn family (some branches of the family added an "e" to their surname) also owned several large farms that were let out to tenants. Some of these too saw the effects of re-building. *Plas Uchaf*, (GR 967716) was owned by the branch of the Wynns living at *Coed Coch*. The farm is located on the foot of the slope of the western side of the hill that is dominated by *Mynydd y Gaer* hillfort and appears to date from the late seventeenth or early eighteenth century.[408] The Victorian windows of the stone farmhouse are mis-leading and the true age of the house is apparent from its blocked up stone mullions windows. *Talhaearn Farm* (GR 929702), which gave its name to a medieval township, was re-built at some time in the early seventeenth century. *Old Foxhall* (GR 033674) dates from the late seventeenth century and was the home of another branch of the Lloyd family. The house provides a good example of a Jacobean homestead.

---

[408] CADW : "Register of Landscapes, Parks and Gardens of Special Historic Interest in Wales" Part 1.1 Clwyd (1995)

Eighteenth Century Re-building: The process of rebuilding continued into the 18th century as at *Garthewin* (GR 915705), a medieval township centre 2 kms west of Llanfair Talhaearn. The present elegant stuccoed and cream-washed house is a Grade II listed building and the result of a series of re-modelling exercises between 1710 and 1930 The first re-building of the eighteenth century took place around 1710 when Dr. Robert Wynne, Chancellor of St. Asaph and Vicar of Gresford .demolished its seventeenth century predecessor and built a new country house on the same site. The essential features of the house's present day appearance are those of a re-modelling carried out 1767 and 1772 for the chancellor's grandson, Robert Wynne by the Chester architect Joseph Turner designer of Chester's new Bridgegate.[409] The surviving eighteenth century house has three storeys and nine bays. It stands on a south-facing slope on the south side of the Elwy valley nestled between the steep slopes of Moelfre Uchaf to the west and Mynydd dir to the east. Nothing is known of the form of the medieval house but part of the layout of a seventeenth century house is still evident towards the rear of the property. We get an insight into the interior of the eighteenth century house from an entry in the diary of a visitor to the house in 1772.The visitor, Miss Jinny Jenks from Enfield, noted that the house had *"two very good parlours and a hall"* and was *"well furnished, particularly a very elegant tea room over the hall hung with fine India paper, gold papier mache beads"*[410] This brief description makes it apparent that the gentry in this small Welsh valley kept abreast of London fashions. The house remained in the hands of the Wynne family until the late twentieth century. In 1930, the owner, R.O.F. Wynne, commissioned the eminent architect CloughWilliams-Ellis of Port Meirion fame, to carry out further changes since the house was

---

[409] E. Hubbard (ibid) (1986) p57
[410] "A Tour of North Wales by Jinny Jenks 1772" National Library of Wales MS 227538 p16

showing the signs of some years of neglect. The most evident of these was the addition of another loggia to the east side of the house to balance the earlier one created by Joseph Turner on the west side. (see Plate IV)

New Eighteenth Century Farmhouses: New farmhouses were also constructed during the eighteenth century as in Llanfair Talhaearn parish at *Ty Gwyn* (GR 958705) built in 1726 and *Pen yr Allt* (GR 952751) built in 1710. Another example of eighteenth century re-building of homesteads can be seen at *Tal y Bryn* (GR 998706) in Llannefydd parish.

Farm Out-buildings: The eighteenth century interest in agriculture also finds expression in another ancient site that was a former township, this being *Melai* owned by another branch of the Wynne family and set on a tributary of the Elwy in Llanfair Talhaearn parish (GR 902678). The site has an example of fashionable farm buildings in the form of elliptically arched entrances to farm buildings. At *Garthewin* too, another branch of the family built an elaborate cobbled stable yard and barns accessed through an arch bearing a clock tower and dating from 1722. Jinny Jenks, who visited the house in that year, gives an insight into the use of these farm buildings. She describes *"two teams of eight oxen which fetch stone from the quarry, eight or twelve cart horses for ploughing, dragging timber etc., four coach horses and sixteen others including horses for their own riding, hack horses for the servants, mules for going errands and some few training for runners."* Other animals kept included *"never fewer than fourteen milk cows, fifteen to twenty young cattle , shilling beef, sheep and hogs, a pack of dogs and ten common dogs of various sorts."* Such developments indicate that the Wynne family were not just country squires in a Welsh backwater but in touch with the latest in national fashions and developments. In 1938, the owner, R O F Wynne, converted the main barn at

Garthewin into a theatre. The *Garthewin* players, based at the barn put on regular performances of Welsh plays. Kate Roberts and Saunders-Lewis, the well known protagonist of Welsh Nationalism and a friend of Wynne, were closely involved in productions at *Garthewin* as were the Welsh National Theatre Company. *Garthewin* has been described as "*a major centre of Welsh cultural expression*" [411]

The Nineteenth Century: *Plas Heaton*, a classical stone house of up to three storeys, standing on the south eastern rim of the Elwy river basin (GR 032692), is a good example of the re-building that continued into the nineteenth century. The house dates from 1805 and was re-named after the Heaton family who occupied it from that time. The present facade conceals an earlier house of the early eighteenth century while traces of an even earlier house dating from the Great Re-building of the sixteenth and early seventeenth centuries have been recorded on the site.[412]

Some later nineteenth century rebuilding also occurred in the valley making use of leading architects indicating that the local gentry were still very much aware of current fashions in home building. The house at *Wigfair* (GR 028713), another ancient township site was rebuilt 1882 in the Neo-Jacobean style by the eminent Chester architect, John Douglas (see Plate 28) A manor house had presumably stood on the site that was occupied by Sion Tudor

---

[411] (i) A Tour of North Wales by Jinny Jenks 1772" National Library of Wales MS 227528 p 17
(ii) CADW : "Register of Landscapes, Parks and Gardens of Special Historic Interest in Wales" Part 1.1 Conwy, Gwynedd and the Isle of Anglesey (1995)
[412] C.P.A.T. SMR 22974

(1522-1602) an eminent poet and a courtier of Elizabeth I. By the eighteenth century, the house was in occupation by a branch of the Lloyd family.

Plate 27 Hafodunos (before the 2004 fire)

There were also changes to the landscape of the upper reaches of the valley brought about by the influence of "new" commercially-derived money from outside Wales particularly from the fortune of the Sandbach family. *Hafodunos*, the most important estate in Llangernyw parish, (GR 868671) was originally established by Bleddyn Llwyd, a local chieftain around 1100. The medieval house which possibly had a monastic connection at one time was replaced by a new manor house built by Llwyd's descendants, the Lloyds, in 1674. Traces of the religious foundation are said to be still visible[413]. The house was visited in 1772 by the traveller Jinny Jenks who described it as *"a very good old white house sited on an eminence"*[414]. On the death of John Lloyd in 1821, the estate passed to his daughter and son-in-law, the Reverend Thomas Hugh Clough in whose hands it remained until 1833 when it was purchased by Samuel Sandbach (1769 - 1851), a rich Liverpool sugar merchant and former mayor of that city, with huge estates in "Demerary", now

---

[413] CPAT SMR 22953
[414] "A Tour of North Wales by Jinny Jenks, 1772" Nat. Library of Wales MS 22753B p40

Guyana. Samuel's son, Henry Robertson Sandbach (1806 - 1895) rebuilt the house at a cost of over £30,000 in 1865.

The new *Hafodunos* Mansion (see Plate 27) was built in the 14th century Venetian Gothic style to a design by the nationally known architect Gilbert Scott (1811-1878) and laid out extensive gardens[415]. Within the house itself is a seventeenth century secondary staircase, a survivor of the earlier house on the site. The Sandbach family were patrons of the internationally known Welsh sculptor John Gibson (1790-1866). He created five marble reliefs for the house which have now been removed to the Walker Art Gallery in Liverpool. However, examples of Gibson's reliefs survive in the main hall and sculpture room. Today, this impressive house, a Grade I listed building, has lain empty since 1990 having been used for some years after 1945 as a girls' boarding school and subsequently as a nursing home. A 1998 survey of the house which is still owned privately by the executors of the last owner revealed that the stone work is in good condition but the timbers have been seriously damaged by wet rot and dry rot. To repair the damaged timbers would cost as much as £0.75m. Hence an urgent appeal is being made to find ways of preserving this unique property.[416] *Late postscript: Hafodunos was seriously damaged by a fire in October 2004.*

---

[415] R.H. Teague & R.L. Brown: "Griffith Jones' Pious Minister - The Reverend John Kenrick, Vicar of Llangernyw 1730 - 1755" Trans. Denbs. Hist. Soc. Vol. 49 (2000) p17
[416] J Piddington and J Nicholson : Draft Prospectus for the future of Hafodunos (2001)

The Laying out of Parks: In the eighteenth and nineteenth centuries, the laying out of ornamental emparked landscapes around a gentleman's home was a means of proclaiming his status since very few could afford such enhancements to their homes.[417] Consequently, such work was carried out on a relatively limited scale around the valley's major homes of the lesser gentry at *Wigfair, Plas yn Cefn Hall, Gallt Faenan, Garthewin, Plas Heaton* and *Hafodunos*.

Plate 28: Wigfair Hall

Garthewin had what has been described as a medium-sized park around the house. In 1772, a visitor noted that the house had lawns *"down to the meadow through which the River Elwy winds"*.[418] The present grounds are cut off from the Elwy by the turnpike road opened in the mud nineteenth century. The boundaries of the present park are demarcated by iron park railings in places up to twelve bars in height, the enclosed area includes much of Mynydd dir and the lower slopes of

---

[417] Richard Muir "The New Reading of the Landscape" Exeter Univ. Press, Exeter (2000) pp 133-136
[418] "A Tour of North Wales by Jinny Jenks 1772" National Library of Wales MS 227528 p 16

Moelfre Uchaf. The park appears to have been laid out in the nineteenth century which is borne out by the use of iron park railing fencing to enclose the park The fence is not shown on an estate plan of 1784 but in 1844, six does from the park of *Garthewin* were given as a gift to the owner of *Bodelwyddan*.[419] Little decorative or amenity planting was carried out in the park. A group of limes is shown in a field to the south of the house in the plan of 1784 but only two of these remain. The park is crossed by three entrance drives each of which had an entrance lodge.

At *Plas Heaton*, a small park was probably laid out at the time of the 1805 rebuilding of the house. A plan of 1812 shows a line of perimeter planting although some dry stone walling was also used to mark the boundary in places[420]. Some group planting of oak trees appears to have been carried out but today only single trees remain to mark the sites of former grouped plantings. Several ponds were incorporated into the landscape, possibly for use by stock.

Hafodunos was the last park to be laid out in the river basin dating from the third quarter of the nineteenth century. Little landscaping planting was carried out other than some groups of oaks and a line of monkey puzzle trees close to the now un-used west drive, Some natural woodland was left in place to enhance the vistas from the house. The

---

[419] CADW: "Register of Landscapes, Parks and Gardens of Special Historic Interest in Wales" Part 1. : Conwy, Gwynedd and the Isle of Anglesey (1995) p89
[420] CPAT SMR 22974

monkey puzzle trees remain and were seen in the outstanding HTV Wales series *"Fishlock's Wild Tracks"* in the late 1990s. In the accompanying book, the presenter of the series describes them as *"like a row of bottle brushes against the sky"*.[421] An arboretum was established close to the house, probably with the help of the eminent botanist and plant collector, Joseph Dalton Hooker, Director of Kew Gardens, who was on close contact with the Sandbach family. The grounds contain 1020 different species of trees.[422]

Garden Design: All the major houses of the valley also had extensive gardens including walled gardens for the production of household vegetables and fruit. At *Garthewin*, the Wynne family's pleasure gardens are contemporary with the house as is made clear in Jinny Jenks' diary of 1772 which records a flower garden, kitchen garden, a pinery and a *"pretty white dove house"*. There were some new plantings, particularly of during the nineteenth century. Some layout changes were made in the twentieth century when Clough Williams-Ellis converted the carriage sweep in front of the house to a raised terrace. Open views across the Elwy valley to Moel Unben were maintained by the use of a ha-ha. Walled paths lead to a fishpond, an arched gazebo, a dovecote (c1710) and walled garden all of which had a utility role supplying food for the household.[423].

---

[421] Trevor Fishlock : "Fishlock's Wild Tracks" Poetry Wales Press, Bridgend (1998) p137
[422] J Piddington and J Nicholson : Draft Prospectus for the future of Hafodunos (2001)
[423] (i) A Tour of North Wales by Jinny Jenks 1772" National Library of Wales MS 227528 p 16
(ii) CPAT SMR 22945

The garden at *Plas Heaton* dates from the 1860s and is surrounded in its entirety by a ha-ha. . Apart from small lawns close to the house, the garden is made up of woodland accessed by circular walks. Tree plantings in the garden include ash, yews, sycamore, oak and box. A terrace cut into the limestone on the north side of the wooded circular walks gives views to the Irish Sea and the Clwydian Hills. Early photographs indicate that the garden once contained far more flowering plants than exist at present. An early nineteenth century ice house survived from an earlier garden layout to the north west of the house. Two walled gardens survive, one provided vegetables the other fruit.

Elsewhere in the valley walled gardens still survive but are in an advanced state of decay. Such is the case at *Plas Uchaf* in Llannefydd where a walled garden stood on the south side of the house. Today parts of the terracing have collapsed and the retaining walls are derelict. A summer house survives as do the remains of a five-seater privy adjacent to it.[424]

Garden layouts in the river basin reached their peak at *Hafodunos*. The heyday of these gardens was in the time of the house's occupation by the Sandbach family during the second half of the nineteenth century. The garden contained many exotic ornamental plants said to have been introduced there under the influence of Joseph Dalton Hooker. Hooker, a close friend of Charles Darwin was a leading nineteenth century botanist and plant collector. The gardens were made up of two distinct sections. To the south of the house lie formal terraced gardens with planted

---

[424] CPAT SMR 22978

borders whilst to the south east is a planted wooded area with informal walks (now heavily overgrown) leading to the Nant Rhan-hir which flows through this section of the grounds. The stream has been used to provide a visual impact through ravines and cascades. Grottoes and follies were added for additional effect. Two stone bridges over the stream allowed for circular walks to be taken from the house. A walled garden containing fruit trees and derelict greenhouses is divided into two by a stream that flows through it, lies close to the house[425]. The garden is now being surveyed under a partially EC funded project known as *"Paradisos"* to restore dilapidated gardens of international importance to their former glory.

The Housing of the Poor: In the face of evidence of such affluence, it must not be forgotten that the majority of the population was made up of agricultural labourers, the descendants of the medieval bondmen. In the Lordship of Denbigh, the remaining bondmen were freed from service and their traditional ties under a royal charter of 1506 (which significantly also freed their lands for sale to others). It has been argued that the demise of bond tenure led to increased affluence for the lowest social classes in the Welsh countryside in the years after 1480 since they had more bargaining power and were not tied by customary dues and services[426]. However, life for the labouring classes and small farmers of the valley was harsh throughout the period between medieval times and the early twentieth century.

---

[425] CPAT SMR 22953

[426] John Davies "A History of Wales" Penguin, London (1993) p213

It has been estimated that between one-third and one-half of the population of Wales lived at subsistence level during the sixteenth century[427], these figures would have been increased significantly in times of failed harvests and low wages. The lot of the poor changed little in succeeding centuries. By 1750, the expectancy of life at birth in rural Wales was around 35. The rising prosperity that accompanied the high rates of economic growth in the late eighteenth century did not have much impact on the rural working classes since any increases in wages were more than offset by the impact of inflationary prices.[428] The enclosure of common lands in the Elwy valley imposed even further hardship on this class in the first half of the following century depriving them of grazing lands and fuel supplies.

The living quarters of the poorer elements of Welsh rural society differed markedly from those of the gentry. Workers cottages were still built on a basically medieval pattern until the nineteenth century. Such houses were open to the roof with a loft accessed by a ladder at one end of the main room[429]. Documentary evidence from the nineteenth century indicates that many single men were accommodated in farm outbuildings while married couples frequently lived in an earth-floored single room cottage. In some cases such dwellings were made up of a longhouse *(ty hir)* where animal quarters adjoined the single storey living accommodation[430]. The longhouse can still be

---

[427] G.E. Jones ""Modern Wales - A Concise History" CUP Cambridge (1984) p 40
[428] Geraint H Jenkins "The Making of Modern Wales 1642-1780" OUP Oxford (1993) p273
[429] A J Parkinson "Vernacular Architecture" in J Manley et al (ed) "The Archaeology of Clwyd" Clwyd CC., Mold (1991) p218
[430] A.H. Dodd "The Industrial Revolution in North Wales" Bridge, Wrexham (1990) p3

identified on many farmsteads in the valley, now usually modified or in use as a barn or cowshed. However, it should be noted that in the Late Middle Ages, the longhouse was the most widespread form of farm dwelling in upland Britain and was also widely found in lowland locations where they continued to be built until the sixteenth century. In Cheshire, farmers and animals were sometimes housed under the same roof into the seventeenth century.[431]

A contemporary writer described the cottages of rural North Wales as *"habitations of wretchedness"*.[432] At some time during the late 18th and in the 19th centuries, terraced cottage accommodation for agricultural workers and other labourers appears to have been built in the villages of Llanfair Talhaearn and Llangernyw creating the first sizeable nucleation of settlement in the valley.

Building Materials: House building made use of locally derived materials. In the upper Elwy valley, there was access to local stone and slate for the roofs of these simple village dwellings. Leland confirms that in the early sixteenth century, local slate was being quarried in *Isdulas* commote for the roofing of houses.[433] There is documentary evidence that some cottages were roofed with thatch as was the case in Llangernyw in the mid

---

[431] Nigel Harvey : "A History of Farm Buildings in England and Wales" Newton Abbot (1970) pp41-45
[432] Walter Davies "General View of the Agriculture and Domestic Economy of North Wales" London, (1810) p82.
[433] Lucy Toulmin Smith " Leland's Itinerary in Wales 1536-1539" Bell, London (1906) p94

eighteenth century[434]. Small upland farms were better built than labourer's cottages and often had two storeys with latticed windows. The rebuilding of farmhouses large and small and the use of stone to wall estate and farm boundaries would have given employment to local men in the small roadside quarries that occur throughout the area. The estates themselves provided employment for local people in the kitchens and gardens of their houses as well as on the home farms.

Despite the emerging affluence of local landowners and the building of estates, the landscape of Wales still gave visitors the impression of a wild, bleak and joyless wilderness in the late seventeenth and early eighteenth centuries. The insulation of poor road links and language barriers limited contact with the outside world and many of the local people would not have ventured beyond the local market centres of Denbigh, Llanrwst and Abergele in their short life times. This led one authority to describe mid seventeenth century Wales as *"a remote and inaccessible federation of small communities"*[435]

Cultural Development: The eighteenth century saw the blooming of Welsh culture through poetry, drama and music. The area drained by the Elwy and its tributary streams spawned many important Welsh language writers and poets reflecting the retention of the Welsh language and culture within the valley. Robert Thomas, sexton of Llanfair

---

[434] R.H. Teague & R.L. Brown: "Griffith Jones' Pious Minister - The Reverend John Kenrick, Vicar of Llangernyw 1730 - 1755" Trans. Denbs. Hist. Soc. Vol. 49 (2000) p 34

[435] Geraint H Jenkins "The Foundations of Modern Wales 1642-1750" OUP, Oxford (1993)   p 88

Talhaearn was part of the influential "Morris Circle" of writers and poets that had an important part to play in the renaissance of Welsh culture in the middle years of the eighteenth century.[436]

A popular form of entertainment in the rural settings of the valleys of the Dee, Clwyd, Conwy and, no doubt, the Elwy were short satirical interludes played out by amateur actors in front of paying local audiences in barns, tavern yards and streets. The parish of Llannefydd was the birthplace of perhaps the greatest exponent of this form of the dramatic arts, Thomas Edwards (1739-1810) alias "Twm o'r Nant". The poet was born on the farm known as Lower Penporchell (GR 996681), part of a medieval bonded hamlet where the landowner was once Iolo Goch, bard to the court of Owain Glyndwr in the late fourteenth century. Tom was the eldest of ten children of an illiterate agricultural worker and was taught to read by a local smith living in *Waendwysog* (GR996661) around two and a half kilometres south west of Henllan.[437] The leading villeins of Twm's satire and irony were dissolute priests, parasitic lawyers and self-righteous evangelists; he would not have been short of similar subject matter in the Wales of the twenty first century!! He was so popular that in true Welsh hyperbole he was dubbed the "Cambrian Shakespeare" by some of his contemporaries

---

[436] Geraint H Jenkins "The Foundations of Modern Wales 1642-1750" OUP, Oxford (1993) pp 396-7
[437] R Morris Roberts "Twm o'r Nant" Clwyd Historian No.47 autumn 2001 pp14 -15

CHAPTER 13: INDUSTRY AND TRANSPORT

The Industrial Revolution in North East Wales: By 1750, only one sixth of the Welsh population lived in towns[439] but the urban market for agricultural produce and raw materials for industry and the building trade had some economic impact even on remote communities such as those of the Elwy basin. There was also, as we have seen in the previous chapter, awareness among the wealthier elements of society of changing fashions in house design. It is therefore worth examining what impact the "Industrial Revolution" had on the valley since it was transforming the landscape of the Dee Estuary along the Flintshire coast, only 25 kms (16 miles) to the east and the coalfield area around Wrexham, 40 kms (25 miles) to the south east from the early eighteenth century onwards. Within the local communities in the river valleys there was some well-established cottage industry such as shoemaking, the knitting of stockings, corn milling, black smithing and woollen weaving. This was a far cry from the highly capitalised, labour-intensive methods of industrial production being applied in industrial North East Wales.

The mineral wealth that underpinned the rise of industry elsewhere in North East Wales did not exist in sufficient quantity to stimulate industrial development on any scale within the Elwy basin. However, there was no shortage of effort to rectify the situation by local landowners. From the late 17th century the Wynne family was making

---

[439] Geraint H Jenkins "The Foundations of Modern Wales 1642-1780" OUP Oxford (1993) p88

strenuous efforts to discover lead and copper in their lands in the Conwy valley.[440] In this, they eventually met with some success for productive lead mines were established to the west of Llanrwst in the mid nineteenth century[441] when demand for lead was very buoyant to meet the needs for roofing and water pipes in the expanding urban areas of Britain.

The Exploitation of Local Lead and Copper Ores: The heavily faulted Silurian rocks of the Elwy and Aled valleys had been subject to mineralisation on a small scale by ores of lead, zinc and copper but most workings were small scale. Known locations of old workings are shown in Figure 11 which reveals that lead and copper ores were mined in a five kilometre wide band of country running from Cefn Meiriadog in the north east to Gilfach south of Llansannan in the south west.. The 1880 OS map reveals that the most westerly mine was a lead mining shaft at Llangernyw just to the north of *Hendre Ddu* farm (GR 8746664. This mine was on the estates of the Sandbach family of *Hafodunos* but their interest in the venture had waned by the late 1860s[442]. However, the *Dyffryn Aled Mining Company* took a renewed interest in the mine which was worked again for a short period between 1883 and 1884.[443]

---

[440] A H Dodd (ibid) p18
[441] C. J. Williams "Metal Mines of North Wales" Bridge Books, Wrexham (1980)
[442] .H. Teague & R.L. Brown: "Griffith Jones' Pious Minister - The Reverend John Kenrick, Vicar of Llangernyw 1730 - 1755" Trans. Denbs. Hist. Soc. Vol. 49 (2000) p21
[443] CPAT SMR 18097

FIG. 11

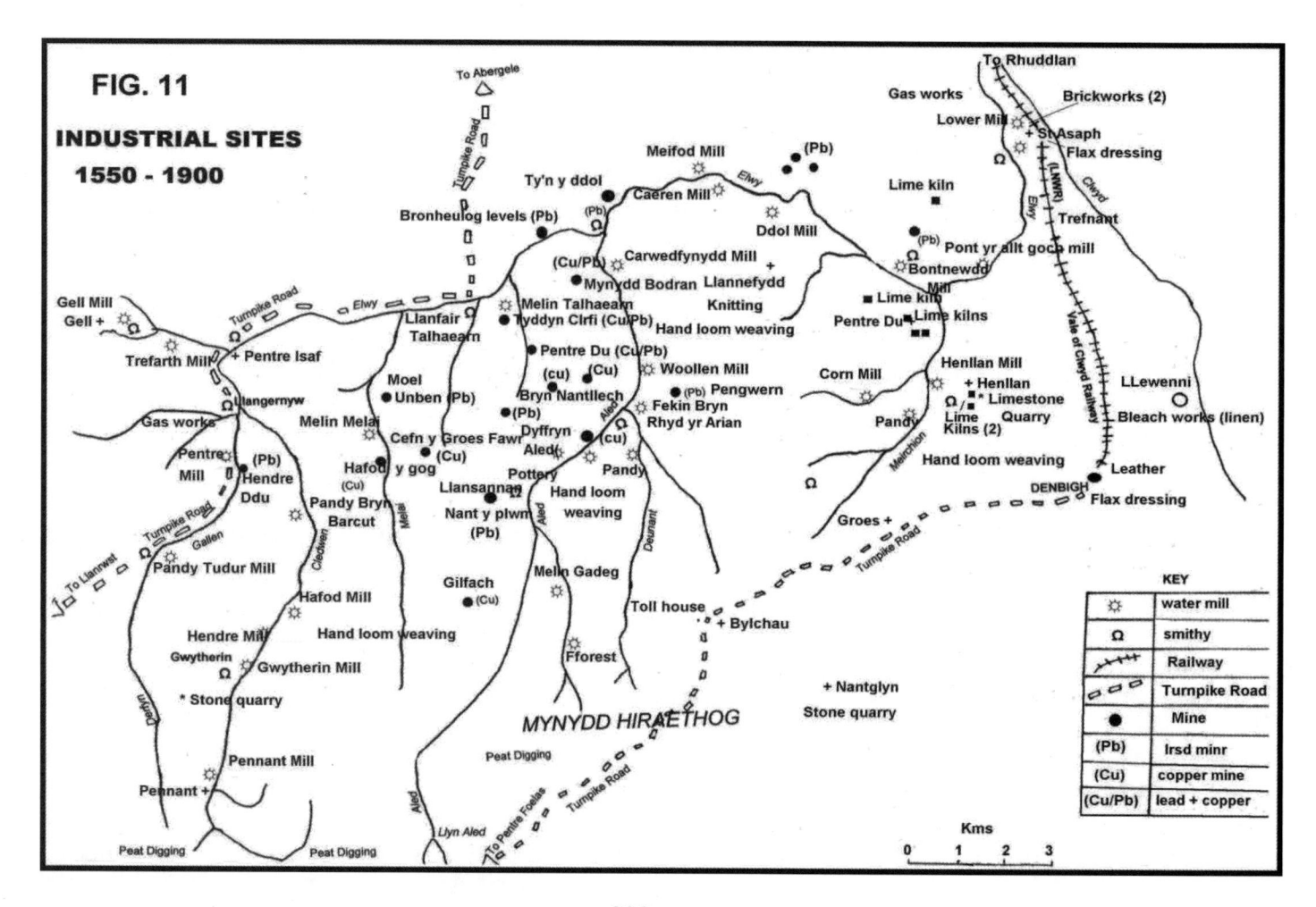

INDUSTRIAL SITES 1550 - 1900

More extensive workings, mainly for copper ore in the "Lower Ludlow" series of Silurian rocks, were located in the Aled valley 2 kms north west of Llansannan at *Dyffryn Aled* (GR 959670) on lands owned by the Yorke family, a branch of the Yorkes of *Erddig* near Wrexham, who had acquired lands in the valley following a marriage to a Wynne heiress. This mine was worked from the early nineteenth century until 1895. The ores were worked from a level beginning on the bank of the river Aled and several shafts.[444] Other small-scale workings existed in the hill country between the middle Aled valley and Llanfair Talhaearn. A shaft and some ruined buildings related to a late nineteenth century copper mine exist at *Rhyd yr eirin* (GR 940568). Nearby, two levels are in evidence on the valley sides of *Nant Rhyd yr eirin.* (GR 941681) with a further level cut into the hillside at GR939686.[445] To the east of *Rhyd yr eirin* a cooper mine was in existence at *Bryn Nantllech* from the early years of the nineteenth century until 1887. Three abandoned shafts are identifiable at the site (GR 940685). Trial shafts, probably for lead, were sunk at *Pentre Du* (GR 943690) and to the east of the Aled valley at *Pengwern* (see Fig. 11) at GR 964682.

The Welsh lead mining industry reached a peak of activity in 1862 but three years later a prospectus was issued proposing the establishment of a mine to extract copper and lead from a new mine at Llanfair Talhaearn, an area where small scale working of ores on a part time basis had gone on for centuries. Progress was slow but the mine

---

[444] Conwy Borough Council Sites and Monuments Record No. 18062.
[445] CPAT SMR 18193

was established in 1890 on lands at the farms of *Tyddyn Clefi*, *Foel* and *Bryn Kenrick* to the south east of Llanfair Talhaearn village.

Plate 29: Photograph courtesy of Denbighshire Record Office, Ruthin.

Considerable financial outlay was involved. The mine was worked through a series of shafts and levels but the main shaft, known as *"Morgan's"* was sunk to a depth of 83 metres' A thirty five foot water wheel (see Plate 29) was installed to power machinery to dress the ore. The mine worked two lodes on north-south fault lines. These were known as the *Morgan lode* and the *New lode*. The concentrated ore was transported by horse and cart to the railway at Abergele. The venture was a failure with only small quantities of ore being raised between 1891 and 1903.[446] Today only adits and the sites of two

Waterwheel at Llanfair Talhaearn Mine c. 1898
Source DRO 56738

---

[446] C. J. Williams "Metal Mines of North Wales" Bridge Books, Wrexham (1980)

reservoirs remain. To the north east of Llanfair Talhaearn, the remains of trial shafts for lead and copper have been identified on the north western slopes of *Mynydd Bodran* (GR 943708) that no doubt date from the flurry of mining activity in the last two decades of the nineteenth century.

Some ores were extracted on the north side of the Elwy River near *Bron-Heulog* (GR 938715) where two levels were driven into the southern slopes of Mynydd Bodrochwyn for the mining of lead. These levels are shown on the 1880 OS map. A further two late nineteenth century levels used to extract lead ore are visible to the east at *Ty'n y Ddol* (GR 949717). Other small scale lead workings can be traced through a number of shafts sunk into the Carboniferous limestone rocks in Cefn Meiriadog parish.

In the Llansannan area, a mine known as *Nant-y-Plwm* (stream of the lead) worked lead ores from 1883 until 1887. The mine (GR 929660) was worked by a level and three shafts. Three kilometres to the south of this mine, trial shafts for copper were dug at *Gilfach* (GR 921632), the southernmost location of mining activity in the late nineteenth century. North West of Llansannan, shafts sunk for the extraction of copper ores have been identified at *Hafod y Gog* (GR 902670) and *Cefn y Groes Fawr* (GR 914663) which both date to the nineteenth century. Two kilometres to the north of these sites, a trial shaft for lead has been located on the western slopes of *Moel Unben*.

To some extent, geological conditions inhibited large scale exploitation of local copper and lead ores while to some extent, the landowners financing the ventures had missed the boat since prices for both lead and copper had already peaked before they began their activity owing to the discovery of cheaper supplies of both ores in the New World. Fortunately, the landowners were never to realise their dream of creating a new Parys Mountain in the Elwy basin.

The Stone Quarrying Industry: Quarrying always played its part in the industrial activity in the Elwy river basin, In the lower sections of the valley, several lime kilns were built to meet the needs of local farms particularly those farming the acidic soils that developed on the Silurian grits, sandstones and shales of the middle and upper sections of the valley. The Carboniferous limestone could be reached by small quarries in the lower part of the valley. The 1880 first edition of the 1: 10560 County Ordnance Survey map shows three kilns in existence in the hamlet of *Pentre Du* (GR015698) in Llannefydd parish and another (GR 002706) north west of Tal *y Bryn farm*. Other limekilns were located close to the village of Henllan and on the limestone ridge in Cefn Meiriadog parish. One of the best surviving examples lies just outside the watershed of the Elwy river system at *Foxhall* near Henllan (GR 031673). Here, the remains of a lime kiln stand to a height of 3.5m. together with its stone built loading ramp. A small limestone quarry is located nearby.[447]

Elsewhere local stone was extracted for the building of houses, barns, sheepfolds and field walls. Such quarries were small and often adjacent to the farms that made use of them or in road-side locations. Stone was not produced systematically but only as local needs dictated. Track ways to upland pastures and peat workings were often surfaced with locally quarried stone. At intervals along the 1825 turnpike road from Denbigh to Pentre Foelas, (now

---

[447] CPAT PRN 13339

the A543) are dis-used small stone quarries used to provide hard stone for the new road but which still form a distinctive feature in the landscape of the moors. Slate was quarried in Llansannan parish in the Aled valley during the eighteenth century.[448] Stone quarrying still continued into recent times meeting the needs of the moment as at Llyn Aled Isaf where locally quarried stone was used in the construction of the reservoir dam and access roads,

Peat Digging: .Another extractive industry that left its mark on the landscape of the source areas of the rivers Elwy and Aled was the digging of peat. The boggy uplands on the northern edge of Mynydd Hiraethog were an important source of fuel in the form of peat. Numerous sites of former peat digging, peat stacks and drying platforms can still be seen throughout the area.[449] The cutting of peat traditionally began in May and formed an important activity on the moors particularly during the eighteenth and nineteenth centuries. However, there are references to "rights of turbary" for the community of Gwytherin in the 1334 Survey of the Honour of Denbigh. . What remains of this activity in today's landscapes are the remains of track ways leading on to the moors from lowland farms and water filled hollows along stream course as in the valley of *Nant Bach* (GR 906588). Elsewhere digging has left rectangular depressions on the surface of the moor. In some cases small lakes now occupy depressions left by peat cutting as on *Fawnog Fawr* (GR859584) close to the southern boundary of the tithe parish of Gwytherin (*fawnog* translates as "peat bog"). Further evidence of peat cutting is found along the valley of *Nant Goch* (GR 887571), a

---

[448] A.H. Dodd (ibid) (1990) p 16

[449] WG Owen & R J Silvester "The Mynydd Hiraethog Survey, Clwyd" (64) CPAT Welshpool (1993) p 3

headwater tributary of the Elwy which forms part of the Gwytherin tithe parish boundary. Peat continued to be cut for fuel on Mynydd Hiraethog until the 1950s.

The Application of Water Power in the Local Woollen Textile Industry: Looms to convert locally spun woollen yarns into cloth were expensive pieces of equipment and often housed in outhouses known as "*tai gwydd*" on the more substantial farms. Production took place mainly in the slack winter months and the spinning and weaving of woollens brought in a useful supplement to family incomes in the upper valley. Without a doubt the key to potential industrial development within the river basin was not mineral ores but water power which was available along the many fast flowing streams including the Elwy itself. Fulling mills set along the valleys of small streams first appeared in Denbighshire from the early fourteenth century.[450] Their purpose was to wash out dirt and grime and treat the woollen textiles by inducing the material to "felt" using water power. Many of the early fulling mills were financed by local landowners.[451] The trade was disrupted by the Glyndwr uprising and most of the fulling mills that are known in Denbighshire came into existence in the sixteenth and early seventeenth centuries. These numbers expanded further in the eighteenth century with a new surge in demand for woollen cloths for export. Until the end of the eighteenth century, Denbighshire was the most important woollen manufacturing county in Wales.

---

[450] J Geraint Jenkins "The Welsh Woollen Industry" Nat. Museum of Wales, Cardiff (1969) p 216
[451] A D Carr "Medieval Wales" Macmillan, Basingstoke (1995) p 98

***"Pandy"* Place Names in the Elwy Basin:** The place name *"Pandy Tudur"*, a small hamlet on the Afon Derfyn, a tributary of the upper Elwy some 4 kms (2.5 miles) south west of Llangernyw (GR 858643), bears witness to the existence of a local woollen industry since the name *"pandy"* means a fulling mill. This fulling mill is recorded on several occasions in the *Wigfair Manuscript* housed at the National Library of Wales. These references span the period 1589 - 1860 indicating that the woollen industry was active in the upper reaches of the valley for the best part of three centuries. Like many other former woollen mills in the area, the fulling mill was transformed into a corn mill at some stage in its history. Spinning and weaving were mainly carried out in farmhouses by women although parish registers for Gwytherin record the names of several male weavers in the seventeenth and eighteenth centuries.

Older OS maps also identify a *"pandy"* on the Afon Cledwen in Llanfair Talhaearn parish (GR 889658) roughly mid-way on the river's course between Gwytherin and Llangernyw listed as *"Pandy Brynbarcut,"* the oldest evidence for this mill dates from 1839 although it is probably of earlier origin. The 1881 Census reveals that this fulling mill was still in use (The fuller was John Edwards, 56 born Llanfair Talhaearn) confirming the survival of the woollen industry in the river basin until the latter years of the nineteenth century. Fulling was the only mechanised process in this cottage industry until the eighteenth century with water power being used to power large hammers which pounded the cloth to tighten the weave and raise the nap. These two fulling mills stood a relatively short distance (3 kms) apart in the headwaters of the Elwy. There were at least three other fulling mills in the river basin. One of these lay 7 kms to the east of *Pandy Brynbarcut* in Llansannan parish on the Afon Deunant, a tributary of the Afon Aled (GR 958670) and was in use by 1625. .Another was located 6 kms further east on the Afon Meirchion 1 km south west of Henllan (GR 019680) was in use by 1795. The final example lay a little way downstream in

Llannefydd parish (GR 953713) and was in use in 1839. Just outside of our study area, in the neighbouring river basin of the Afon Ystrad, another tributary of the Clwyd, a fulling mill was still being worked as a woollen mill in 1881. This mill *"Pandy Bodeiliog"* in Henllan parish, (GR 023641) was being worked by John Davies (54) and his son.[452]

The Stocking Knitting Industry: The above examples indicate that at least in the upper parts of the valleys of the Elwy and its tributaries, local wool was being processed at a domestic level with the spinning of yarn being a common practice in small farmhouses. Several fifteenth or sixteenth century spindle whorls were recovered from excavations of abandoned dwellings along *Nant Criafolen* on the eastern edge of Mynydd Hiraethog[453]. Locally produced woollen yarn was knitted into stockings during the eighteenth and early years of the nineteenth centuries when this activity was commonplace in upland areas of Denbighshire. Knitting was often carried out in communal groups gathered in a local farmhouse to save on fuel and light. The local market centre for the trade was Llanrwst, a key link in an "Atlantic "stocking trade which exported stockings to the ports of Charleston and the Gulf of Mexico in the American colonies. The port from which these exports were made was Barmouth.[454] The knitting trade

---

[452] PRO RG11 Piece 5533

[453] CPAT "Historic Landscape Characterisation - Mynydd Hiraethog" Welshpool, 2001.

[454] Gwyn A Williams "When was Wales?" Black Raven Press, London (1985) p144

centred on Bala may also have created a local outlet for woollen yarns since the industry flourished around Llannefydd[455]

The Weaving of Woollen Cloth: A document has survived describing one of the small weaving establishments that existed in the river basin during the early nineteenth century. It describes the weaving shop of Thomas Jones of *Dan y Fron*, Llansannan. The weaver had two narrow width looms in an outhouse on his farm and employed one weaver. Thomas had other strings to his financial bow since he was also a shopkeeper and chapel caretaker (presumably at Tan y fron chapel). The main product of this small weaving establishment was flannel but he also produced quality specialised cloth with a warp of linen and a weft of untwisted wool. The cloth produced was used to manufacture fine bedcovers known as *Cwrlidau Stwff*.[456]

The marketing of woollen cloths from the valley may well have been in the hands of wool factors from Liverpool who were expanding their operations in the late eighteenth century[457]. Water power was also used to produce woollen cloth (flannel) in the valley. The cloth industry in rural Wales developed from the late fourteenth century[458]

---

[455] Dewi Roberts "The Old Villages of Denbighshire and Flintshire" Careg Gwalch. Llanrwst (1999) p42
[456] Quoted from Gweirydd ap Rhys MS (UCNW) in J Geraint Jenkins "The Welsh Woollen Industry" Nat. Museum of Wales, Cardiff (1969) p 219
[457] Geraint H Jenkins "The Foundations of Modern Wales 1642-1780" OUP Oxford (1993) p285.
[458] A D Carr "Medieval Wales" Macmillan, Basingstoke (1995) p97

Plate 30

Former watermill : Felin Pont-yr-allt-goch, Wigfair

making use of locally produced wool becoming more available following the expansion of sheep farming in the upland areas. Each area of Wales tended to produce a distinctive local type of cloth. Denbighshire weavers specialised in a thick white woollen cloth.[459] Three mills survived into the nineteenth century and two are recorded as such in the 1881 Census returns. One mill lay on the Afon Cledwen at Gwytherin (GR 878617) and is recorded as *"Factory House."* Another lay downstream on the Elwy at Bontnewydd (GR 013708) where, in 1881, a flannel manufacturer, Robert Jones (68) employed one man and a boy. Jones had been born in Tryfan, Caernarvonshire, a small centre for woollen manufacture A third woollen mill, this time on the Aled river just before its confluence with the Elwy, is identifiable from the first (County) edition 1: 10560 scale OS map of 1880. On the modern OS map (GR 953713, the site bears the name *"Felin Pandy"* (fulling mill) which perhaps testifies to its original role in the woollen industry. The exact date of origin for these water-

---

[459] Geraint H Jenkins "The Foundations of Modern Wales 1642-1780" OUP Oxford (1993) p120.

powered woollen mills is not known but it is possible that they may date from the years between 1797 and 1837 when suitable waterside sites for woollen factories became a common subject for advertisement in the local press.[460]

Plate 31

Water Powered Corn Mills: Almost every small tributary of the Elwy had a water powered corn mill along its course many dating from medieval times. (See Fig. 11) The *Henllan water mill* on the Afon Meirchion is mentioned by the locally-born bard Iolo Goch in a tract written around 1380. Flour mills such as this were so prolific that they give an insight into the internal economy of the valley and provide us with a clue as to why, even in the twenty first century, the Elwy valley remains a bastion of the Welsh language and culture. It is clear that these mills served a limited local market in processing locally grown grains (mainly oats, rye and barley) into flour for bread making or cattle feed. It has been claimed that in some parts of medieval Wales, many kindred groups had their own mill

---

[460] A.H. Dodd "The Industrial Revolution in North Wales" Bridge, Wrexham (1990) p249

[461] which may explain their widespread distribution. They speak of a self sufficient agricultural economy where the technology of water power was harnessed to meet essentially local needs. Such mills cannot have been very profitable but played an important role in local life and represent a key element in the valley landscapes many being served by their own weirs, sluices and often quite long mill races.

Re-erected mill sluice, St. Asaph

Plate 32

Many of the former corn mills are now private houses as is the case with the eighteenth century building known as *Melin Dolhaearn* east of Llanfair Talhaearn (GR 932705) which ceased to produce flour around 1950. The breast shot water wheel remains in situ.[462] Some corn mills served very sparsely populated areas as was the case at *Ty Felin* on *Fforest Farm* (GR 945628) sited on the river Aled 3.5 kms to the south east of Llansannan. The mill dates

---

[461] A D Carr "Medieval Wales" Macmillan, Basingstoke (1995) p97
[462] CPAT SMR 104561

from the 1840s and went out of use during the late 1940s. The site was converted into a dwelling in the late 1990s. *Felin Pont yr Allt Goch* (Plate 32) is now three cottages.

The Lack of Transport Links: Perhaps the biggest barrier to the economic development of the valley was its physical isolation from main route ways. Even today, no single route way traverses the whole of the Elwy valley which in the main is still served by single track hollow-ways, some dating back to prehistoric times. Local people made use of well established track ways leading across the hills. We know, for instance, that the eighteenth century writer *Twm o'r Nant* walked 14 kms (9 miles) across the hills from his home near Henllan to Pentre Foelas to receive instruction in Welsh verse from an eminent local poet (and clog maker), *Sion Dafydd*.

The threat of floods in the narrow valley floor of the valley led Pennant to describe the Elwy as *"a turbulent stream,"* flash floods destroyed the bridge at St. Asaph on several occasions. To the south of St. Asaph, *Pont yr Allt Goch* (GR039715) was rebuilt in 1671 following flood damage[463] only to be rebuilt again in 1706 along with *Pont y Gwyddel* (GR 952717) some way upstream. The bridges were rebuilt with money from the County rate[464]. The single arch of *Pont-yr-allt-goch* was said by Jinny Jenks in 1772 to be *".the largest* (arch) *even in England except the centre arch at Black friars"*.[465]

---

[463] D. Leslie Davies "County Bridge Building in Denbighshire in the mid 17th Century" Trans. Denbs. Hist. Soc. Vol.13 (1964) p187
[464] Bryn Ellis "Denbighshire Quarter Sessions Rolls in the Eighteenth Century" Trans. Denbs. Hist. Soc. Vol. 50 (2001) p78
[465] "A Tour in North Wales by Jinny Jenks, 1772" Nat. Lib. Of Wales MS 22753B p45

Y Dwr Mawr" the great floods of 17th August 1879 following several days if heavy rain were perhaps the worst in recent times but parts of the valley are still rendered impassable for days at a time following persistent heavy rain. Consequently route ways tended to avoid the valley bottoms. The main Roman road from Chester to Segontium passed along the ridge to the north of the valley and the main roads tend to cross the valley from North West to south east passing across rather than along it. One of these routes to cross the valley was once important, Peterson's "*Description of Roads in Britain*" (1772) describes the route of the mail coach from London to Bangor as going through Denbigh, Henllan, Llannefydd, Pont y Gwyddel, Betws yn Rhos, Dolwen, Croesfordd and Conwy Ferry. The road is shown clearly on the map of Denbighshire published in the second quarter of the nineteenth century and reproduced as Fig. 12 No doubt, Jinny Jenks travelling from Denbigh to Garthewin, Llanfair Talhaearn, in 1772, used at least part of this route. She describes passing

"up and down such hills that seemed almost straight (down) at which we almost wondered how we got up or down, though the roads wind round them like a corkscrew to make the ascent easier, and the roads are perfectly good many of which have terrace or shelf roads cut on the sides of the hills, where the outer wheels of the carriage is not half a yard from the precipice, so they are alarming until one is used to them"[466]

---

[466]"A Tour of North Wales by Jinny Jenks, 1772" Nat. Library of Wales MS 22753B p 14

The only other east-west route in the river basin ran from Denbigh to Llansannan where it crossed the Aled before running on to cross the Elwy at Llangernyw at *Pont Faen*, a three arched bridge dating from the eighteenth century. From Llangernyw the road split into two separate routes heading for the Conwy Valley crossings at *Tal-y-Cafn* and *Llanrwst*. This road was the subject of an Act pf Parliament in 1759 that led to widening and repairs to be undertaken on the Denbigh to Tal y Cafn section.

Turnpike Roads: A turnpike dating from 1825 was built by Thomas Telford running along the watershed in the southern limits of the Elwy basin linking Denbigh to Pentre Foelas. The new road (now the A543) was 26 kms (16 miles) long and 7.4m (8 yards) wide. The toll house known as *"Bylchau Gate"* survives in much altered form as does an inn built mid route. The inn was initially called *Bryntrillyn* (hill of three lakes) but was changed to the *"Sportsman's Arms"* following the rise of grouse shooting on the moor in the mid nineteenth century.

The only turnpike road using the valley of the River Elwy was a 26 km. (16 mile) stretch connecting Abergele to Llanrwst. It was built in 1858 but served only the central section of the Elwy valley between Llanfair Talhaearn and

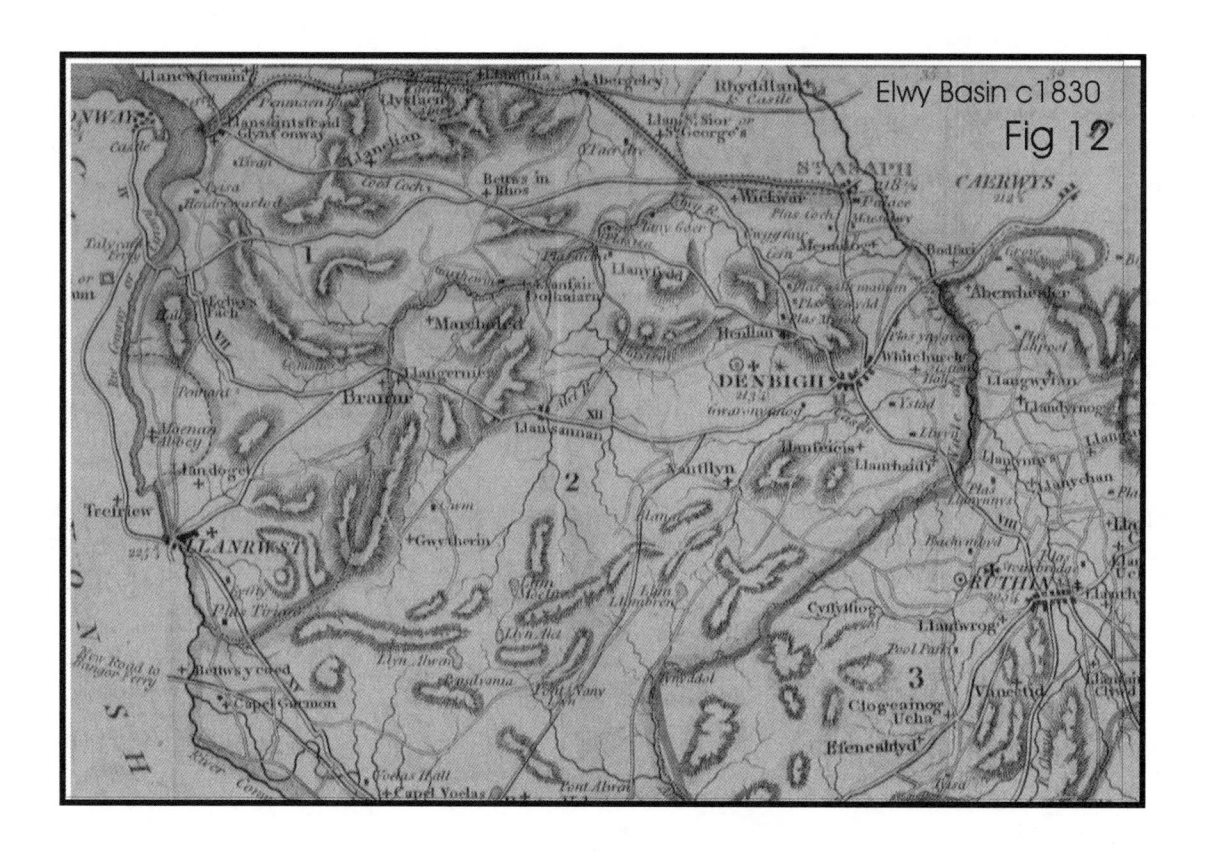

Elwy Basin c1830
Fig 12

Llangernyw. The 1881 Census indicates that a tollhouse north of Llangernyw was still in use. This road brought about some improvement in communications with the outside world and was infinitely better than what had existed before. A local clergyman reminiscing about 19th century roads in the area described the road from Abergele to Llanfair Talhaearn as having *"steep gradients and a rock bottom in places"* [467] This was the road that was later replaced by the new turnpike but its course can still be traced along lanes running parallel to, and about 300 metres to the west of the main road (A 548) that follows the line of the turnpike road. Between Llanfair Talhaearn and Llangernyw, the old road crossed the river through fords on six occasions. In wet weather, this would have been dangerous and at times impossible. There is evidence that the local parish authorities at least tried to maintain the early roads. Llanfair Talhaearn Churchwarden accounts for 1734 record the levying of a rate of two pence in the pound towards road repairs in the parish. The Sandbach family, owners of the *Hafodunos* estate near Llangernyw from the 1830s, was the main promoters of the new turnpike investing over £12000 in the venture[468]

Railways: No railway was ever built within the river basin although the Vale of Clwyd line from St. Asaph to Denbigh built in 1856 runs for part of its length along the watershed between the Elwy and Clwyd rivers. The lack of road and rail communication has its advantages in that it has helped preserve the charm of the valley landscape and preserve its distinctive Welsh culture.

---

[467] J.R. Ellis "A History of Abergele and District" Clwyd CC., (1991) p123.
[468] .H. Teague & R.L. Brown: "Griffith Jones' Pious Minister - The Reverend John Kenrick, Vicar of Llangernyw 1730 - 1755" Trans. Denbs. Hist. Soc. Vol. 49 (2000) p20

CHAPTER 14: THE LANDCAPE OF RELIGIOUS CHANGE 1750 - 1910

CAPEL Y GRORSFFORDD

On a bleak hillside crossroad,
The dis-used chapel stands alone
A victim of depopulation
Its message lost upon the young.

No smoke drifts from *Ty Capel's* chimney,
No upturned heads in the *"Set Fawr"*
No words of God flow from the pulpit
No congregation fills the floor.

Once they came by foot and pony
Along the lanes that cross the moor
Braving Hiraethog's snows and tempests
Seeking shelter through God's front door

They felt the *"hwyl"* flow from the pulpit
Inspired by Matthew, Luke and John,
The stirring lines of hymns immortal
Tydi a'r Rhoddaist, Calon Lan!!

Today, the grey stone walls are silent
But on a misty Sabbath morn
Perceptive ears may hear the echoes
Of harmonies from times long gone.

Jonathan Jones III

From around 1730, the person of Wales began to experience a new force that was to bring about significant social and cultural changes in their everyday lives and was also to bring about a national consciousness that had been lacking since the days of the medieval princes. The force responsible for these dramatic changes was the rise of Nonconformism. The rise of Nonconformism was such that it has been likened by one writer to *"the passing of a hurricane"*[469] An eminent Welsh historian has described the movement as *"one of the most remarkable cultural transformations in the history of any people"*[470]

This movement found expression in the landscape through the building of new chapels particularly by the Calvinistic Methodists and Baptists (See Figure 13) in every village, hamlet and on many cross roads of quiet country lanes throughout the Elwy basin. A recent study of the "chapel" phenomenon has noted that these *"Palaces of the Oral Arts"* that once trembled at the passionate preaching of an inspired minister, and shook to the resonance of massed congregational hymn-singing are now fast disappearing from the landscape of rural Wales. However, in the Elwy river basin, the majority of these eighteenth and nineteenth century buildings still survive although a number lie empty and as such are slowly deteriorating...

---

[469] Jan Morris "Wales : Epiv Views of a Small Country" Penguin, Harmondsworth (1986) p119
[470] Gwyn A Williams "When was Wales? " Black Raven Press, London. (1985) p 159

FIG. 13

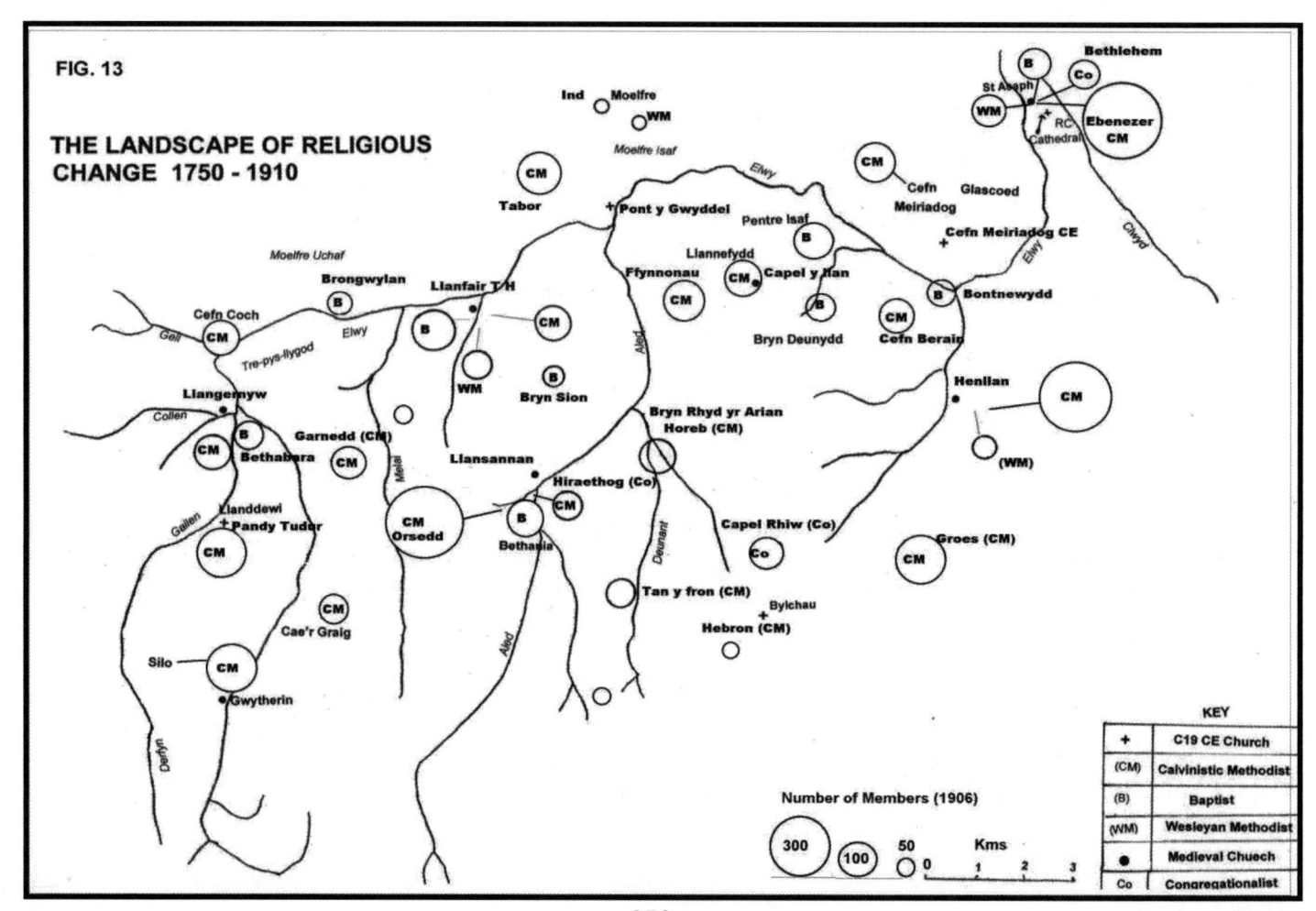

THE LANDSCAPE OF RELIGIOUS CHANGE 1750 - 1910

Number of Members (1906)
300 / 100 / 50
Kms 0 1 2 3

KEY
+	C19 CE Church
(CM)	Calvinistic Methodist
(B)	Baptist
(WM)	Wesleyan Methodist
●	Medieval Church
Co	Congregationalist

256

Sadly, throughout the Principality, the majority of Welsh chapels are now out of use which led one writer to observe how *"The streets and byways of Wales are nowadays littered with the decomposing hulks of chapels, hundreds of abandoned Bethels and Bethesdas"* [471] Despite forming an important element in the built landscapes of Wales, chapels have until recently received little attention from landscape historians. The poet John Betjeman, writing in characteristic nostalgic mode about chapels in England, observed that they were *"designed by architects but ignored by guide books"*[472], The same is true in Wales although many of the most interesting early chapels in rural Wales were designed and built by members of the congregation thus forming an important element in Wales' cultural heritage..

Initially the rise of Nonconformism in Wales was unspectacular and did not really accelerate in the Elwy basin until the final decade of the eighteenth century. Until the Reformation of 1536, the Welsh, like their English neighbours were Roman Catholic in religion. After that date, they also followed the English into the Anglican faith after Henry VIII's schism with Rome. Although embraced with enthusiasm by the larger landowning families, the local agricultural communities in North Wales showed little enthusiasm for the new structure for worship. Nor, in general, did they show any support for the old religion of Roman Catholicism which, in North Wales, survived only in parts of Flintshire and to a lesser extent in the town of Denbigh.

---

[471] Anthony Jones : "Welsh Chapels" Alan Sutton Publishing Ltd Stroud, (1984) pIX

[472] J Betjeman "First and Last House" John Murray, London (1969)

One factor to be considered in this negative change in attitude to the newly established Anglican Church was the suppression of the cults of Welsh saints in the Reformation. Also unpopular was the banning of the use of holy wells which were abundant throughout North Wales and in many cases had served as sites of religious veneration since pre Christian times.[473] Traditions of superstition and magic still had a strong influence on life in the remoter valleys of Wales into the seventeenth century.[474] Consequently, the hold of Anglicanism over the rural Welsh in areas such as the Elwy basin was tenuous and never really recovered from the changes of the Reformation. Thus the appeal of the established church gradually diminished after 1770 as alternative forms of worship became available. .

It has been claimed with some justification that Welsh Nonconformity provided a spiritual leadership in Wales that had been absent since the time of the early Christian saints[475]. However, the Puritan movement was initially slow to attract the Welsh and the transfer of worship from the parish church to the chapels was a protracted process. This reflects Wales' economic isolation and poor communications with the outside world meaning that new ideas and news travelled into the communities of the heartlands very slowly. It also reflects the impact of a series of laws, termed the *Clarendon Code* passed following the Restoration of the monarchy in 1660 designed to impair the expansion of Dissenting sects. These Acts, were not repealed until 1828, included the infamous *Test Act* of 1673

---

[473] Jan Morris "Wales : Epic Views of a Small Country" Penguin, Harmondsworth (1986) p112
[474] Geraint H Jenkins "The Foundations of Modern Wales 1642-1780" OUP Oxford (1993) p43
[475] Francis Jones "The Holy Wells of Wales" Univ. Of Wales Press, Cardiff (1992) p58

which excluded Dissenters from holding a Crown office. These restrictions, together with widespread persecution, led a leading Welsh historian to dub the period 1660-1689 *"The heroic age of Welsh Dissent"*.[476]

By 1715, there were only about seventy Nonconformist chapels in the whole of Wales with only eight recorded in North East Wales.[477] Dissenters were subject to both physical and psychological abuse in nearby towns such as Denbigh, thus much worship was led by itinerant preachers in remote parts of the countryside away from prying eyes. This was apparently the case in the hills around the Elwy valley. John Kenrick, the vicar of Llangernyw 1730 - 1755, noted that the Methodists (Calvinistic) held meetings in the hills surrounding the parish but claimed that all of the 105 families in his parish were staunch Anglicans.[478] This is doubtful and it was probably the fear of persecution and possibly eviction that drove devotees to hear clandestine sermons in the remote parts of the upper valley. The reference is nevertheless important as it narks the beginnings of the impact of Methodism in the upper Elwy valley. The opposition to travelling Nonconformist preachers was not merely confined to the Anglican clergy. The lesser gentry also opposed the movement on the grounds that it undermined their position in society and weakened bonds of deference.

---

[476] Geraint H Jenkins "The Foundations of Modern Wales 1642-1780" OUP Oxford (1993) pp 193-4
[477] John Davies "A History of Wales" Penguin, London (1993) p293
[478] R.H. Teague & R.L. Brown: "Griffith Jones' Pious Minister - The Reverend John Kenrick, Vicar of Llangernyw 1730 - 1755" Trans. Denbs. Hist. Soc. Vol. 49 (2000) p 32

Following the Toleration Act of 1689, many of the legal and social pressures to attend Anglican services were removed and Dissenters could build their own meeting houses provided that they were licensed. As a consequence itinerant Nonconformist worship gradually gave way to the establishment of permanent licensed meeting houses in several parts of Wales. Nonconformism achieved much greater initial success in South Wales rather than in the North during the earlier years of the eighteenth century. The Calvinistic Methodists operated as local societies known as a *"seiat"* meeting in the open or in houses or barns. The earliest such society in Wales dates from 1737 and typically, a society would have between ten and thirty members.[479] Thus, no places of permanent worship were established in the Elwy basin until late in the eighteenth century. During the mid eighteenth century, itinerant Nonconformist preachers visited the area on a regular basis and from around 1780, Calvinistic Methodism began to establish a firm foothold in the villages previously untouched by Dissent[480] The use of the Welsh language was central in its services although The Welsh language was also used in Anglican services all the Anglican churches of the valley until the first half of the twentieth century.[481] The layout of chapels was in line with the early Nonconformist dislike of ostentatious interiors of some larger Anglican churches. Their chapels were served by with rows of simple pews facing the pulpit rather than an altar for preaching was now the main focus of activity.

---

[479] Gareth Elwyn Jones "Modern Wales - A Concise History" CUP, Cambridge 2nd Ed. (1994) p 132

[480] Philip Jenkins "Between the Two Revolutions, Wales 1642 - 1780" in G E Jones & D Smith (ed) "The People of Wales" Gomer, Llandysul (1999) p101

[481] W T R Pryce "Approaches to the Linguistic Geography of North East Wales 1750-1846" National Library of Wales Journal 71 (1972) pp343-363

Early Chapels (1780-1825) in the vernacular style

Bethabbara Baptist Llangernyw

Cefn Coch CM near Gell

Silo CM, Gwytherin

Tan-y-fron CM

Capel Rhiw Independent nr. Bylchau

Garnedd CM, near Llangernyw

Plate 33

The chapels, often converted from barns, also lacked the symbols of class division that existed in many Anglican churches with their elaborate private pews for the gentry while the remainder of the congregation sat behind them in a strict social pecking order.

Initially, the Calvinistic Methodists had no intention of founding a new denomination and their separate existence was not formalised until 1811. Services were frequently conducted by itinerant preachers some of whom were well known throughout Wales. These events which were lively affairs, often attracted hundreds and, in such cases, took place in the open air. One of the best known preachers was a Carmarthenshire man, William Williams *Pantycelyn* (1717 - 17901), who has been described as *"Wales' greatest hymn writer"*[482]. Certainly the singing of hymns in Welsh was a central attraction of Methodist services and contributed to their popular appeal.[483]

By the second half of the eighteenth century the first chapels were being built initially in nearby larger settlements such as Abergele.[484] Places of worship were also later established in the Elwy river basin itself during the last decade of the eighteenth century, a time when non-Anglican groups throughout Wales were taking part in what has been described as *"an intellectual cauldron of competing ideologies"*[485]. In rural North Wales, it was the message of

---

[482] R Garlick & R Mathias "Anglo-Welsh Poetry 1480 - 1980" Poetry Wales Press, Bridgend. (1984) p 6
[483] Gareth Elwyn Jones "Modern Wales - A Concise History" CUP, Cambridge 2nd Ed. (1994) p132
[484] J.R. Ellis "A History of Abergele and District" Clwyd CC., (1991) p38.
[485] Gwyn A Williams "When was Wales?" Black Raven Press, London (1985) p 152

the Calvinistic Methodists that most inspired the local population. An Anglican clergyman in Anglesey complained loudly in the 1790s that hordes of Methodists were over-running North Wales[486]. In the Elwy basin, the Calvinist Methodist chapels at *Ffynnonau* in Llannefydd (1795), *Capel Cefn Meiriadog* (1796), and *Capel Tanyfron* (1777) date from this period. All three were remote from the main villages and their parish churches. Significantly perhaps, the last named (and oldest) lay high in the hills in a remote valley close to a bridge over the river Deunant reflecting perhaps that initially Calvinists built chapels to replace the open air preaching sites that were previously used.

Other Calvinistic Methodist chapels were established in the Elwy basin in the opening decades of the nineteenth century particularly in the decade following the formal break away from the Anglican Church in 1811. These included Capel *Seion* in Henllan (1805), *Capel Silo* in Gwytherin (1815), *Garnedd* chapel (open by 1822) and *Capel Cefn Coch* opened in a rural part of Llangernyw parish in 1818. A Calvinistic Methodist chapel was even established in the cathedral city of St. Asaph in 1807 when the first chapel on the site of *Ebenezer* in Gering Street was opened. The present chapel building, (now closed), dates from 1845. Despite its egalitarian structure, not all landowners were opposed to Nonconformism and frequently sold or leased land to them for the building of chapels. This may reflect the fact that Methodism supported a labour force that was *"disciplined to suffer hardships and forego rewards in this world by the thought of spiritual glories to come"* [487]

---

[486] Quoted by Gwyn A Williams in "When was Wales?" Black Raven Press, London (1985) p 162

[487] A.H. Dodd ibid (1990) p 31

The Baptists, whose activities in Wales began in the 1640s,[488] also built some of the oldest surviving chapel in the Elwy river basin. Records survive relating to the Baptist chapel of *Pennel* at Pentre Isaf (Llannefydd) that show the community was in existence by 1805 although the date stone on the chapel indicates that the present building has stood there since 1815. This may indicate that temporary accommodation was used while cash was raised for the building of the main chapel. Similarly, the earliest records of the *Bethania* Baptist chapel at Llansannan date from 1814 when a barn was used to hold services. The *Bethabara* Baptist chapel in Llangernyw is still in use with the present building dating from 1830, although the 1881 Census Return describes the building as being under construction, possibly a restoration. However, a stone plaque on the building records that a Baptist community had been worshiping in the village since 1785. The Baptists further expanded their activities in the Elwy valley after 1830 and were able to gain sufficient support to build several other small chapels in the valley later in the nineteenth century. (See Figure13) These included *"Soar"* (GR 909675) high on the southern slopes of Moel Unben and *Bodgynwch* (GR 884698) on the toll road from Llanfair Talhaearn to Llangernyw. Both chapels had just 50 members recorded in 1906.

Wesleyan Methodism was also expanding in North Wales during the early years of the nineteenth century and the break with the Church of England in 1811 led to both the main strands of Methodism becoming religious denominations in their own right forming part of the wider Nonconformist movement. Before 1811, both the early Wesleyans and Calvinists saw themselves as forces for the renewal of faith within the umbrella of the Established

---

[488] Geraint H Jenkins "The Foundations of Modern Wales 1642 - 1780" OUP Oxford (1993) p64

Church. The Wesleyans had their origins in England and thus chapels holding services in English were established in the coalfields and industrial areas attracting labour from English-speaking areas. In Welsh-speaking areas such as the Elwy valley, the Calvinists were in the ascendancy. Initially, the area was served by two itinerant Wesleyan preachers based in Ruthin who travelled on horseback and preached in the open air. However, a small chapel was built at Henllan in 1818 with another early chapel being established by 1812 at Llanfair Talhaearn at the edge of the village on the old road to Llansannan. Others were built in Moelfre (GR 961743) and St. Asaph.

The Congregationalists (also known as "Independents") too were establishing their first chapels in North East Wales in the first quarter of the 19th century. Their chapel in Llansannan was known as *"Hiraethog"* but only had just over 60 members in 1905. This was in contrast to their rural chapel known as *"Capel Rhiw"* on a lonely crossroads at an altitude of over 300m. (1000 feet) above sea level on the southern slopes of Moel Tywysog (GR 981647).which boasted 112 members in the same year. The Congregationalists also had a chapel built in 1850, serving a small rural community on the northern slopes of Moelfre Isaf (GR 955744) and a larger one *"Bethlehem"* in St. Asaph. However, neither the Congregationalists nor the Wesleyans were able to rival the dominance of Calvinistic Methodism within the Elwy and Aled valleys.

The chapels that were built in the Elwy and Aled valleys throughout the late eighteenth and nineteenth centuries were essentially expressions of the permanence of Nonconformism within the local communities. They were financed and often built by the independent communities of local people (hence the name "chapel") who were to worship there. The funding for local chapels took some time to be raised in poor agricultural areas, what resulted was a building that is truly local and representative of the community it served. Land had to be either bought or leased over a 999 year period.[489] This was the case at Gwytherin, where the land for *Capel Silo* was leased in 1815.[490] Until 1850, the members used local people rather than specialist architects to design their chapels and thus their style can be correctly defined as "vernacular". In some cases, their design was similar to those found in domestic architecture such as the long house (see *Bethabara*; *Capel Rhiw* and *Garnedd*).

One of these simple early chapels survived in Abergele until the nineteenth century. *Capel y Bryngwyn* was a simple thatched structure with mud walls erected around 1715. Some of the earliest chapels in the Elwy basin were of similar structure and are still in use in some cases. These include the simple stone-built one storey Baptist chapel of *Bethabara* in Llangernyw; *Capel Rhiw* near Bylchau; *Capel Ffynnonau* and *Capel Pennel* near Llannefydd; *Capel Garnedd* near Llangernyw and *Capel Cefn Coch* near Gell these chapels had a simple single storey design employed locally in the late eighteenth and early nineteenth centuries when they were first built. A number of early chapels in the area were built to a common design (see Fig. 34). The success of Nonconformism in Wales owed much to a series of evangelical religious "revivals" that boosted the number of local "converts" and eventually led to these

---

[489] Anthony Jones : "Welsh Chapels" Alan Sutton Publishing Ltd Stroud, (1984) p10

[490] Denbighshire Record Office DRO/DD/GA/184

groups seeking to establish their own local meeting house or chapel. Successive revivals throughout Wales each fed a chapel-building boom as membership soared.[491]

Plate 34

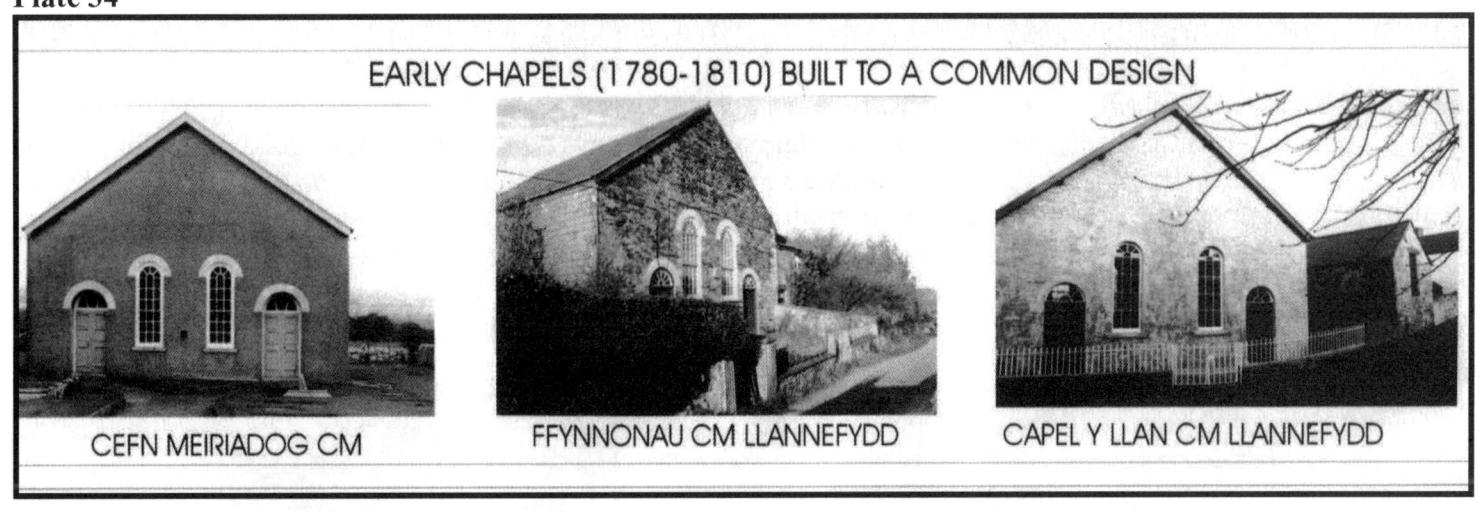

EARLY CHAPELS (1780-1810) BUILT TO A COMMON DESIGN

CEFN MEIRIADOG CM   FFYNNONAU CM LLANNEFYDD   CAPEL Y LLAN CM LLANNEFYDD

---

[491] Anthony Jones : "Welsh Chapels" Alan Sutton Publishing Ltd Stroud, (1984) p23

PLATE 35 — Extended Chapels

Pandy Tudur CM Chapel

Pennel Baptist Chapel Pentre Isaf Llannefydd

Horeb CM Chapel Rhyd yr Arian

Groes CM Chapel

Bethania Baptist Chapel Llansannan

In some cases existing chapels were demolished and a larger chapel was built on the same site to accommodate new members. Thus we find that chapels such as *Capel Horeb* at Bryn Rhyd yr Arian built in 1841 was altered or extended in 1871; 1891 and 1906.

The earliest of these "revivals" in Wales is recorded in 1730 at Trefeca in Breconshire. For the most part, the revivals were fairly local in their impact although they were experienced on a national scale in 1859 and 1905. Often the preachers at the heart of these revivals preached outdoor to audiences of thousands gathered on the hillside. An important relatively local revival occurred in the upper Elwy valley in 1828 when 80 new "converts" joined the ranks of the Calvinistic Methodists at *Silo* chapel in Gwytherin within a two month period while at the nearby Calvinist chapel at *Garnedd* on the Llangernyw - Llansannan road, the preaching of Cadwaladr Owen brought in 40 new converts in the same year. The 1828 revival is not classed as a "national" revival but nevertheless accounted for between 20,000 and 25,000 conversions across Wales in that year.

By 1851, a Nonconformist chapel; building boom was well underway leading to 2813 chapels being in existence throughout Wales by that year, most having been built over the preceding half century. Between 1800 and 1850 (on average) a new chapel was opened in Wales every eight days.[492] The religious census of 1851 indicated that some 80 per cent of worshipers in Wales attended a Nonconformist chapel.[493]

---

[492] John Davies "The Making of Wales" Cadw/Alan Sutton, Stroud (1996) p114

[493] John Davies "A History of Wales" Penguin, London (1993) p 319

Plate 36

Capel-y-Cwm (CM 1836), Llangernyw

Most chapels of the period were rectangular in plan with gable ends, one of which contained the main door. Windows were mostly round-arched. Occasionally larger chapels had a square plan with a pyramidal roof. Many of the chapels built in the 1800 - 1850 period had a small dwelling house at one end to accommodate either the minister or the chapel keeper. Such an extension was known as the "*Ty Capel*". These survive at *Capel Rhiw*; *Garnedd, Pennel* and *Cefn Coch*. Materials used to build the early chapels were mainly of local origin mostly stone obtained from nearby quarries. Slate was imported from further afield while the bricks employed in *Cefn Berain* chapel were probably made in St. Asaph. However, the Wesleyan chapel in St. Asaph used red glazed bricks from Ruabon probably brought into the town by rail. Many of the new chapels had a small graveyard adjacent to the building.

Plate 37

LATE (POST 1850) RURAL CHAPELS

BRYN DEUNYDD BAPTIST, LLANNEFYDD  CEFN BERAIN CM  TABOR CM, MYNYDD BODROCHWYN

This reflects the prohibition of Nonconformist burials according to their own rites in some Anglican churchyards. The chapels of *Garnedd, Silo* (Gwytherin) *Bryn Deunydd* (Llannefydd) and *Pandy Tudur* have their own graveyards. After the 1840s, many architects specialised in the design of chapels often influenced by chapel plans printed in English architectural journals. Such designs were often beyond the scope of builders drawn from members of the congregations although the ministers and deacons agreed on a final design with the architect meaning that the new chapels retained some individuality.[494] Perhaps the best known chapel architect in North Wales was Richard Owen (1831 - 1891), a Caernarfonshire man who operated from offices in Liverpool. Owen was responsible for the design of many chapels throughout Wales. In rural areas where the services of an architect could not be afforded, the vernacular style persisted for longer. The architects fulfilled a brief to maximise the density of seating within the chapel area. The names of the new chapels were drawn from the Holy Land and represented places named in the Old Testament in particular hence the profusion of *"Herons"*, *"Bethels"*, *"Salesma*n *"Seion"*.

Classical styles of architecture based on the buildings of ancient Greece or Rome spread into Wales from England and were preferred to Gothic in most Welsh speaking areas,[495] although the Wesleyans who built their chapels in the more anglicised parts of Wales preferred the Gothic style. After c1860, chapels built in the classical style often had their main entrance on a gable end which was decorated with relief features such as Doric columns. Designs based on the Italian sixteenth century Renaissance found favour in some areas. Here, the gable end was often decorated with a Palladian round window above the main door flanked by two smaller ones. Alternatively, a large arched window was placed above the main gable end door flanked by two smaller ones. From around 1860, Romanesque arched doorways and windows were also introduced. Larger chapels showing classical influences in their design include *Capel Ebenezer* in St. Asaph and *Capel Cofia Henry Rees* in Llansannan.

---

[494] Anthony Jones : "Welsh Chapels" Alan Sutton Publishing Ltd Stroud, (1984) p52

[495] Hubbard "The Buildings of Wales: Clwyd" Penguin Harmondsworth. P79

Plate 38

The second half of the nineteenth century saw another innovation in chapel design - larger chapels were built higher to allow for the provision of a gallery an example being at *Bethlehem* chapel in St. Asaph. This vastly raised the seating capacity and allowed these chapels to host preaching festivals (*Cymanfa Pregethu*) and singing festivals (*Cymanfa Ganu*) that attracted visitors to the chapel from a wide area. Such activities were central to Welsh culture and did much to promote the popularity of choral singing and local eisteddfoddau. The

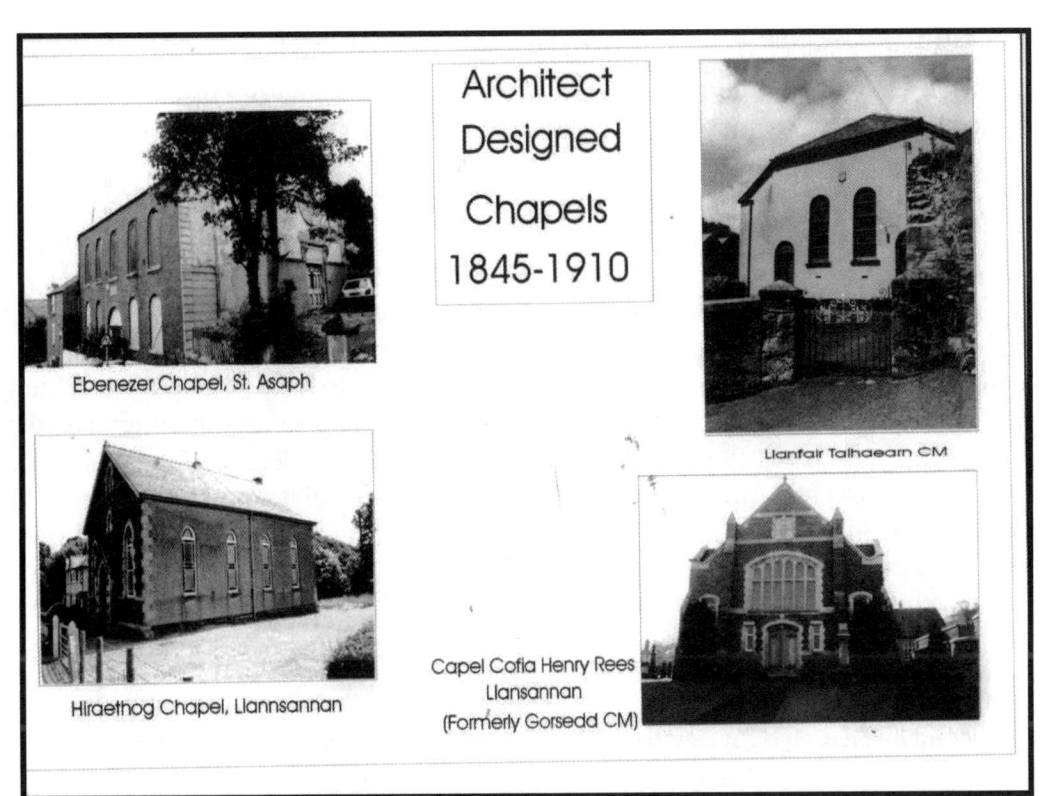

Architect Designed Chapels 1845-1910

Ebenezer Chapel, St. Asaph

Llanfair Talhaearn CM

Hiraethog Chapel, Llannsannan

Capel Cofia Henry Rees Llansannan (Formerly Gorsedd CM)

chapels built between 1870 and 1910 reflect the new found confidence of Nonconformist worshippers and conform their presence in their communities through often ornate and imposing chapels facades. Examples in the Elwy and Aled river valleys include the two Llansannan chapels of *Hiraethog* and *Capel Cofia Henry Rees*, the largest chapel in the whole river basin which is still flourishing today. Not all chapels built in the later decades of the nineteenth century were large or ornate; the small Calvinistic Methodist chapels of *Tabor* on the North West slopes of Mynydd Bodrochwyn and *Hebron* chapel near Bylchau were of a simple functional design.

To some extent, the success of Nonconformism reflects the fact that the Anglican Church had a decreasing attraction to the local population from the early years of the nineteenth century this found expression in the deplorable condition of the fabric of some Welsh churches owing to lack of funds[496]. At Llangernyw, a visit by the rural Dean of St. Asaph in 1749 noted some broken and missing flagstones but otherwise, the church was in a reasonable state of repair. From the early years of the nineteenth century, a degree of antagonism developed in Wales between the Nonconformists and the Anglicans where the gentry-led class structure prevailed[497]. The autobiography of Sir Henry Jones (1852 - 1923), the son of a Llangernyw shoemaker who achieved great repute in the academic world, indicates that this was not always the case although there was always some pressure from the local squirearchy (the Sandbach family) for those who wished to receive their patronage to become Anglicans[498]. It is also significant that

---

[496] Geraint H Jenkins "The Foundations of Modern Wales 1642 - 1780" OUP Oxford (1993) p175
[497] Richard Moore-Colyer "Welsh Cattle Drovers" Landmark, Ashbourne (2002) p11
[498] Sir Henry Jones "Old Memories" (1923)

there was no Welsh speaking bishop in Wales between 1716 and 1870.[499] One notorious bishop of St. Asaph, Bishop Drummond (1748-61) actively attacked the use of the Welsh language in church services.[500] However, it seems that some priests in the diocese took a more pragmatic view since it is recorded that in the mid eighteenth century, services in Llangernyw parish church were conducted in Welsh[501].

Plate 39

An often overlooked phenomenon is that Anglican churches also saw increased attendances in times of religious revivals, particularly following the great national revival of 1859. Thus, despite Nonconformist successes, the Anglicans, with the support of the local gentry "restored" or rebuilt their churches in the valley during the second half of the nineteenth century as at Llansannan (1878), Llangernyw (1849 and 1881) and Gwytherin (1869). This may be an indicator that the Elwy and Aled valleys shared in the wider Anglican revival which occurred in Wales during the 1860s and 1870s.[502] The

---

[499] G.E. Jones ""Modern Wales - A Concise History" CUP Cambridge (1984) p 127

[500] Geraint H Jenkins "The Foundations of Modern Wales 1642 - 1780" OUP Oxford (1993) p343

[501] R.H. Teague & R.L. Brown: "Griffith Jones' Pious Minister - The Reverend John Kenrick, Vicar of Llangernyw 1730 - 1755" Trans. Denbs. Hist. Soc. Vol. 49 (2000) p 34.

[502] John Davies "A History of Wales" Penguin, London (1993) p 435

Anglicans even built three new churches to serve the needs of two newly created parishes. The parish church of St. Mary's, Cefn Meiriadog (1864) was built from limestone quarried in an adjacent field. A new church to serve the new parish of Llanddewi was built in 1867 to meet the needs of the northern half of Llangernyw parish. There is some evidence that the new church where services were held in English may have been created to meet the needs of the English speaking Sandbach family of Hafodunos and their non-Welsh tenants and household[503]. A further new church dedicated to St. Thomas was built in 1857 to serve the new parish of Bylchau. In addition, a new Anglican church was built in 1882 at Pont y Gwyddel.to serve the needs of outlying farms between Llannefydd and Llanfair Talhaearn. This church remained in use until 1982 and has since been skilfully converted into a private house.

Plate 40

The late nineteenth century flurry in church building was too late to stem the tide of Nonconformism in the valley. The increasingly anglicised landowning classes continued to embrace Anglicism as can be seen from the monuments to the Wynne family in the church at Llanfair Talhaearn and the Sandbach family in Llangernyw church.

---

[503] R.H.Teague & R.L. Brown (ibid) p20

To their tenants and labourers, the egalitarian regime of the Nonconformist chapels where the congregation rather than social standing influenced decision-making proved a very attractive alternative despite the fact that neither the Baptists nor the Independents (Congregationalists) established an organisational structure for Wales until the third quarter of the nineteenth century. One writer has pointed out that, contrary to popular belief, Nonconformist communities were not totally egalitarian in their structure since the deacons were usually drawn from the ranks of the middle classes or skilled workers.[504]

During the course of the nineteenth century, over 5000 Nonconformist chapels were built in Wales, more new chapels than the whole of the rest of Britain put together.[505] The chapel building movement in Wales had its final impact with the last great national religious revival in 1905 when several very large chapels and often grandiose buildings were constructed such as *Capel Cofia Henry Rees* at Llansannan. In the Elwy basin several chapels were altered to accommodate larger congregations after the 1905 Revival, these include *Pandy Tudur*; *"Horeb"* at Bryn Rhyd yr Arian and *"Bethania"* in Llansannan. As the fervour for religious involvement slowly waned after 1905, only rarely were the largest chapels filled to capacity and after 1910, few new chapels were built.

During the last two decades of the twentieth century, many of the chapels that marked the evidence of social and cultural change in the landscape of Wales were beginning to disappear. Some were demolished; some still lie empty

---

[504] Gareth Elwyn Jones "Modern Wales - A Concise History" CUP, Cambridge 2nd Ed. (1994) p279

[505] Anthony Jones : "Welsh Chapels" Alan Sutton Publishing Ltd Stroud, (1984) p131

and un-used while others have been put to other uses as village halls or, in the case of *"Ebenezer"* in St. Asaph, converted into an antiques saleroom **(see Plate 41).** Many were converted into residential property as is the case with the Baptist chapels at *Bryngwylan* and *Capel Bryn Sion* the Calvinistic Methodist chapels of *Hebron* in Bylchau, *Cefn Coch* and *Cae'r Graig* (Gwytherin). Amongst the chapels currently lying empty in the river basin is *Salem* Calvinistic Methodist chapel in Llanfair Talhaearn which was built in 1862 at the height of the boom in chapel building following the 1859 National Revival. Others have been the subject of recent rationalisation notably *Capel Hiraethog* in Llansannan (built 1902) which has now closed following the transfer of its members to the larger *Capel Cofia Henry Rees* in the centre of the village. However, not all the rural chapels have fallen into dis-use; many are still in regular use and cared for by their members. This is certainly the case with *Capel Cefn Meiriadog, Capel Pandy Tudur* and *Capel Bryn Deunydd*. Fortunately, in the past decade, there has been a growing awareness of the importance of these humble buildings to the national heritage of Wales and their presence is now being recorded for enlighten future generations about a phenomenon that changed the cultural identity and landscape of a small nation.

CHAPTER 15: THE INFLUENCE OF THE PAST IN THE PLANS OF PRESENT DAY VILLAGES AND HAMLETS

The late Wynford Vaughan-Thomas, one of the outstanding Welsh-born literary and media celebrities of the twentieth century, observed that the villages of Wales did not grow up like their English counterparts as tight clusters of buildings lying close to the church and manor house. Instead, rural settlement in Wales was made up of scattered communities often remote from their parish churches[506]. Yet, today's visitor to the villages of the Elwy valley could be excused for thinking that the villages of Llannefydd, Llangernyw, Llansannan and Llanfair Talhaearn had also developed around their ancient church sites because in all three villages, the churches are surrounded by tight clusters of cottages dating from the seventeenth century onwards. In this chapter, the changing shape of the villages in the valley will be examined with a view to explaining how and when the villages achieved their present layouts.

Gwytherin: The village of Gwytherin is a nucleated settlement lying on a gentle slope above the reach of flooding from the River Cledwen which flows north-south through the area. (See Fig. 14) To the south of the village the valley narrows sharply and its sides steepen markedly as the stream nears its headwaters in Mynydd Hiraethog. The former parish is located in the hundred of Isaled about 3.2 kms (2 miles) from the source of the Elwy known at this point as the Afon Cledwen. The parish was formerly made up of four townships none of which are mentioned in the

---

[506] Wynford Vaughan-Thomas : "Wynford Vaughan-Thomas' Wales", Michael Joseph, London (1981) p 130

FIG. 14

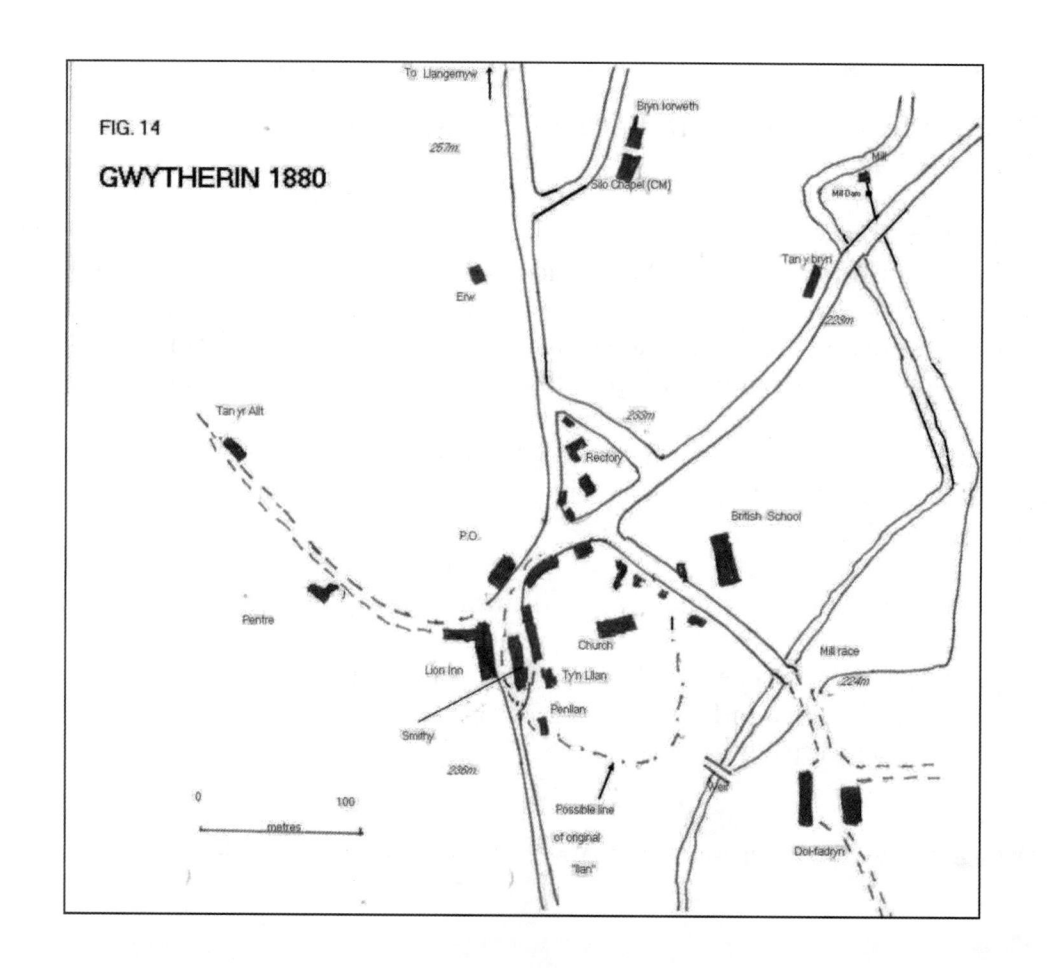

GWYTHERIN 1880

1334 Survey although the village itself is mentioned. The townships of *Is-llan* (below the church enclosure) and *Uwch-llan* (above the church enclosure) survived. The hamlet of *Pennant was* once a township but had lost township status by the 19th century. The former township of *Cornwal* was transferred to Llanfair Talhaearn.

There is field name evidence that arable sharelands once lay to the west of the village centre although no trace of ridge and furrow remains. It is possible that Gwytherin role as a medieval *clas* centre in early medieval times was responsible for its nucleated shape which has survived through to the present day possibly making this the only true medieval village layout in the whole of the Elwy basin although it was probably more of a hamlet than a village in size before the nineteenth century.

Site of smithy

The original village developed on the northern fringes of the curvilinear churchyard which formed the focus and raison d'etre of the settlement. (See Fig. 14) The curved street that follows the line of the north side of the churchyard may well have originated as the road serving the cottages of bonded tenants of the *clas* and tilling the arable sharelands noted to the west of the village. A permanently tilled area known as an *"ardd"* (garden) surrounded the "llan" of the church and even today one old cottage on the street is still called *"Ty'n yr ardd"*.
Plate 42

Ty'n Llan, Gwytherin

Plate 43
In post-medieval times, the rising demand for wool led to an expansion of settlement in the hills around the valley and the village may have survived as a service centre for this area housing a smithy and other tradesmen, together with agricultural labour for the surrounding farms. The parish registers record several tradesmen as resident in the village in the seventeenth and eighteenth centuries; these include weavers, shoemakers and stone masons. The size and shape of the village have changed very little since the drawing of the Tithe map in 1841. The oldest secular building in the village is probably the Lion public house that dates from 1694 and perhaps served droving and pack horse routes up the valley to the tracks leading across Mynydd Hiraethog to the south west.(see Plate 44) The smithy, which was sited in front of the inn, probably served the same trade since although the village is now a backwater away from main routes, in the days before motor cars pack horse routes converged on the village. Other than the church school (now closed), little new building took place during the late nineteenth century. On the slopes to the west of the Lion Inn, a group of four cottages known as *Pentre Uchaf* were built, probably around 1790, to house working people. (See Fig. 14). By 1810, the cottages were being

recorded as simply *"Pentre"* The centre of the village had two relatively small working farms in this period: *Ty'n y Llan* occupying 50 acres (20 ha) in 1881 and *Penllan*, the latter being un-occupied by the time of the 1881 Census.

Plate 44

Capel Silo an early nineteenth century Calvinistic Methodist chapel located on a low hill on the north side of the village, partially clad partly in slate to protect it from the weather, still serves the community. Otherwise, today's village economy is fragile. A number of the cottages are holiday homes; the village inn is closed as are the school and village shop. Even the church has an uncertain future. The village retains air of peace and tranquility in keeping with a site that began as a centre of religious devotion over one and a half millennia ago. In the narrow valley above the village (see Fig 7) stand ancient farmsteads with names strangely evocative in this age when interest in wizards, Celtic mysticism and magic have been re-kindled in popular literature. The farm names concerned are *Merddyn* (Merlin); *Llwyn Saint* (Grove of the Saint) *Bryn y Clochydd* (Hill of the Sextant) and *Dolfrwynog* (Meadow of the bridle)

Fig. 15

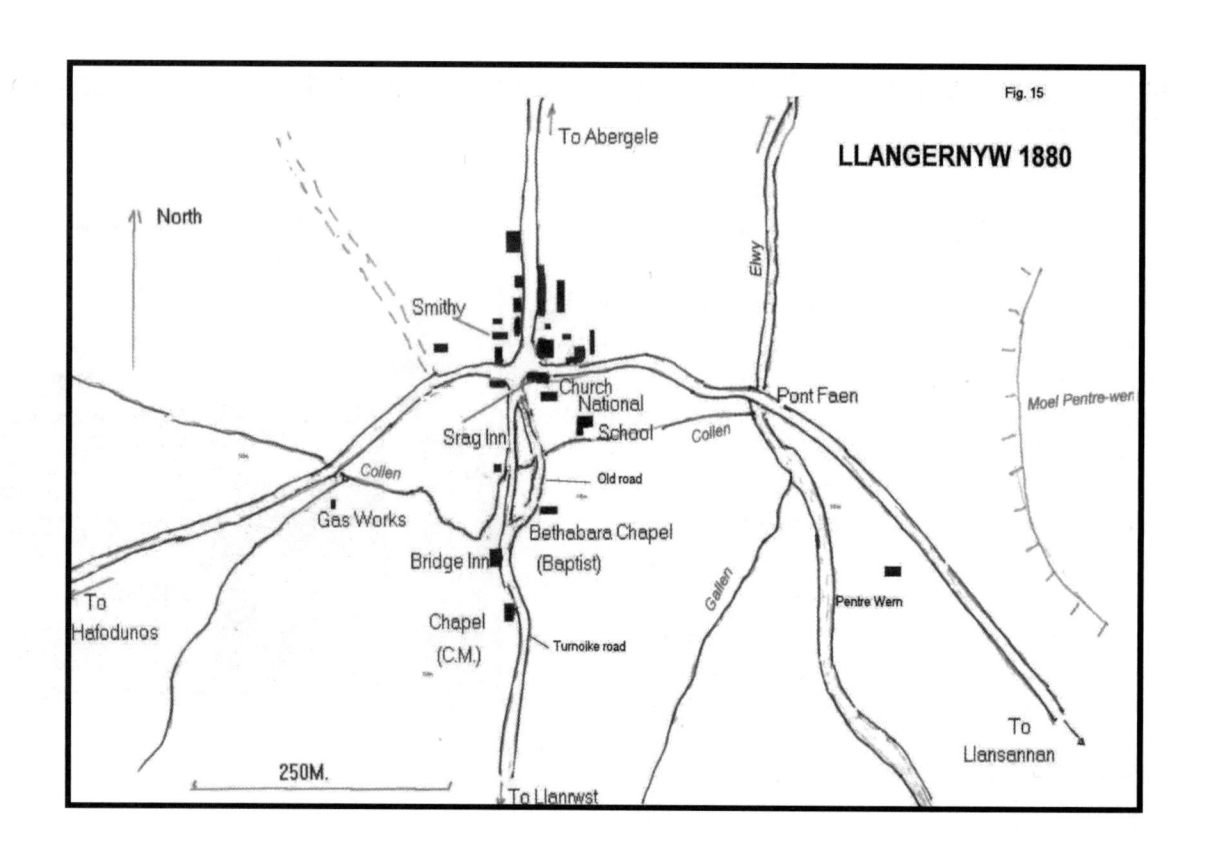

LLANGERNYW 1880

- To Abergele
- North
- Smithy
- Church
- Srag Inn
- National School
- Pont Faen
- Elwy
- Collen
- Gas Works
- Old road
- Bridge Inn
- Bethabara Chapel (Baptist)
- Collen
- Gallen
- Pentre Wern
- Moel Pentre-wen
- Chapel (C.M.)
- Turnpike road
- To Hafodunos
- To Llanrwst
- To Llansannan
- 250M.

Llangernyw 1881   Plate 45
(Plate included by permission of Llyfrgell Genedkaethol Cymry/ The National Library of Wales Ref JTH 02451)

The present day village of Llangernyw is located in the Elwy valley at a point where the river is joined by two small left bank tributaries the Afon Gallen and the Afon Collen. There is a tradition that the area that makes up the parish of Llangernyw was given to *St. Kentigern's* monastic community in St. Asaph by *Maelgwn* of Gwynedd in the early sixth century.[507] Presumably the lands

Village from west 1881 (Source NLW)

---
[507] "St. Digain's, Llangernyw" Parish church history pamphlet. Llangernyw (1997)

passed on to the Diocese of St. Asaph with the passing of the monastery which may explain why the townships of the parish were excluded from the medieval Lordship of Denbigh. Certainly the bishops of St. Asaph were patrons of the priest's living in the parish of Llangernyw during the eighteenth century. Thus, none of the original nine medieval townships of the parish are mentioned in 1334 Survey of the Honour of Denbigh. Like Llanfair Talhaearn, the parish lay within two commotes: Isaled and Isdulas. The nine townships were: *Bodrach; Nannerth; Pantymanus; Pentrewern; Rhanhir' Hafodunos; Dwyafon; Branar; Marchaled* and *Bodgynwch*.

The church served as a focal spot for the hamlets and isolated farms of the medieval parish. The village which is set around a central crossroads above the reach of flooding from the River Elwy is a fairly recent development (see Fig. 15). However, the church site clearly dates from early Christian times or even earlier. The five annual fairs were centred on this cross roads and even into the churchyard where fleeces, earthenware, horse gear (including packsaddles), ropes and wooden goods were displayed for sale and meat hung and sold in the "*Churchyard porch.*"[508] The church font still bears the scars from the sharpening of butchers' knives on its sandstone bowl. After complaints from the bishop of St. Asaph, the churchyard market venue was abandoned in 1750. A letter from the Vicar to the Bishop of St. Asaph dated 1750 indicates how small the village was at that time since it is described as a "*little pitiful village where are not above three or four thatched houses*"[509] Among these would have been the

---

[508] St. Asaph Diocesan Records - Rural Dean's Visitation Report (1749)
[509] R.H. Teague & R.L. Brown: "Griffith Jones' Pious Minister - The Reverend John Kenrick, Vicar of Llangernyw 1730 - 1755" Trans. Denbs. Hist. Soc. Vol. 49 (2000) p 34.

smithy located across the road from the Stag Inn that stood on the cross roads close to the church on land that was formerly part of the churchyard. The smithy would possibly have produced the iron shoes that were attached to the feet of cattle before being driven away to English markets by drovers.

(Plate included by permission of Llyfrgell Genedkaethol Cymry/ The National Library of Wales Ref JTH 02459)
Plate 46

The Tithe Map of 1841 shows that some expansion had taken place in the previous 90 years since by then linear development was apparent along the north-south main street that was to be later turnpiked. There was little housing along the roads leading east over the Elwy or west towards *Hafodunos*. By 1880, the OS Map shows that north-south growth had continued with further housing development along the new turnpike road from Abergele to Llanrwst that passed through the cross roads in the village. Seven "village cottages" are listed along this road in the 1881 Census. These were inhabited at that time by three widows, an

Bridge Inn 1880 (Source NLW)

agricultural labourer, a sawyer, a boot maker and a corn miller.

The 1881 Census also provides evidence of the growth of service functions in the village serving the needs of the surrounding rural area. Plate 45 shows the village at around the time of the 1881 Census. There was a shop known as "*Siop Llan*" close to the crossroads the owner being a substantial farmer employing six men and farming 250 acres (101.2 ha) .The blacksmith's shop was designated the "*Boar's Head*" and sold general produce alongside its metal working trade. The name suggests that it once served also as an inn. The *Stag Inn* was functioning as a public house but the landlord also farmed 80 acres (32.4 ha) and employed four men. The *Bridge Inn*, at the southern end of the village (see Plate 22) on the turnpike road was named as an inn in the 1879 Ordnance Survey map but by 1881 had ceased to be an inn. The village by this time had its own small gas works to the west of the village on the road to *Hafodunos*. The owners of this house, recently rebuilt by the eminent architect Sir Gilbert Scott were the Sandbach family, then the leading family in the village with an estate of over 4000 acres (1620 ha), who no doubt had some influence in this innovative development. The twentieth century saw a further expansion of building in the village with new housing sited on the south and west sides.

Llanfair Talhaearn: The heart of the village is located on the valley bottom and steep sides of a small south bank tributary of the Elwy just to the south west of the confluence of the two streams (see Fig. 16) Llanfair Talhaearn was described by Samuel Lewis in 1833 as "*an ancient parish in the hundreds of Isaled and Isdulas*" (the latter commote lay on the north side of the Elwy river). The parish had twelve townships. The townships of *Barog; Bodrychwyn; Garthewin; Melai; Petrual* and *Talhaearn* were all described in the 1334 Survey of the Honour of Denbigh.

Plate 47

Llanfair Talhaearn village from church

Cornwal was formerly a township of Gwytherin later transferred to Llanfair Talhaearn; *Cynnant* and *Ciliau* lie north of the Elwy and are not mentioned in the 1334 Survey while the remaining townships of *Dolganner, Bont* and *Prysllygoed* were not mentioned in 1334.

In medieval times the church probably stood in isolation on the west side of the valley while the township of *Talhaearn* and its associated bond hamlet would have been located on the east side of the valley above the reach of floods close to the site of *Talhaearn* farmhouse.(see Fig. 16). The present *Talhaearn* farmhouse dates from the early seventeenth century and doubtlessly had a medieval predecessor on the site. Exactly when the village itself developed on its present site close to the valley bottom between the church and *Talhaearn Farm* is difficult to establish but none of the houses in this part of the village appear to pre-date the eighteenth century. Jinny Jenks remarked on the appearance (and existence) of a nucleated village on the site in 1772. Miss Jenks described the view of the village from the terrace at Garthewin:

Plate 48

"from whence you see the village and church and a very pretty stone bridge with three arches which, being all white, have a very pleasing effect." [510]

Most of the present houses probably date from the nineteenth century even the misleadingly named Plas *yn Llan*, a large early Victorian house close to the Elwy Bridge.

Former National School Llanfair TH

The bridge over the Elwy dates from the eighteenth century and there are still signs of the ford that preceded it. The bridge carried all traffic from the direction of Abergele through the village since the present road to the north of the Elwy did not exist before 1860. Thus the village served as a small route centre with roads converging on the bridge from Abergele, Denbigh, Llanrwst and Llansannan. It is therefore possible that from at least the seventeenth century the first inns, smithy and shops serving the needs of travellers developed.

---

[510] "A Tour of North Wales by Jinny Jenks, 1772 " Nat. Library of Wales MS 22753B p 18

Fig. 16

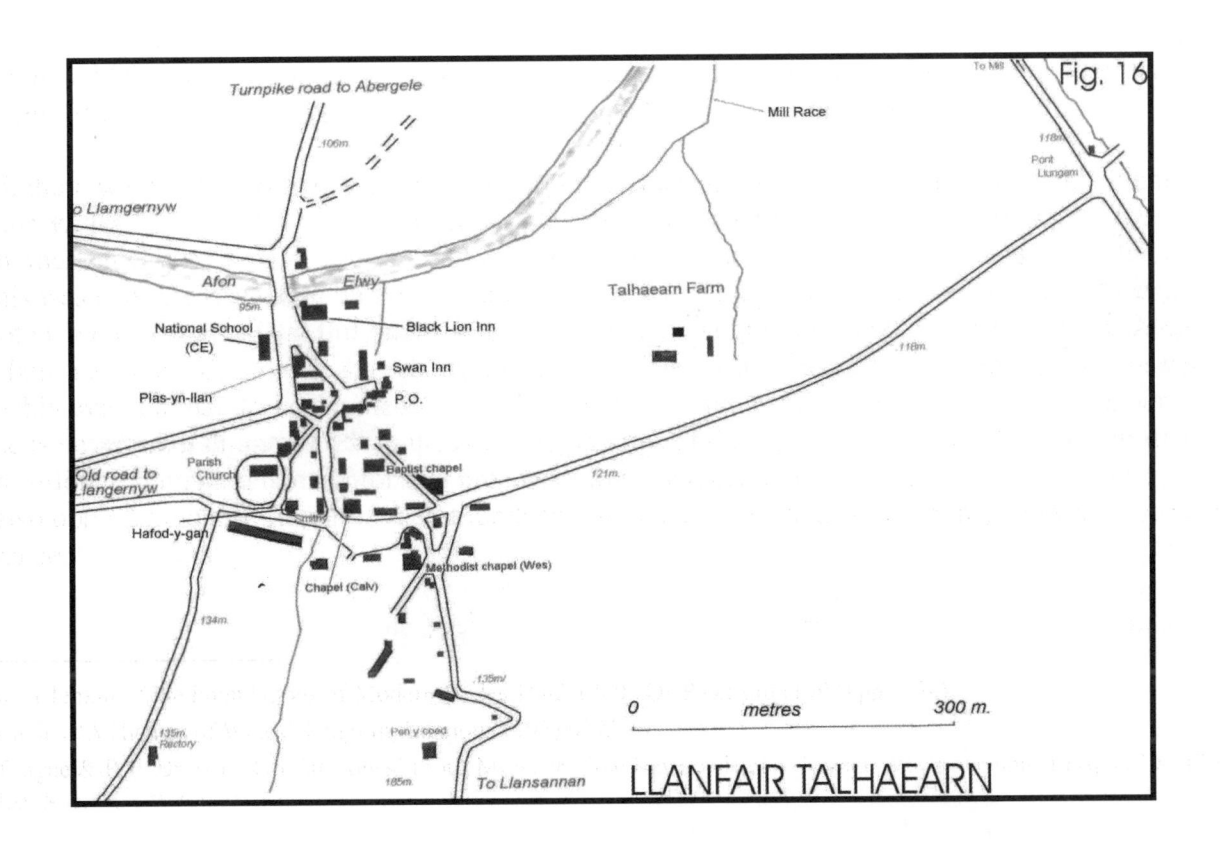

Turnpike road to Abergele
To Mill
Mill Race
Pont Llungam
To Llamgernyw
Afon Elwy
Talhaearn Farm
National School (CE)
Black Lion Inn
Swan Inn
Plas-yn-llan
P.O.
Old road to Llangernyw
Parish Church
Baptist chapel
Hafod-y-gan
Methodist chapel (Wes)
Chapel (Calv)
Rectory
Pen y coed
To Llansannan

0   metres   300 m.

LLANFAIR TALHAEARN

At some stage in the nineteenth century the small stream running through the centre of the village was culverted. It can still be seen entering the Elwy about 100m east of the bridge. It enters the culvert below Water Street at the south end of the village opposite the Methodist chapel. The Tithe map of 1842 shows that by that date a fairly compact village had developed to the east of the church. Figure 16, which is based on an early Ordnance Survey map, shows the village in 1880. The two surviving inns in the village, the *Swan* and the *Black Lion* inns were still the main inns at that time together with the *Crown Inn* which no longer exists.

The 1881 Census gives an accurate snapshot of the socio-economic make up of the village in that year. It is clear that a wide range of providers of professional services and craftsmen were settled here meeting the needs of the population of the village, its surrounding rural area and travellers passing through the village. A range of skilled crafts were represented and included a master shoemaker employing three people at *Tan y Bryn*; four tailors, a smithy employing three men, a wheelwright's shop employing two, a carpenter and four stone masons. A range of shops existed including a post office which also sold groceries and drapery, another grocery/drapery at *Elwy House*, three other small grocer's shops and a china dealer. In Water Street was the home of a pedlar, Edgar Dwyer (35) who informed the census enumerator that he was born in the USA. The village policeman lived in a lodging house on Denbigh Road.

Plate 49

Morris St. Llanfair TH

By far the most numerous occupational group in the village were agricultural labourers who travelled out daily from their homes to surrounding farms. This represents a change in tradition since married farm workers had formerly lived in cottages close to their places of work while single men often lived on the farms themselves. This development clearly contributed to the development of village communities in the valley from the eighteenth century onwards and may reflect changes in hiring arrangements for farm workers.

A small number of professional people also served the needs of the villagers. Their spiritual needs were met by a Calvinist minister, and an Anglican rector. There were also chapels in the village set up by the Baptists and Wesleyan Methodists although no resident minister is recorded for either. The educational needs of the village children were met at the Board school by the schoolmaster George Foulkes Jones, a Flintshire man. The health care needs of the villagers were met through a general practitioner's surgery in *Hafod y Gan* while social care for those who fell on hard tomes were met by the workhouse union based in St. Asaph which had an assistant overseer resident at *1, Rose Hill*, Llanfair Talhaearn. A car proprietor lived in School Lane no doubt provided some form of public transport including perhaps the day trips to the village by tourists from the popular growing coastal resorts of Abergele and Rhyl.

Today, the village has a population of just less than 1000 of whom about half are Welsh speaking. It still retains its main focus along the streets leading from the Elwy bridge but has seen some twentieth century building of properties on higher land on the east side of the village. In Llanfair Talhaearn main street, the village hall built in 1933, was sponsored by a leading member of the local gentry, Robert Wynne of *Garthewin* indicating that the influence of the local; gentry continued to be felt here well into the twentieth century.

Llanfair Talhaearn has the feel of a Cornish village with its alleyways and back lanes such as Morris Street (Plate 49) and School Street. The National School building in the centre of the village survives as a private house but still bears the date 1836. The growth of the village during the last years of the nineteenth century led to the establishment of a new school building which is still in use on a lane to the west of the parish church.

Llannefydd: The village is sited on a gentle north-facing slope to the south of the River Elwy with its centre less than two kilometres south east of Mynydd y Gaer hillfort. The village, with a tiny nucleus around the church, (see Plate 24) is set within a labyrinth of lanes and footpaths (see Fig. 17) linking the ten townships in the parish with the ancient church and its cemetery. The 1334 Survey of the Honour of Denbigh mentions the townships of *Llechryd; Berain; Tal y bryn; Myfoniog; Bodysgaw; Penporchell* and *Carwednewydd* all of which survive today as farms. The township of *Dinascadfel* stood on the site of the hillfort but was not mentioned in 1334. The two remaining townships of *Tycelyn* and the tantalisingly named *Tiryrabad* ("land of the abbot") were not mentioned in 1334, neither was the name Llannefydd itself although the church, a chapel of St. Asaph cathedral, certainly existed perhaps in isolation from other settlement.

The ancient sites of the church and graveyard still partly dedicated to its fifth century founder St. Nefydd with the holy well of *Ffynnon Nefydd* 270 metres to the north of the church. The church was re-dedicated to St. Mary possibly at the time of its re-building in the fifteenth century. Interestingly, the well of St. Nefydd was also replaced by a well dedicated to Mary. This well lay closer to the church in the farmyard of *Gwyndy Farm* where it survives as a spring (see Fig. 17). Tradition though dies hard in Wales and the original well of St. Nefydd seems to have retained its attraction as the centre of the well cult until the reforms of Henry VIII in the first half of the sixteenth century. The church probably stood alone in medieval times linked by lanes or footpaths to its community

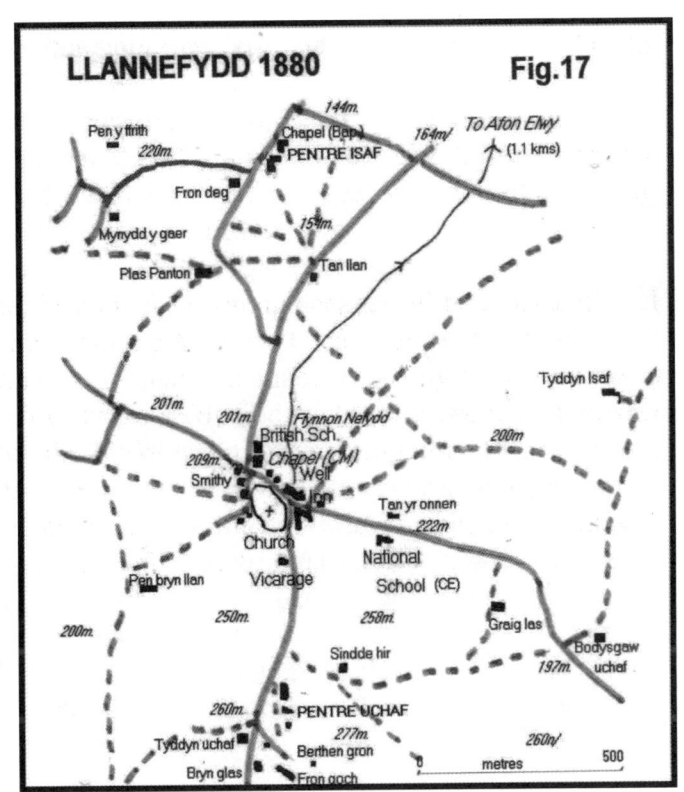

Fig. 17 LLANNEFYDD 1880

living in surrounding hamlets and farms. This was in accordance with the customs described in the medieval Laws of Hywel Dda whereby all houses had a footpath leading to the church and cemetery.

The pattern of lanes and paths focusing upon the church site is shown in Fig. 17 which shows the shape of the village around 1880: Even by the time of the earlier Tithe survey in 1844, the centre of the village was tightly nucleated around the church with a few cottages lying close to the churchyard. Diocesan records indicate that there were only six houses in the village in 1700. Surrounding the village the land in fields surrounding the church nucleus was laid down to arable crops, hay, clover and pasture suggesting relatively intensive land use for an upland area. This settlement pattern may have its origins in medieval times since in order to conserve the best arable land, homesteads were often located around the edges of the arable sharelands (rhandiroedd). This produced a distinctive pattern of rural settlement in the form of a girdle of dispersed dwellings around a central arable core as appears to have possibly been the case at Llannefydd. Farms forming part of the girdle of homesteads around the edges of the arable sharelands may have included the sites of the present farmsteads of *Tyddyn uchaf*: *Sindde hir*; *Graig las*; *Tyddyn isaf*; *Tan llan*; *Plas Panton* and *Pen bryn llan*. The *"llan"* referred to in the names of *Tan llan* (below the enclosure) and *Pen bryn llan* (top of the hill of the enclosure) may well have been the lands formed by the arable

Plate 50

Llannefydd village, from church (Note curvilinear church wall)

sharelands that would have been fenced in to avoid damage from grazing animals. The two farms closer to the village: *Tan yr onnen* and *Gwyndy farm* in the village itself may date from after the enclosure of the arable sharelands in post medieval times.

It is difficult to say exactly when any degree of nucleation developed around the church. The oldest of the stone built cottages at the heart of the village date only from the eighteenth century and may have developed to serve the needs of travellers passing along the route through the village from Denbigh to the Conwy ferries. This is almost certainly the raison d'etre for the *Hawk and Buckle* Inn which the owners claim to be of seventeenth century date. In 1881, there also appears to have been a further public house in the village. The centre of the village was the site of four annual fairs in which locally produced hand knitted items were sold alongside the usual cattle and other agricultural produce.

The 1881 Census Return gives us a clear picture of the functions of the buildings around the church. One of the largest buildings was *Plas yn Llan* that housed a draper's shop run by the Salisbury family. The

Hawk & Buckle Inn, Llannefydd

Plate 51

building also housed three other households two of which were headed by ageing agricultural labourers and the other by a tailor presumably working for the business. The village post office also occupied a central site and was also in multiple occupation. The postmaster was Moses Jones, a native of Penmachno who also described himself as a shopkeeper. Also living in the same building was an 81 year old retired schoolmaster and a mother and daughter described as "shop women". By this time there was also a village police constabulary. The vicarage at the south end of the village was occupied by the Reverend Ebenezer Jones, a Cardiganshire man. The *Hawk and Buckle* inn was in the hands of a local man, Thomas Lloyd. There were five other small cottages in the village centre occupied by a bake house keeper, a shoemaker, a horse trainer, a shop woman and a gamekeeper's widow and her agricultural labourer son. One sizeable farm was located in the centre of the village, this being *Gwyndy Farm*, a 100 acre (40.5 ha) establishment run by Hugh Evans, a Llansannan man possibly farming part of the former shareland that once surrounded the village. There was a smithy in the centre of the village run by William Williams and his two sons.

The OS map shows two schools at either end of the village centre. To the North West stood the British School (Nonconformist) and at the eastern end the National School (Anglican). The existence of two schools in such a small village may reflect the division between the two religious bodies heightened by resentment of the burden of tithes which contributed to the Llannefydd riots in the 1880s that required military intervention to subdue the outraged villagers.[511] The events perhaps can be seen as an expression of the link between Nonconformism, land reform agitation and radical Liberalism that was to break the political dominance of the Wynn family in the area within a few years.

---

[511] Tim Jones "Rioting in North East Wales 1536 - 1918!" Bridge Books, Wrexham (1997) pp 56- 74

The Calvinistic Methodist chapel stood adjacent to the British school. These two schools were not the first to serve the village. The building housing the *Llaeth y Llan* dairy once housed one of Griffith Jones' *"Circulating"* schools. Griffith Jones (1684 - 1761) founded these schools (others existed at Llanfair Talhaearn and Llangernyw) to teach pupils in Welsh enabling up to thirty pupils to gain some degree of literacy in their native tongue and access the scriptures. Between 1733 and 1761, 3325 of these schools were established throughout Wales. They operated seasonally for three monthly periods and were taught by itinerant teachers.[512] The movement was described by Professor Gwyn Williams as *"a brilliant success"* [513] and certainly contributed a great deal to the spread of Nonconformist ideology in the area.

The shape of the central village was relatively stable from the eighteenth until the twentieth century when new housing was built at the North West end of the village nucleus. However, there were some interesting settlement patterns beyond the circle of better quality agricultural land that surrounded the village. Half a kilometre south of the village centre stood a small cluster of dwellings known as *"Pentre Uchaf"* (higher village or hamlet). These stood above the village at a point close to where the land steepened to rise to former upland grazing and common land. These houses were occupied by working people of limited means in 1881. The six households were headed by an ageing charwoman, three agricultural labourers and a retired laundress and housekeeper. A similar group of dwellings for poorer people stood one kilometre north of the village at the eastern end of Mynydd y Gaer hill. This

---

[512] Gareth Elwyn Jones "Modern Wales - A Concise History" CUP, Cambridge 2nd Ed. (1994) p144

[513] Gwyn A Williams "When was Wales?" Black Raven Press, London (1985) p 154

cluster of houses was (is) known as *"Pentre Isaf"* (lower village). In 1881 three stood empty with the remaining five dwellings being occupied by agricultural labourers and a labourer's widow. The hamlet had its own Baptist chapel: *Pennel* now dis-used.

Llansannan: The village is located in the valley of the River Aled with the original nucleus and medieval church being located on the west bank of the stream above the reach of flooding. A small tributary stream, the Afon Bach, flows into the Aled from the west and marked the southern limit of settlement in the village until around the mid nineteenth century (see Fig. 18). As with other village churches in the river basin, the church, dedicated to St Sannan developed on the site of the cell and later curvilinear cemetery enclosure *(llan)* of the sixth century saint and probably initially stood alone on the present village site. The 1334 Survey of the Honour of Denbigh mentions a Llansannan township indicating perhaps that by this time a small hamlet had developed here either close to the ancient site of the church or some 400 metres to the south west around the farm known as *"Hendre Llan"* (GR931657).

The parish of Llansannan is of medieval origin and was large originally covering 18,473 acres (7474 ha) made up of the thirteen townships of. *Treflach; Llansannan; Rhydeidon; Beidiog; Pennant Aled; Llysaled; Archwediog; Chwibren; Mostyn and Hendrennig; Hescin; Deunant; Arllwyd* and *Grugor*. With the growth of trade in the later Middle Ages it is likely that some service functions developed close to the church and the nearby crossing of the River Aled. The *Saracen's Head Inn* appears to have been built on land that was formerly part of the churchyard perhaps to serve the needs of travellers passing through the village. The river bridge acted as a focus for routes from

FIGURE 18

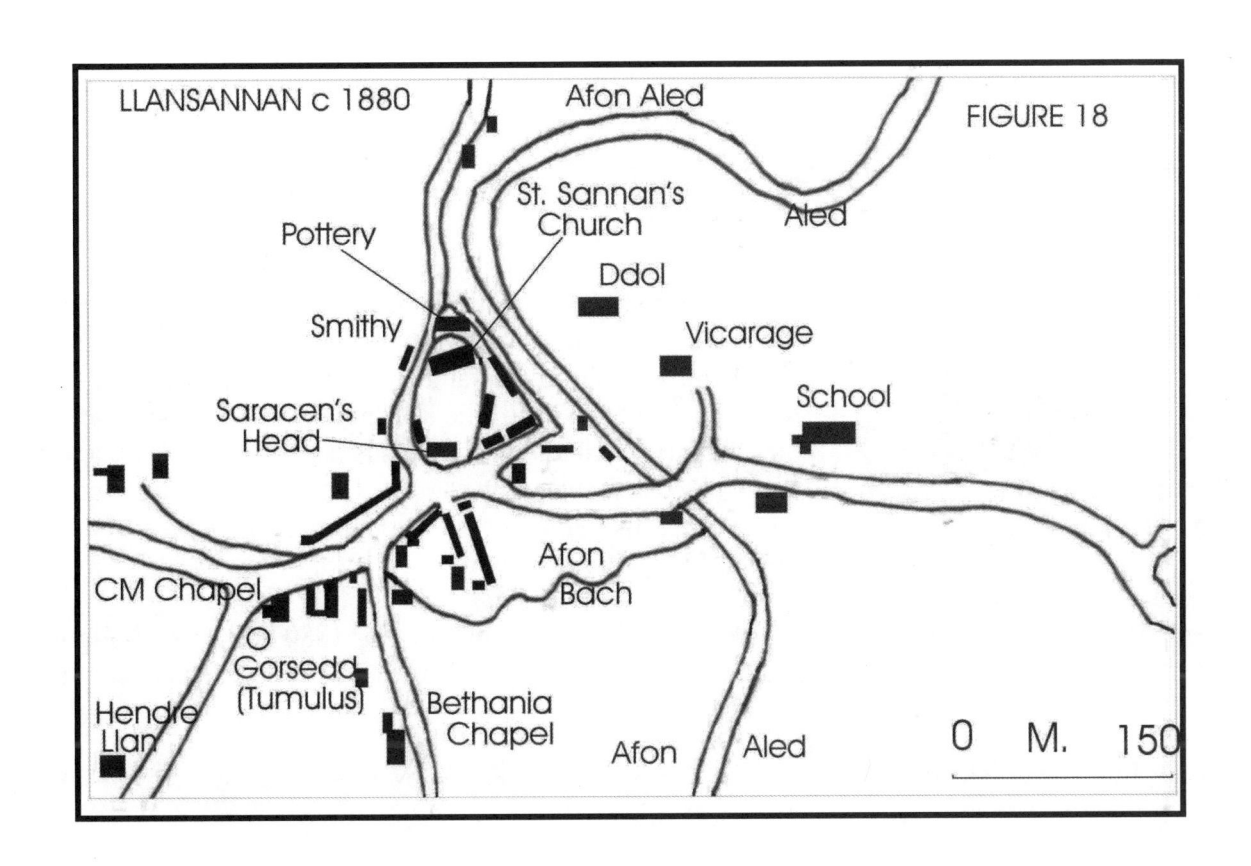

LLANSANNAN c 1880

Afon Aled
Aled
Pottery
St. Sannan's Church
Ddol
Smithy
Vicarage
Saracen's Head
School
CM Chapel
Afon Bach
Hendre Llan
O Gorsedd (Tumulus)
Bethania Chapel
Afon Aled

0 M. 150

Llangernyw and Gwytherin to the west, Llanfair Talhaearn to the north, Pentre Foelas and Cerrig y Druidion to the south and Henllan and Denbigh to the east.

Plate 52

Saracen's Head Inn

The coming together of routes in the village encouraged trade to develop and fairs were held in the village for there is a mid eighteenth century reference to the use of the churchyard for this purpose.[514] The first map of the village is the Tithe survey of 1841 that shows that the village was very nucleated in shape close to the west side of the Aled bridge. Both the Tithe map and the first large scale edition of the Ordnance Survey maps of the later nineteenth century give strong clues that medieval arable sharelands lay to the south west of the village close to *Hendre Llan Farm*. The field boundaries are very elongated at this point and the name of the farm "*Dalar Bach*" can be translated as "little headland".

The growth of the village by the year 1880 is shown on Figure 18. The compactness of the village centre still remained as it was in the 1840s but there had been some expansion to the

---

[514] R.H. Teague & R.L. Brown: "Griffith Jones' Pious Minister - The Reverend John Kenrick, Vicar of Llangernyw 1730 - 1755" Trans. Denbs. Hist. Soc. Vol. 49 (2000) p 34.

Plate 53 *(Plate included by permission of Llyfrgell Genedkaethol Cymry/ The National Library of Wales Ref JTH 02575)*

south of Afon Bach where Calvinistic Methodist and Baptist chapels had been built. On the east side of the Aled, a vicarage and school had been added.

The 1881 Census return indicates that the people of the village lived in four main parts of the village centre namely Water Street, Church Street, Cogar Street and Exchange Passages. Three public houses: the

Saracen's Head, *the Crown* and the *Red Lion served* the needs of travellers and local customers. A range of tradesmen lived in the village serving the needs of the people of the upper Aled valley, these included a thatcher, two tailors five carpenters, two shoemakers, a baker, a letter carrier, police constable, a stone mason and two blacksmiths (brothers) working the smithy that stood close to the church. . Also close to the church was a pottery at the house known as *Ty Hwnt i'r Fynwent* (House next to the graveyard). Three shops are identified at *Aled House, Manchester House* and *Siop Issa*. A copper miner and flannel weaver presumably commuted to places of work outside the village as did the many agricultural labourers who made up by far the most numerous element in the working population.[515]

The Census gives an impression of a relatively self-sufficient but poor community in the village in the closing decades of the nineteenth century. The document identifies a much larger number of mostly elderly paupers receiving outdoor relief from the Poor Law authorities than was the case in neighbouring villages. In fact, the Census also shows that at the Union Workhouse at St. Asaph, there were more paupers in residence from Llansannan than any of the neighbouring villages in the Aled and Elwy valleys. The majority of the paupers in the village lived in Water Street and the Exchange No doubt many of the villagers were finding solace in their places of worship which had been established since the early nineteenth century. The Baptists chapel of *Bethania* has records dating back to 1814. . By far the most successful was the Calvinistic Methodist Chapel at *Bryn yr Orsedd* which had

---

[515] PRO : RG11/5563/83

over 320 members by the end of the century. Fewer than 100 members attended the *Bethania* Baptist Chapel[516]. Numbers attending Anglican services are unknown.

The main change to the plan of the village since 1880 has been the addition of a new main road, the A5544 which passes through the village linking Llanfair Talhaearn to Bylchau. In the twentieth century, new housing developed adjacent to the road at the west and east ends of the old village. New housing was also added on the south side of the village on the west bank of the River Aled.

Henllan: This present day village does not wholly lie within the catchment of the Elwy river system but part of the village site is drained by the Afon Meirchion, a tributary of the Elwy. The village is actually sited on a spur of Carboniferous limestone rock that is the watershed between the river basins (catchment areas) of the Elwy and River Clwyd. The church itself lies wholly within the Elwy basin. The name of the village translates as "old enclosure" and this, together with the dedication of the church to St. Sadwrn, suggests an early medieval date, possibly as early as the sixth century, for the first settlement here. The village church is first mentioned in a taxation return of 1291 as a chapel of St. Asaph cathedral but appears to have achieved parish church status soon after that date. The church

---

[516] Welsh Church Commission - County of Denbigh - The Statistics for Nonconformist Chapels (1901)

FIG. 19

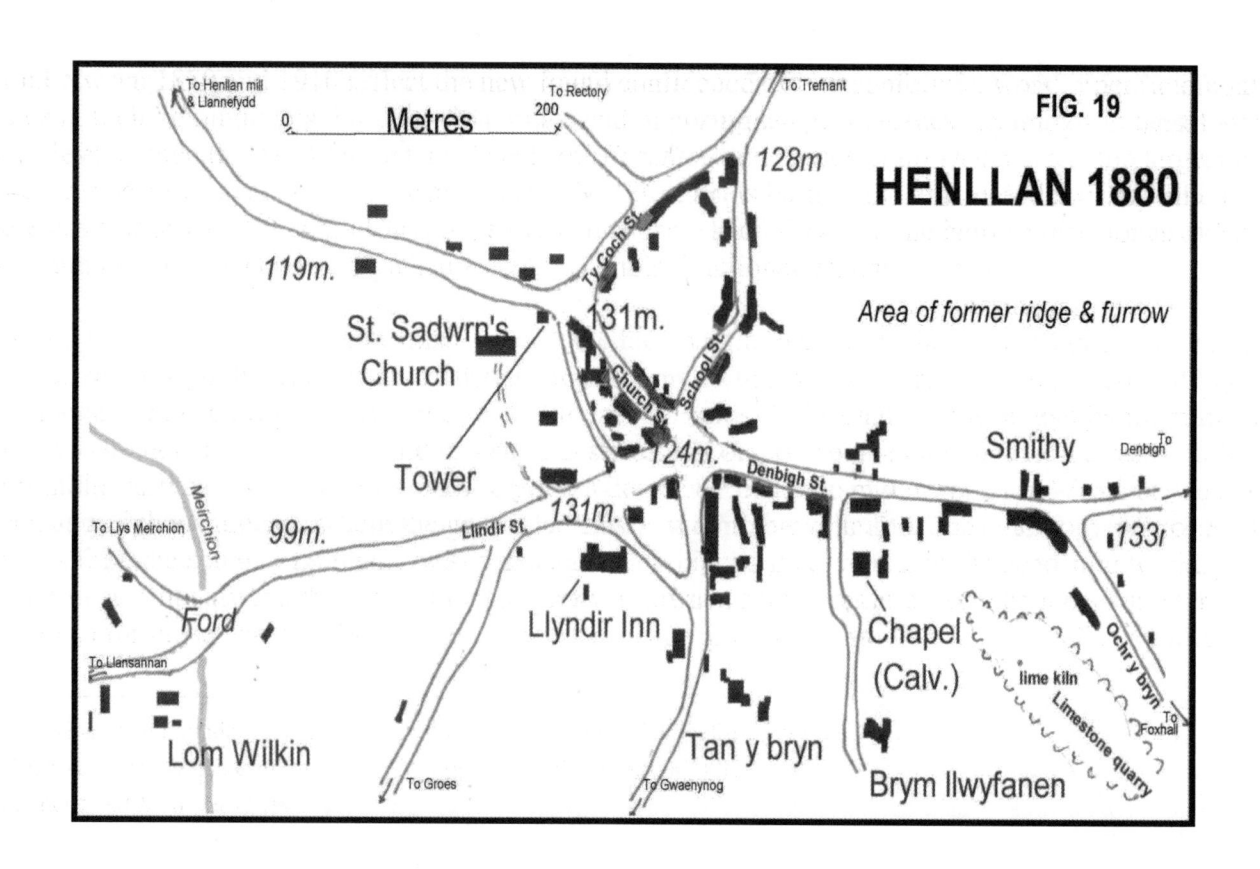

HENLLAN 1880

Area of former ridge & furrow

served a huge medieval parish of around 100 square kilometres containing twelve townships: (*Banister Isaf; Banister Uchaf; Brynysgub; Erifiat; Gwenynog Llan; Llewenni Isaf; Llewenni Uchaf; Rhanfawr; Tywysog; Taldrach*; *Tre'r parc; Uwchcaeron*). The majority of these lay outside the Elwy river catchment area.

The core of the village seems to have been located on the watershed itself, on the hill close to the detached church tower. In the late seventeenth century, the cartographer John Ogilby noted its location on an "eminence" At the end of the century Llwyd was more informative and alluded to thirteen houses around the church with another eighteen "not far off". This implies that settlement in the village was growing around two separate nuclei. The second nucleus is not identifiable with certainty but probably lay south east of the church close to the junction of Church Street and Denbigh Street. (See Fig. 19) Six different routes converge close to this point and no doubt this site proved attractive to tradesmen and shopkeepers. One such building was the *Llindir Inn*; a Grade II listed building, possibly of late fifteenth century origin but was much altered in the nineteenth century.[517] The village lay along an important local coaching route to Abergele from Denbigh. The large scale OS map of 1880 shows that a smithy was in operation on Denbigh Street on what was the eastern edge of the built-up area at the time. Two Nonconformist chapels had been established on the south eastern edge of the village, Seion Calvinistic Methodist chapel (Plate 56) and a Baptist chapel on the road to Foxhall, now a residential street known as *Ochr y Bryn*.

---

[517] Denbighshire Sites and Monuments Record.

Plate 54

The area lying between the church and *Llindir Inn* centred on Church Street was probably built over in the eighteenth and nineteenth centuries. The street pattern of this area is intriguing and may give a clue as to the early development of the village perhaps around a piece of unenclosed common land on which a number of local and long distance routes converged. One of the two nuclei of settlement described by Llwyd at the end of the seventeenth century was possibly on the site of the hamlet of the bondmen who tilled arable sharelands close to the village. This was probably (but not necessarily) the nucleus of settlement around the site of the church recorded in the Survey of Denbigh 1334. In this case the second larger cluster of seventeenth century dwellings at the other end of Church Street possibly developed as long distance commerce was re-established from the late fifteenth century hence the location of the *Llindir Inn*.

Ty coch Street Henllan

On the eastern side of the village core (GR 025682), aerial photographs taken in 1949 revealed the former existence of ridge and furrow, part of an open field strip system[518]. The area has since been built upon. However, the 1880 map shows that this area of possible medieval arable sharelands was still not built upon and housed two lime kilns. The boundaries of this former area of open field is still preserved in the village street pattern since it is bounded by School Street, Denbigh Road, Ffordd Meifod, Bryn y Garn and the road to Trefnant. A further interesting aspect of the street plan of Henllan is the existence of a triangular area bounded by Church Street, Ty Coch Street and School Street. The course of each of these streets curves slightly around this triangular space for no apparent reason. It may indicate that some kind of enclosure on this site pre-dates the street system. It leads us to the question as to whether this was an ancient enclosure - perhaps the *"hen llan"* that gave its name to the village or perhaps it represents the enclosed croft lands farmed on a personal basis by the medieval bondmen. By 1880, the area was surrounded by buildings but still has a partly open core.

The 1881 Census tells us more about the people who inhabited this large village.[519] The village was still broadly agricultural in its economic make-up with agricultural labourers being by far the largest occupational group. There were several working farms within the limits of the village notably *Bryn-llwyfanen* which farmed 40.5 hectares (100 acres); *Tan y Bryn* 6.5 ha (16 acres); *Truan* 5.25 ha (13 acres); *Plas Meifod* 39.25 ha (92 acres) and, just outside the village, *Pandy* 24 ha (60 acres). The inn keeper at the *Llindir Inn* was also a cow keeper (milk supplier). Today, the

---

[518] CPAT PRN 19753
[519] PRO RG 11 Pieces 5532/3

Llindir Inn is the only inn in the village, but in 1881, local drinkers had more choice since there were four other public houses such as the *Cross Foxes* and *Cross Keys* in the Denbigh Street area and others located in dwelling houses in Church Street and Ty Coch Street.

Plate 55

Industry was small scale, the largest being quarrying for local limestone at a quarry located south of Denbigh Street (GR 026679). The quarry proprietor was Margaret Griffiths, a widow living at 29, Denbigh Street. Several village men were employed at the quarry. There were several limekilns within the village area supplying a local market for lime for agriculture and cement. Outside the village at *Pandy Bodeiliog*, the Davies family manufactured woollen cloth on this site with a long history in textile production. There were a number of small shops in the village mostly general stores but there was a Post Office and a grocers/flour dealer's shop in Llindir Street and a draper in Denbigh Street.

Almshouses Henllan

A range of specialist craftsmen lived in the village notably a blacksmith working the smithy on Denbigh Street who employed one journeyman and a wheelwright/ carpenter's business at 16 School Street run by Thomas Jones and his two sons. Other crafts within the village included stonemasons, joiners, plasterers/ slaters (the two trades seemed to be combined), tailors, shoemakers and a clogger: Henry Chippendale born in Accrington but living with his wife and child at 18 Ty Coch Street.

The presence of a clogger in the village is interesting in that it may tell us something about social and economic conditions in the village in 1881. From George Borrow's conversation with John Jones, the Llangollen weaver, some 25 years earlier, it appears that clogs were not generally worn in Denbighshire.[520] Clogs were only 20% of the price of a pair of shoes and were widely used in the textile areas of Lancashire. Is the presence of a clogger in Henllan an indicator that the local working population had fallen upon hard times and could no longer afford to buy shoes? We know that economic hardship existed in the 1880s to such an extent that in 1888, disturbances in the neighbouring village of Llannefydd, led to the reading of the Riot Act. Nevertheless, the 1881 Census indicates that there were very few paupers in Henllan compared with neighbouring villages such as Llansannan, and six shoemakers plied their trade in the village at that time. George Borrow's writings may provide the answer. Borrow visited the home of a clogger born in Bolton, Lancashire in another unlikely venue, the upper reaches of the Ceiriog valley in the south of Denbighshire. It seems that the "clogger" concerned did not actually make clogs but fashioned locally cut alder wood into squares that were collected by a middle man and taken for manufacture to Lancashire. This indicates an organised trade in alder wood to supply the heavy demand for clogs in Lancashire and perhaps also reflects that supplies of alder wood were becoming scarce in that county, hence a wider search for raw materials.

---

[520] George Borrow : "Wild Wales" (1862) Collins, London (1962 edition) p115

Certainly, the valley of the Afon Meirchion would have had plentiful supplies of alder wood and thus it raises the question as to whether Henry Chippendale was employed in supplying this demand.

Plate 56

The professions were not well represented: amongst the population there was the rector, a Calvinistic Methodist minister whose chapel was described as "being built", two teachers and a police officer. At the top of the social scale were a number of owners of larger properties on the fringes of the village who described themselves as "landed proprietors" or "Justices of the Peace". Of these, the most affluent was probably the Mainwaring family of *Galltfaenan* but the owners of smaller, but still substantial properties such as the Griffiths family of *Garn* were more typical. The employment of villagers as domestic servants at these houses is reflected in the 1881 Census which records domestic servants, gardeners and a coachman living in the village. Even, the modest farm of *Brynllwyfau* employed a live-in governess, groom, dairymaid and housemaid. At the other end of the scale of prosperity, a group of alms houses (Plate 55) provided village accommodation for those who no longer earned a regular wage.

In comparison to other villages in the area, a large number of the inhabitants of Henllan in 1881 were born outside of the village, some from as far afield as Scotland Liverpool, Lancashire, Dolgellau, Oswestry and Chester. In today's village, those who have settled in the expanding village in the past twenty years are described as the "new people"; it seems that the changing make-up of the village population is something that Henllan has had a long time to come to terms with!

Cefn Meiriadog: Lying 3 kms south west of Llanelwy (St. Asaph), Cefn Meiriadog is not really a village since it is made up of a number of dispersed farms and cottages lying in a network of lanes on the southern edge of a limestone ridge which gives its name to the parish. The parish of Cefn Meiriadog is relatively new having been created from part of the parish of Llanelwy in 1865. The new parish included two ancient townships of *Cefn* and *Wigfair*. The parish Church of St. Mary (GR 018716) was consecrated in 1864 having been built at the expense of local landowner Sir Watkin Williams-Wynn. (see Plate 21) The spiritual needs of the Nonconformist population were met at the chapel (Plate 19) named "*Tabernacl*" which, in 1905, had 165 worshippers[521]. In the twentieth century, some nucleation developed around *Cefn Mairwen* (GR 017714) where a row of council houses and some private dwellings were built.

Bontnewydd: As the translation of the place name implies ("new bridge"), Bontnewydd is a hamlet clustered around the eighteenth century bridge over the Elwy. It seems likely that the settlement here developed to serve the needs of travellers passing over the bridge. The *Dolben Arms Inn* dates from the eighteenth century and still serves

---

[521] Welsh Church Commission - County of Denbigh - The Statistics for Nonconformist Chapels (1905)

Fig. 20 Bontnewydd

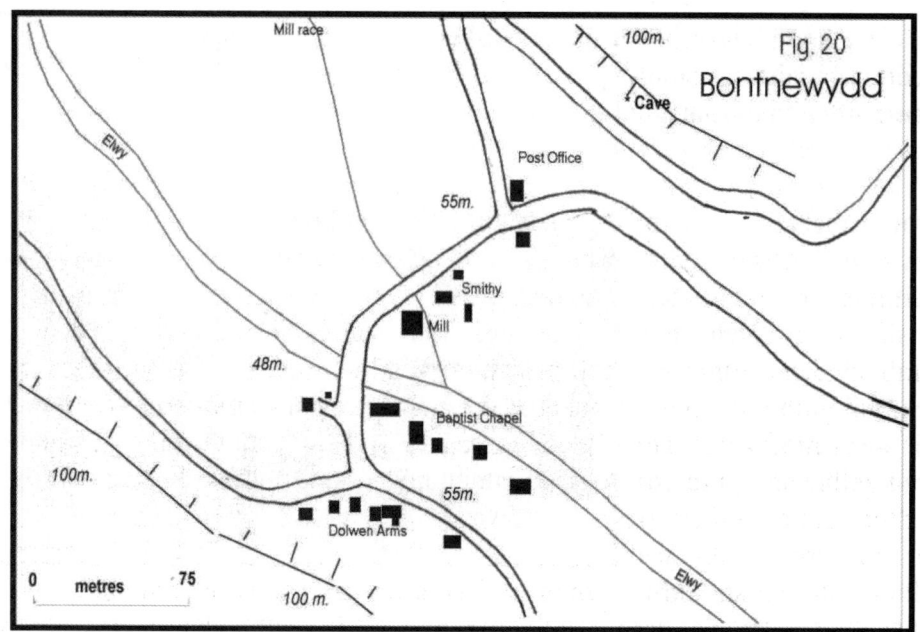

the needs of customers passing along the narrow lanes that converge on the bridge. The Tithe Map of the 1840s and the first large scale OS map dating from 30 years later show that most cottages stood on the south side of the river on the opposite side of the road to the *Dolben Arms*. North of the river stood the water mill and an adjacent smithy. The water mill remains as a house conversion but the smithy has disappeared apart from its name which survives as the name of the nearby *Smithy Farm*. A Baptist chapel served the population in 1906, this stood across the road from the Dolben Arms (see Fig.20)

Cefn Berain: The hamlet of Cefn Berain lies mainly to the north of an intersection of minor roads two kilometres south east of Llannefydd village. It is a small hamlet of scattered farms and cottages running in a loosely linear pattern from SSW to NNE for over one kilometre along a ridge top lane. (See Fig. 21) The name Cefn Berain translates as "Berain Ridge" and the hamlet is strung along the crest of rising land reaching an altitude of around 200 m.(650 feet) backed to the west by a steep descent into a valley cut by a small tributary of the River Elwy which flows two kilometres to the north.

There is no extant record that throws light on the origins of the hamlet but the presence of the nearby medieval hall of *Berain* that lends its name to a medieval township as well as the hamlet is probably of significance. One description of the hamlet speculates that the elongated fields close to each homestead may be of medieval origin perhaps the remnants of former strip cultivation.[522] It may be speculated that the area of gently sloping fields that separates the hamlet from *Berain House* about 0.7 kms to the north west possibly

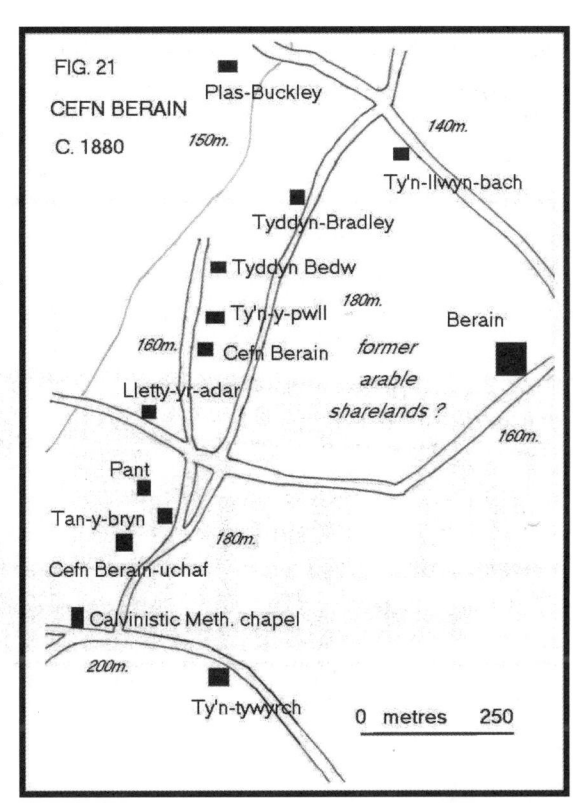

---

[522] Conwy Sites and monuments Record CPAT 105491

represents former arable sharelands and the hamlet the medieval settlement of bondmen who formerly worked these fields from their cottages at the edge of the cultivable area of the township The lands concerned lie on Carboniferous limestone on which traces of medieval ridge and furrow have been identified a little to the north east of Cefn Berain.

The Tithe Map of 1844 and the large scale OS map of 1880 show that all the present day roads were in existence but several present day public footpaths are shown as lanes. The 1881 Census Return shows that all the farms that made up this settlement, other than *Tyddyn Bartley* - 15 acres (6 ha) were very small, either of two or four acres (0,81 - 1.62 ha) in size and that their householders had secondary occupation as labourers. This suggests that if the hamlet is not the result of bondmen occupation in late medieval times, it either began in post medieval times as a squatter settlement on the waste or as a planned settlement for those forced to leave their homes by the process of enclosure.

Gell: Gell is a small hamlet with its nucleus close to a minor cross roads in the valley of the Afon Gell, the only significant left bank tributary of the Elwy. In 1871 the two routes meeting here crossed the Afon Gell by two fords. One of these routes is clearly an ancient one and linked the Elwy Valley to that of the Conwy. This was guarded at the Elwy end by the Llangernyw motte described in Chapter 8 which was close to the confluence of the Afon Gell and the Elwy.2 kms ESE of the village. The fast flowing stream was used to drive a local water mill in the village while across the ford over the stream was a smithy.

Pandy Tudur: This small village stands on the steep sided valley of the Afon Derfyn, a tributary of the upper Elwy some 4 kms (2.5 miles) south west of Llangernyw (GR 858643). The name *"pandy"* means a fulling mill. This fulling mill is recorded on several occasions in the *Wigfair Manuscript* housed at the National Library of Wales with the earliest record dating from 1589. It is of interest that the fulling mill is given the name *"Pandy Budr"* until the mid nineteenth century. This translates as "dirty fulling mill," at some stage in the last 150 years *"Budr"* became *Tudur"* obviously much more acceptable as an address for local householders. By the late nineteenth century the fulling mill had been transformed into a corn mill. The present two storey stone building dates from the eighteenth century and has been converted into a dwelling since its closure in 1932. Its overshot water wheel has been removed. Only the weir and leat remain as a reminder of the site's former role.

The nearby bridge over the Derfyn is known as *"Pont Pandy"* and also dates from the eighteenth century. A cluster of houses were built close to the bridge to form the nucleus of the present settlement in the nineteenth century. This community was served by a Calvinistic Methodist chapel (Plate 20) shown on the 1879 OS map, in 1881, this chapel was referred to as the *"Water Mill" CM Chapel*. The present large chapel is later and dates from 1907 no doubt the result of the religious revival of 1906. The new chapel reflects the fact that the Calvinistic Methodist community was clearly very strong in the village since in 1905 the chapel had 240 members at a tome when the population of the parish (Llanddewi) was 434. [523]The late nineteenth century community of the village does not appear to have been prosperous. The 1881 Census reveals that four of the cottages in the village were uninhabited together with a

---

[523]"Welsh Church Commission : "The Statistics of the Nonconformist Churches (Denbighshire)" (1905)

shop. Two shops remained open as did a smithy. Most of the village inhabitants were agricultural labourers although there were also two slate quarrymen living in this tiny community. There were eight elderly paupers living in the village, an unusually high proportion of the community. They were perhaps being partly sustained by the local Methodist community and outdoor relief from the Poor Law rather than being consigned to the workhouse in Llanrwst. The strength of the Methodist cause in the village may also explain the absence of a public house in 1881.[524]

In 1867, the Anglicans built a new church, St. David's, 0.5 kilometres north east of the village (GR862648) to serve the newly created parish of Llanddewi. The parish was short-lived revering to Llangernyw in 1974. The church was closed in 1963 and now forms a dwelling house.

Pennant: This small hamlet is a former township of Gwytherin. The hamlet is made up of a number of farms clustered at the head of this U-shaped steep sided valley (see Fig. 6) its name translates as "head of the brook". Above this point the stream flows through a fairly narrow gorge before the valley gives way to undulating moorland where the small rivulet known as Nant Caledfryn winds its way down from the upper slopes of Creigiau Llwydion on the western edge of Mynydd Hiraethog.

---

[524] PRO RG11 Piece 5535

Pennant from south

- Moel Gydia
- Tai pellaf
- Ty-draw
- Ty-hwnr-ir-afon

It is difficult to say exactly when man first colonised the head of this lonely valley The 1334 Survey of the Honour of Denbigh makes no mention of the township. However, it is likely that this part of the valley was traversed by herders driving their cattle to the summer pastures on Mynydd Hiraethog. Some 300m. above the hamlet (see Figs. 6 and 8) stands the small upland farm known as *Pant y Fotty* (" hollow of the summer house") the site of which was almost certainly in use in medieval times (although not in permanent occupation at that time). Given the sheltered location of the hamlet and the availability of lowland grazing on the valley floor, it is possible to speculate that at least one small isolated sheep farm stood here in medieval times although no record of such a settlement remains. The first documentary evidence of the place-name Pennant dates from 1667 when Jane, the daughter of Maurice Jones of Pennant was buried in Gwytherin churchyard[525]. The larger farms that occupy the core of the hamlet: *Ty Newydd, Ty Hwnt i'r afon* and *Tai Pellaf* are first recorded in the late eighteenth century. This is also true of the highest farm in the valley, (now abandoned): *Ddolfrwynog* (1776). *Ty Draw*, a 200 acre (81 ha) farm in 1881, does not appear in local records until the nineteenth century but possibly had another name at one stage of its history...

On the hillsides surrounding the hamlet are many sheepfolds some of which may be several centuries old. The expansion of sheep farming to meet the growing demand for wool may account for the establishment of some of the above farms as far back as the sixteenth century. The absence of references to them in parish records does not preclude their earlier existence since Gwytherin records date only from 1667, and even then, most parish priests gave few details of the addresses of the parishioners mentioned. .The 1879 Ordnance Survey map of the hamlet

---

[525] Clwyd Family History Society "Gwytherin Parish Registers 1667 - 1812" Vols. 1 & 2 Ruthin (1996)

shows a small tributary stream drove a corn mill close to *Tai Pellaf*. This indicates that cereal crops were grown in this section of the upper Cledwen valley. These were probably oats used for fodder and bread-making. The population of the hamlet remained too small to support a Calvinistic Methodist chapel or smithy and its remoteness has allowed it to retain its character into the present century.

Bryn Rhyd yr Arian: The village is located at the confluence of the River Aled and its tributary the Afon Deunant 3.2 kilometres (2 miles) north east of Llansannan. Roads following the valley bottoms converged here and the village subsequently developed close to the two crossing points. (See Fig. 22) The 1879 OS map shows the village was made up of a cluster of stone cottages, a smithy and a mill located on a wedge of rising land between the two rivers. The Deunant is crossed by a footbridge to the east of the mill with a further eighteenth century stone bridge but carrying the road to Henllan over the Deunant to the north of the village. The mill is shown as a flour mill but has since been converted into a private house. The remains of a leat and the mill pond can still be seen. Some 300m upstream from the flour mill is a small farm known as

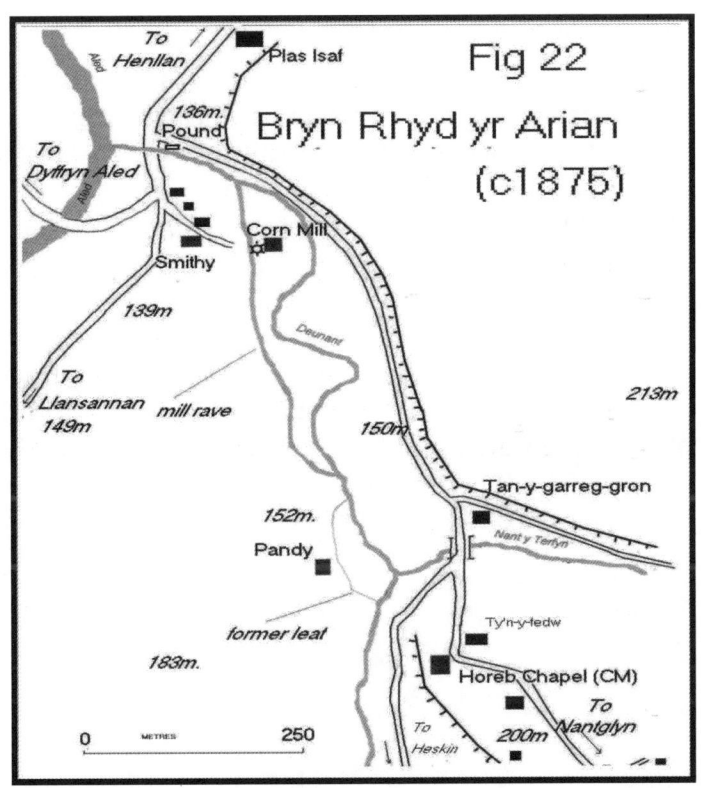

Fig 22 Bryn Rhyd yr Arian (c1875)

"*Pandy*". It lies close to the stream and represents another facet of Bryn Rhyd yr Arian's industrial past: the fulling of woollen cloth. (GR 957670) Close to *Pandy* the Deunant is joined by its tributary, the Afon Terfyn. On the rising land between the two streams stood the local Calvinistic Methodist chapel: "Horeb" built on 1841 but no longer open. (Plate 35)

From the available evidence it appears that the village has its origins in the post medieval period possibly the seventeenth or eighteenth centuries as a small industrial hamlet. The pandy, smithy and mill formed the raison d'etre of the settlement which had probable links to the outside world through drovers using the smithy and clothiers from Shrewsbury or Liverpool taking the products of the fulling mill. In the later nineteenth century a village shop served local needs. The 1881 Census records a *Bryn Shop* run by Elizabeth Jones (46), shopkeeper and farmer born in Llansannan.

Tan y Fron: The small village lies 3.2 kms (2 miles) south east of Llansannan and hugs the steep eastern side of the valley of the Afon Deunant. It is located at a point where two old roads from Llansannan to Denbigh and a north-south route along the valley bottom converged. It is difficult to establish the origins of the settlement but the date stone on the Calvinistic Methodist chapel close to the crossing point of the Deunant (Plate 33) indicates that it was built in 1779. It is likely that most of the houses also date from the eighteenth century.[526] The village has changed very little since it was first mapped in the Tithe Map of 1841. The 1881 Census indicates that it contained a village

---

[526] CPAT PRN 105518

shop with the shopkeeper's son, Robert Williams (41) serving as the preacher in the local Methodist chapel which had a recorded 168 members in 1905. The village also had a wheelwright's shop. The bulk of the small population found work as agricultural labourers. The Census also gives an indication that the social life of the village was fragile at this time of widespread agricultural distress. Three of the houses in the village were uninhabited and three of the older residents were described as paupers.

Bylchau: The hamlet of Bylchau is located at an altitude of 330 m. on the watershed of the Elwy River basin on a saddle of land separating it from the catchment of the Afon Ystrad, another tributary of the River Clwyd. The Tithe maps show that no settlement existed here in the 1840s. The only building existing at that time was the toll house on the turnpike road to Pentre Foelas opened in 1825. Even by the time of the OS Map of 1879 only three buildings existed at the heart of the hamlet, the meeting of two locally important routes, the road from Denbigh to Llansannan and the turnpike road over Mynydd Hiraethog to Pentre Foelas. The three buildings were the toll house known as the "*Bylchau Gate*"; St. Thomas' Church (1857) built to serve the new parish of Bylchau created in 1855 and the Rectory (1862). The religious needs of the Calvinistic Methodist community were met by a small chapel, *Hebron* now a private house, 2 kms SSW of the village alongside an old track to Pentre Foelas. The chapel dates from the 1870s A former school dated 1856 existed but is not shown on the 1879 map. However, the 1881 Census tells us that the schoolmaster lived on site: Frederick Dunn (21) bore in Caernarfon.

Epilogue

In the past fifty years the villages and hamlets of the Elwy and Aled valleys have undergone further dramatic change. Those in the lower sections of the valleys such as Llanfair Talhaearn, Henllan Llansannan and Llannefydd have become attractive as places of residence for those seeking to commute to work in the coastal strip or to Denbigh and those seeking to retire in a place of relative tranquility. No longer does agriculture sustain the majority of the population. The Welsh language, although still widely spoken, has declined with the influx of a non-Welsh-speaking population. Further up the valley around Llangernyw, Gwytherin and Pandy Tudur, Welsh is still widely spoken and agriculture remains an important mainstay of the communities but has experienced hard times in recent years. Much of the area ha seen a population decline as young people leave to seek educational and employment opportunities elsewhere and never return.

Village houses that become empty are increasingly bought as holiday homes and local services decline. Rural communities such as Gwytherin become increasingly fragile as local schools, shops, chapels and public houses close their doors and are converted to dwelling houses often occupied for only part of the year Thus these upland communities present a challenge to planners at a local level in Conwy and at national level in Cardiff to produce a continuing strategy for economic and social development that will sustain these ancient communities through the twenty first century. The intensification of agriculture was a major influence on the character of the landscape until the mid-1980s. The need to maximise farming profits led to drainage of moorland, the filling-in of ponds and the removal of trees and hedgerows. Fortunately, the last two decades have seen incentives to farmers and landowners to manage the landscape more sensitively

Some degree of planning support has aided this process through creating specially designated areas of landscape interest which can be offered some level of protection[527]. Such is the case with the *Blaen y Weinglodd Nature Reserve*, three kilometres south east of Llansannan. This 4 ha (10 acres) example of a peat bog habitat has been designated an SSSI (Site of Special Scientific Interest). Otherwise, little has been achieved to date in the Elwy basin and perhaps a case can be made for a more radical approach to planning in order to control the threats to the landscape posed by the excesses of over-grazing, reservoir construction, wind farms and off- road damage by trail bikes and four-wheel drive vehicles. Conwy Borough Council, the main local authority in the area, have a sound appreciation of what needs to be achieved in planning terms but face limits imposed by planning constraints and finance. The future economy of the area could be sustained by planned "green" tourism which could in turn help provide a market for local farms. This could be achieved by including both the Elwy river basin and Mynydd Hiraethog within a new National Park covering these areas of outstanding beauty and historic interest and preserving them for the enjoyment of future generations

---

[527] Conwy BC "A Countryside Strategy for Conwy 1998-2003" Colwyn Bay p 8

CHAPTER 16: St ASAPH (LLANELWY) - THE CITY OF THE VALLEY.

"St. Asaph .... is a neat, pretty town and standing on the side of a hill"   Jinny Jenks 1772

Although the landscape history of the Elwy and its tributaries is essentially a story of change in the rural landscape, no study of the river basin would be complete without at least a brief discussion of the landscape of its only town, St. Asaph, lying close to the confluence of the Elwy and its parent stream the Clwyd. St Asaph, or to give it its older Welsh name of Llanelwy, lies on a ridge made up by a tongue of boulder clay left by ice from the Irish Sea during the last Ice Age which ended about 14,000 years ago. The ridge separates the Elwy from the Clwyd with the oldest part of the city being perched on its summit and western slopes which led steeply down to crossings of the Elwy that appear to have changed in position on a number of occasions throughout the long history of the settlement.

Man's occupation of the city site probably dates back to the first century Roman site of *Varis (Varae)*. The debate about the actual location of this Roman settlement has been rehearsed earlier in these pages but it seems likely that some form of Roman settlement lay high on the ridge relatively close to the site of the cathedral. The majority of Roman finds have come from an area just to the south of the cathedral with the possibility of the Roman post being located at a cross roads of the Roman road from Deva (Chester) to Canovium and a possibly ancient north-south route running along the dry top of the ridge linking the coast at Prestatyn with the Iron Age fortified hilltops of Denbigh and Ruthin. No definite trace of the ramparts or buildings of the Roman settlement have been located but in 1994, the remains of the Roman road were discovered whilst digging a service ditch on the west side of Upper

Denbigh Road to the south of the cathedral (GR 040742). The road was made up of a band of cobbles 6.4m wide (c21 feet) and 0.2m (c 8 inches) deep and had a ditch 0.7m (c27 inches) wide and 0.55m (c 21.5 inches) deep.[528]

Presumably the Roman site fell into dis-use following the loss of Roman control over the area probably in the late fourth century AD. It is therefore difficult to assess the state of the Roman buildings when two centuries later St. Kentigern founded a church and large monastery at Llanelwy between the years 560 and 573 AD. Having arrived from Scotland by sea, one would have expected him to have chosen a site closer to the sea perhaps near Rhuddlan. It is possible that he was attracted to St. Asaph by the rums of what was left of any Roman enclosure at Llanelwy, the name of which suggests that some form of enclosure was created or pre-existed. If this is the case then it is possible that the cathedral site was utilised as that of the monastic church, certainly early monasteries were sited within the walls of Roman forts elsewhere in Wales namely Caer Gybi (Holyhead); Caerwent and Llandaff).

No such establishment could have been formed without the acquiescence of the local ruler. It is possible that the king of Gwynedd donated the former Roman site to Kentigern. There is a string tradition that Maelgwn of Gwynedd donated the Roman site at Holyhead, where he had a palace, to St. Gybi for similar purposes.[529] There is a further tradition that he donated lands in the Llangernyw area to Kentigern. However, traditional dates for the two do not coincide since Maelgwn is said to have died from yellow fever some twenty years before Kentigern's arrival in the

---

[528] CPAT Ref. PRN 26541
[529] Charles Thomas "Christians, Chapels, Churches and Charters – or "Proto-parochial provisions for the Pious in a Peninsular" (Land's End) Landscape History Vol.11 (1989) p21

Elwy valley. This does not preclude the possibility that the land was given to Kentigern by an heir of Maelgwn. Certainly, an extensive monastic estate would have been necessary to support the large number of monks (over 900) said to have been living at the monastery.[530] The monastic community obviously shaped the landscape of the ridge on which St. Asaph stands although it is not possible to say how, other than to suggest that the parish church site of St. Kentigern set in a curvilinear churchyard at the foot of the hill and close to the Elwy river, may date from the days of a monastic *clas* at St. Asaph.

The settlement appears to have survived Viking attacks and the Anglo Saxon invasion of the area in the ninth, tenth and early eleventh centuries for it is recorded as "Llanelwy" in William I's Domesday Survey of 1087. The site presumably retained its ecclesiastical role since it was not fortified by the Normans who built their defensive motte and bailey castle 5 kms (3 miles) to the north close to the site of the Saxon burh at Rhuddlan. The town appears to have had a commercial role in medieval times since there is a reference to a fair in the town in 1344 at which an angry and heavily-taxed Welsh contingent drove the burgesses of Rhuddlan back to the gates of their planted town[531]. The first Norman overlord of Llanelwy was Robert of Rhuddlan, cousin to the Earl of Chester from whom Robert himself held the land.[532]

---

[530] Denbighshire Sites and Monuments Record.

[531] Gwyn A Williams "When was Wales?" Black Raven Press, London (1985) p 96

[532] P. Morgan (ed) "Domesday Book : 26 Cheshire" Phillimore, Chichester (1978) p269

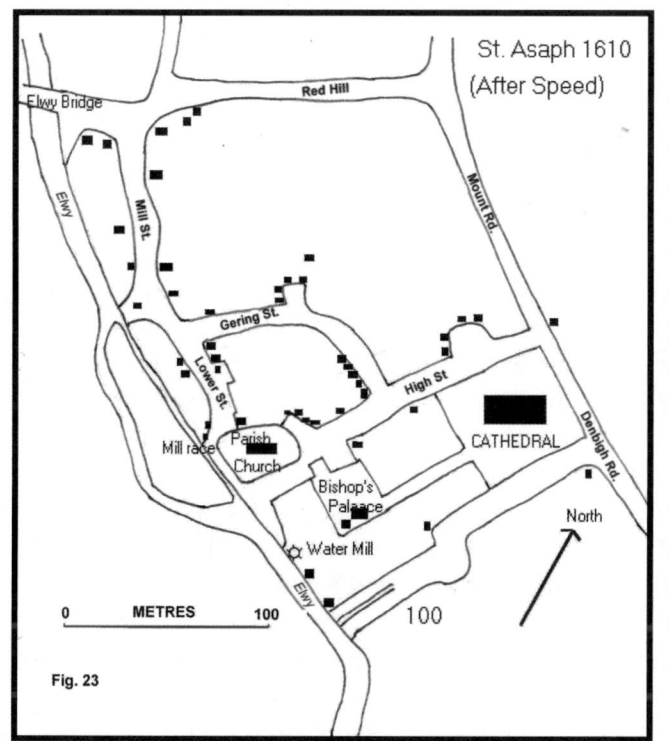

Edward I established a planned town at Rhuddlan in order to consolidate English control of the area, the new town was given borough status and was expected to flourish as the market centre for the northern section of the Vale of Clwyd. Meanwhile St. Asaph was to retain its function as an ecclesiastical centre becoming a Norman bishopric in 1141. A new cathedral church was built in 1152 on the present site (GR 039743) it is unclear as to whether an earlier church stood on this spot. Rhuddlan failed to develop as a successful market centre and thus St. Asaph was able to develop its commercial interests alongside its successful ecclesiastical role and eclipse its atrophied northern neighbour.[533]

Thus by the time that the first known map of St. Asaph was drawn by the Farndon-born cartographer John Speed in 1610, a small settlement of under fifty houses had developed on the western slopes rising from the Elwy valley. Figure 23) is based on Speed's map and shows the plan of St. Asaph at the

Fig. 23

---

[533] H. Carter "The Towns of Wales" University of Wales Press, Cardiff (1965) p66

beginning of the seventeenth century. The cathedral and curvilinear *"llan"* of the parish church are clearly shown together with elements of the present day street plan for the area to the north of High Street. There are few houses on the south side of the High Street perhaps because this area was part of the cathedral precinct but there were several clusters of houses on the north side particularly close to its junction with Gering Street which existed by that time. A further small group of houses lay on a small square opposite to the cathedral close to the junction of High Street and Mount Road.

From Mount Road, Red Hill led down to the Elwy Bridge located 500m downstream from the present bridging point. The bridge appears to have been constructed of wood. Several cottages are shown around the approaches to the bridge at the foot of Red Hill and its junction with Lower Street. A cluster of buildings is shown at the southern end of Lower Street to the north of the parish church. The River Elwy appears to have followed a course to the east of its present one at this time; its channel is shown as being split into two sections creating a small island. It is unclear whether one of the channels is a mill race since one certainly existed at this location during the nineteenth century. The mill at the foot of the High Street is shown but its leat is not, a mill was recorded in this vicinity in 1353. .To the south of the cathedral a street leading south from Upper Denbigh Road (now truncated), is shown leading down to the Elwy. There is no bridge or ford shown but the alignment of this road is close to that of the Roman road leading west to Canovium thus making it possible that the Roman bridging point was close to this point. Chester Street did not exist neither did any form of settlement on the west side of the Elwy. Several buildings in the town survive from the period of Speed's map. The Bishop's Palace was located in what is now Esgoby farmhouse, a timber-framed product of the "Great Re-building" of late sixteenth/early seventeenth century.

Plate 58

Former Alms Houses, St. Asaph High St.

The house was encased in brick during the mid eighteenth century. A seventeenth century dovecote survives on the site. The tithe barn, parts of which may date from the sixteenth century, survives as a private residence. On Lower Street, the Old China Shop and China House may well be among the buildings depicted by Speed and are of possible sixteenth century date. There is a tradition that a convent associated with the parish church once stood on the site. The buildings shown by Speed on Gering Street may have included the Red Lion public house that dates from the turn of the seventeenth century.The key event in shaping the late seventeenth, eighteenth and nineteenth century townscape was the building of a new bridge at the foot of the High Street. A bridge was built here late in the seventeenth century but may have suffered severe damage from flooding. The present bridge was built in 1770 by Joseph Turner, the Hawarden architect also responsible for design of Chester's new Bridgegate and Watergate. The shallowness of the Elwy at this point belies its power; the river is prone to flash floods as is evidenced by the flood defences around the bridge and protecting the Common. In 1772, Jinny Jenks, travelling through St, Asaph as part of a tour of North Wales; described the building of the new bridge:

"At St. Asaph, where the river is much wider, they are building another (bridge) of six arches to the town which will have a fine effect, when finished, and they are making a new road through the meadows to avoid the fords."[534]

The new bridge (Plate 59) carried traffic through the town since it formed an integral part of an important north-south road route through the Vale of Clwyd from the growing settlements on the North Wales coast from the eighteenth century. The route was part of a turnpike road built in the nineteenth century linking Abergele and St. Asaph and today's road (now the A525) still brings a significant flow of traffic through the town.

The obvious beneficiary of the traffic diverted through the town by the new bridge was the High Street. On the north side of the High Street, several of the buildings survive from the late seventeenth century much altered by later additions. These include No. 1 High Street and further up the High Street, the Kentigern Arms (formerly the Kinmel Arms) and Beulah House may date from the same century. The development of the southern side of the High Street also began following the opening of the bridge. Almshouses to house eight widows were built on land formerly part of the cathedral precinct in 1680. The single storey building rebuilt in 1795, survives today as a restaurant (Plate 58)

---

[534] "A Tour of North Wales by Jinny Jenks 1772" Nat. Library of Wales MS 22753B p46

By 1881, the High Street was clearly a bustling thoroughfare containing shops (grocers; linen/woollen drapers; butchers; Post and Telegraph Office) tradesmen's workshops (tailors, shoemakers and a saddler), a solicitor's office and cocoa rooms. In the yard of the Mostyn Arms was the nineteenth century equivalent of the modern day taxi firm - a car proprietor's premises employing three men.

Off the High Street,(see Fig. 24) Gering Street was occupied in 1881 by a mixture of tradesmen and labourers, the most unusual trade being that of fishing tackle maker. A small private boarding school with ten boarders was located on this street. On Lower Street, there were formerly two public houses, the White Horse and the Hand, by 1881, the White Horse's occupant was a plasterer suggesting that it no longer served as a public house. Developments of small houses had been built off Lower Street, these included St. Roger's Court occupied by elderly people; Forge Square and an area of housing called "California". Liverpool House was a large grocer and general dealer's shop with four assistants living on the premises. China House was serving as a china shop.

The position of the new bridging point indicates that the Elwy had shifted to its present course since Speed's time so allowing for the development of Mill Street. A house known as "Rose Gau" was built on the new street in the eighteenth century and survives today as two dwellings. In 1780, a Grammar School to serve the needs of the children of the town's more affluent families was built between Mill Street and Lower Street. This is now a private residence.

Plate 59   St. Asaph Bridge c 1881

(Photograph by permission of Llyfrgell Genedlaethol Cymru?National Library of Wales Ref. NLW JTH01299)

Fig. 24. St. ASAPH c 1881

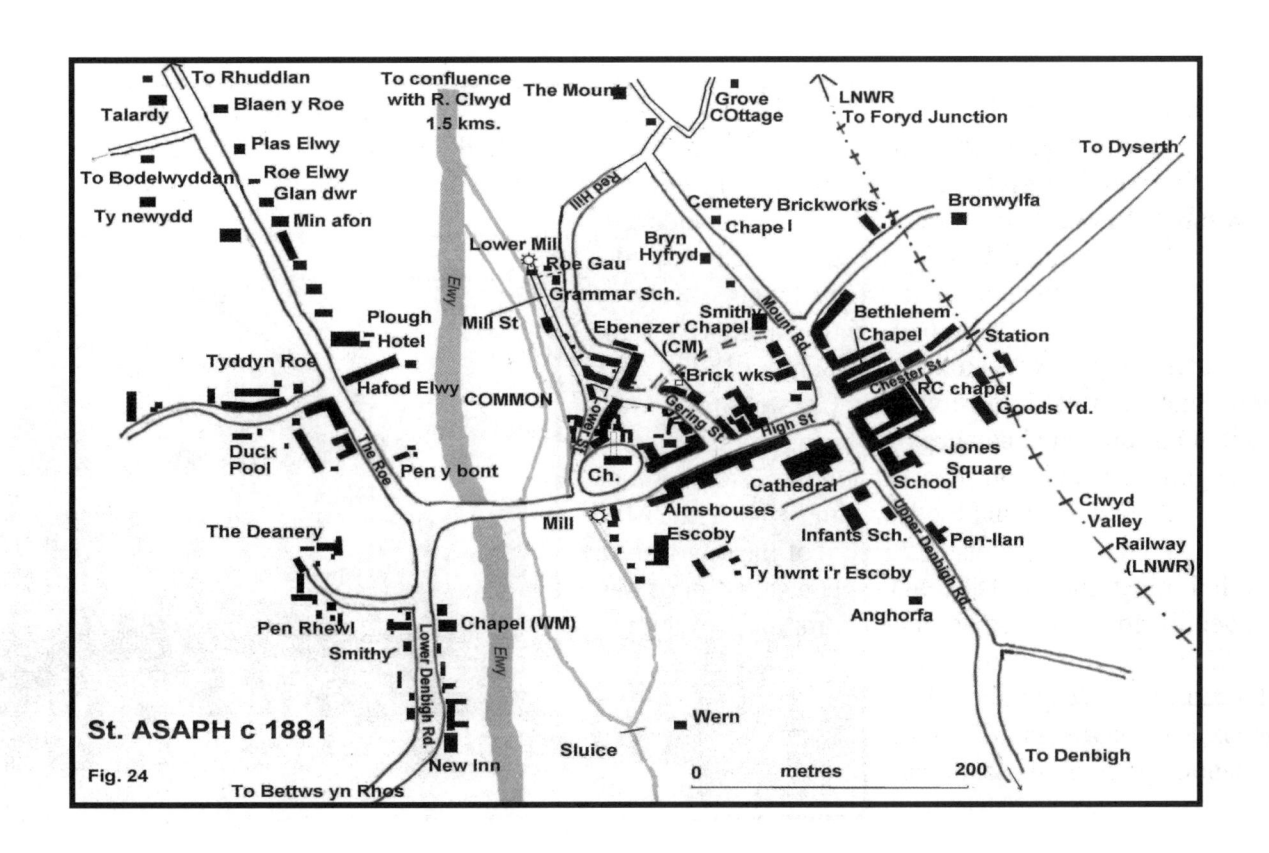

On the High Street, several additional new houses and shops were built during the second half of the eighteenth and early nineteenth centuries, some of the eighteenth century buildings being distinguishable today by the Georgian style sash windows in their upper storeys. The expanding role of the town during the early as a service centre for the surrounding area is reflected in the establishment of two banks in the town. These were the Savings Bank (1818) and a branch of the North and South Wales Bank in 1837. [535] At the top of the High Street, a new street, Chester Street, was built in the early nineteenth century. This new street was described in 1833 as having *"several handsome houses and pleasing cottages"*[536]. Thus by the time the 1845 Tithe Map was drawn, most of the streets in the core of the city were in existence. In the following decade we get a snapshot of the appearance of the town from a contemporary topographer: William Davis :

Plate 60

---

[535] A.H. Dodd "The Industrial Revolution in North Wales" " Univ. Of Wales Press (1933) - new edition by Bridge Books, Wrexham (1990) pp 322, 376.
[536] See CPAT Abstracts 105810 html

"The houses in the principal streets are brick, and in general small, though neatly built; the streets are kept clean. The view of the city from many points around it, is particularly striking; its elevated position on an eminence near the termination of the Vale of Clwyd, crowned on its summit with the Cathedral, and having the parish church at its base, makes it a conspicuous object from every point of view" [537]

The building of a more substantial bridge over the Elwy and traffic to the developing watering places on the coast also stimulated the first developments on the west bank of the river. (See Fig. 24) The Old Deanery (GR 033743) and Plas yn Roe may date from the late seventeenth century During the eighteenth and nineteenth century other building were built on this side of the river along the Roe and the area between the new bridge and the old Roman road to Betws yn Rhos (now the B5381). This area was known as Pen Rhewl. By the time the first large scale OS map was drawn of the area in 1879, a substantial suburb had developed on the west bank of the Elwy. Pen Rhewl the southernmost part of the built up area on the west bank of the Elwy was home to a number of tradesmen (including a tailor, shoemakers, saddler, plumber painter, "tin man" and hawking greengrocer) together with several general labourers and a brick maker. This little community was served by a Wesleyan Methodist Chapel near the river, a smithy and an inn: the New Inn, close by, was an area known as Elwy Square of which four houses were uninhabited and the remainder occupied by general labourers.

---

[537] Quoted from William Davis : "Handbook of the Vale of Clwyd ", (1856)

North of the bridge the houses on southern end of the Roe were for the most part occupied by a number of tradesmen and labourers. A lane leading off the Roe to the west housed the town's gas works. Close by was another group of working class houses that took its name from a nearby pool known as the Duck Pool or Pwll yr Hwyad in Welsh. Close to the river on the opposite side of the Roe lay another group of dwellings for working people known as "Hafod Elwy" of which no less than nine were uninhabited in 1881. This may have been the result of "Y Dwr Mawr" the great floods of 17th August 1879 A number of substantial middle class properties also lined the Roe, particularly at its northern end. These housed a number of professional people in 1881 including a doctor, a retired ship broker, a retired surgeon, a barrister, several annuitants and at Talardy Hall, a County Magistrate: Robert Sisson. Two inns (Swan and Black Lion) and a hotel, the Plough, also occupied roadside locations along the Roe.

Other building development took place on the east side of the town. Along Mount Road, the west side was taken up by the homes of senior clerics notably in the Canonry and the Vicarage. Before the building of Chester Street in the early nineteenth century, the main route to the north east was a lane that led towards Dyserth crossing the Clwyd via the old bridge known as Pont Dafydd. The old bridge survives abandoned by a change in the course of the river; its newer successor further upstream carries the new road from Chester Street across the Clwyd. Along the lane lay a smithy and a seventeenth century gentlemen's residence known as Bronwylfa, the former home of the early nineteenth century poet Felicia Hemans (the house was rebuilt in the 1930s). The old bridge at Pont Dafydd is known locally as "Mrs Hemans' Bridge", since it was a favourite walk of hers from her home and may have inspired the poet to write such poems as *To the River Clwyd in North Wales"* and *"The Vale of Clwyd"* written in the 1820s. The latter poem contains the following verse:

> *"Array'd in every glowing hue,*
> *How varied all the sylvan view,*
> *With tufted woods, romantic glades,*
> *And spires embosom'd in the shades"* [538]

In 1858, the Vale of Clwyd Railway was opened initially connecting Denbigh with the Chester - Holyhead line at Foryd Junction west of Rhyl. St. Asaph had a station in the town on Chester Street. The railway had strong local backing with its first chairman being Townshend Mainwaring of Galltfaenan, Henllan, MP for Denbigh. Significantly the three steam locomotives working the line had local names: *Elwy*, *Galltfaenan* and *Clwyd*. The line had troubled early years and was taken over by the LNWR in 1867. Passenger services ceased on the line in September 1955 with freight services surviving until the line finally closed in January 1968.[539] The railway brought employment to the town, the 1881 Census records around a dozen platelayers living in the town together with a railway porter, a railway carter and two engine drivers. The Station Master lived in a new house built on the station site while a platelayer's family lived in a cottage at the level crossing. A new inn, the Railway Inn, was opened to meet the needs of workers and travellers on the railway.

---

[538] Felicia Dorothea Hemans "Poems - England and Spain, Modern Greece" Garland Publishing, New York (1978)

[539] D. StJ Thomas & J A Patmore "A Regional History of the Railways of Great Britain Vol XI North and Mid Wales" (1979) pp 64 -70

On Upper Denbigh Road two buildings were erected serving the needs of a wider community than that of the town itself. The spiritual centre of North East Wales was also given an important social function to perform in 1838 when a new Union Workhouse was erected on the east side of the Upper Denbigh Road. The building served a population covering a wide area that included Denbigh, the Elwy valley (to Llanfair Talhaearn) and the lower Clwyd valley. The large building was constructed to house 200 inmates. The building was cruciform in plan with a central hub from which each wing housed a different class of inmate (infants, male, female and infirm). The building still survives under the name of H M Stanley Hospital.

Henry Morton Stanley (David Livingstone's contemporary) had been an inmate of the establishment in 1846 at the age of five. He remained there for some years until at the age of seventeen he ran away to sea. On the day of the 1881 Census, the building housed around 120 "inmates". The Workhouse Master was a local man, Robert Jones (41) of Rhuddlan. In the male wing the most common occupation of inmates was agricultural labourer, not surprising given the hard times that local agriculture was experiencing in the 1880s. There were also a number of tradesmen, often elderly or perhaps infirm. These included a number of more unusual trades such as carver and gilder; ship's carpenter; saddler and nail maker. There was also a solicitor and a druggist reminding us that despite its faults, the workhouse served as a safety net for the whole of society. On the female wing, the usual occupation of inmates was domestic servant. Many of the women were young, under thirty years of age. The Census tells us little about how these young women fell on hard times but four of the domestic servants were described as "imbeciles" and presumably found gaining employment difficult. The fate of others can be guessed at through the matching of their surnames with the large number of child inmates. One young inmate, Jane Lovett (18), a domestic servant born in

Rhuddlan was unmarried and had a four week old son named George. Another older unmarried mother, Mary Furmston (40), also from Rhuddlan, had been placed in the workhouse with her four children aged between one and ten.[540]

Closer to the cathedral, the educational needs of children from St. Asaph and its surrounding area were met by a new National School opened in 1863. In its early years, the school served the needs of children aged between seven and fourteen. The school continues to serve the area today and in 1956 became Ysgol Glan Clwyd, the first Welsh Secondary School in Wales. Across the Upper Denbigh Road an infants school stood on the site of the present cathedral car park.

To the north of the schools, close to the junction of Chester Street and Upper Denbigh Road was a square known as Jones Square. This was an area of working class houses the majority of which formed part of an enclave of Irish-born agricultural labourers and hawkers. Four Irish families (possibly inter-related) made up the majority of the Square's inhabitants: bearing the surnames of Collins; Durkin; McManus and Roach. One exception was an Irish born "Chelsea Pensioner", John O'Brien (54).

During the late eighteenth and early nineteenth centuries, the town had developed into a small centre for flax dressing, a trade known as "heckling".[541] This involved preparing raw flax imported from Liverpool for spinning

---

[540] PRO RG11 Piece 5529.

and involved a high degree of skill. The yarn was then woven into linen or mixed with wool to produce "woolsey". The spinning and weaving of flax was carried out in small cottages and farmhouses throughout the area. The workers used their spinning wheels and looms for either linen or wool according to demand. At Llewenni, in the Clwyd valley south of St. Asaph, a large bleach works was built to prepare the woven cloth for market, usually in Chester. The bleachery was in production from around 1780 until 1809 thus giving a timescale for the "heckling" trade in St. Asaph.

By the mid nineteenth century the town appears to have had only two industries: brick making and corn milling. The 1880 OS Map shows two brickworks one off Gering Street and the other adjacent to the railway near Bronwylfa. The works no doubt made use of the red boulder clay that underlies the ridge as a raw material. Both sites are now built upon. Two water mills were served by a leat running from the Elwy to the south of the town. St. Asaph corn mill lay at the foot of High Street but the site has disappeared, another mill known as Lower Mill lay to the north near the site of the Old Grammar School. It too has disappeared although it was still working in 1881. A sluice has been re-constructed on the line of the old leat on the Common as a reminder of this aspect of the town's history.(Plate 32)

The 1881 Census indicates that St. Asaph was enjoying a degree of prosperity serving not only its surrounding area as a shopping and service centre, but also the needs of travellers passing through the town en route to the North

---

[541] A.H. Dodd "The Industrial Revolution in North Wales" Univ. Of Wales Press (1933)- new edition by Bridge, Wrexham (1990} pp293-298

Wales coast or southwards to the towns of the Vale of Clwyd. Its status as a cathedral town and its attractive location had led to many wealthy people of private means settling in the town which was more anglicised than other towns further south in the Vale of Clwyd.

During the twentieth century the town continued to expand its housing southwards along the Upper Denbigh Road and also on the west bank of the river. This was stimulated by the development of an industrial base on the western fringes of the town where the making of specialist glass by Pilkington's Glass brought further expansion of the local economy and new immigrants to the area. At the end of the twentieth century, the building of the A55 trunk road linking directly to the English motorway network brought further housing developments as the town functioned as a dormitory town for commuters to the coastal towns, Deeside, Chester and even Merseyside. Like most other small towns, the retail base of the old core area of the town is undergoing transition as it comes to terms with good road links to out of town retail complexes. The key to the town's future would appear to lie in restoring some tranquility to the city centre. This could be achieved by creating a by-pass for the steady flow of traffic passing through the town's narrow High Street so giving this ancient street the chance to re-establish itself as a thriving retail area based on small specialist shops and freeing shoppers and tourists from the present problem of exhaust gases and noise from passing cars and goods vehicles.

Such levels of environmental pollution were not evident when John Jones of Llanfair Talhaearn wrote one of his few verses in the English language on which we close this book:

While I watch the Yellow wheat
I wander by the river,
To dream a day-dream of my love
For I must love her ever:
I see her in the glassy stream,
Her eyes with sweetness beaming:
Oh how delicious 'tis to me
To be thus ever dreaming.

John Jones (1810 – 1869)   *"Watching the Wheat"*[542]

---

[542] From R. Garlick & R. Mathias "Anglo-Welsh Poetry 1480-1980" Poetry Wales Press, Bridgend (1984) p115

INDEX of PLACES

Aberconwy Abbey:126, 147, 214
Abergele: 91, 202, 203, 216, 232, 238, 251, 253, 262, 266, 281, 307
Bardsey Island: 103
Barmouth: 244
Bedd y Cawr (fortified settlement): 66, 68, 71, 73 , 82
Berain (house, township): 151, 162, 216, 294, 315
Betws yn Rhos: 44, 250
Bodfari hill fort): 78, 102
Bodgynwch (township, chapel): 52, 264, 286
Bodrach (township): 163, 286
,Bontnewydd: 150, 151, 246, 313-314
Brenig valley: 206
Bron Heulog (lead mines): 239
Bryn Rhyd yr Arian (village): 269, 277, 322-3
Bylchau (parish): 56, 152, 251, 251, 265, 274-5, 304, 323
Caer Gybi (Holyhead): 86, 94, 97, 104, 326
Carwedfynydd (township): 170, 294
Castell Cawr (hillfort): 68, 70, 157
Cefn Berain (village): 270, 315-6
Cefn Mawr (peat bog): 34, 41, 51
258, Cefn Meiriadog (parish): 38, 52, 61, 66, 71, 115, 151, 201, 235, 24005, 248 276, 278, 313
Cefn rocks: 22, 23, 30, 31
Cerrig y Druidion: 195, 302
Chester: 77 78, 220, 250, 293, 326, 328, 331, 339, 342-3
Cornwall (county): 16, 50, 101, 107, 115, 130, 1349 289
Cornwal (township): 195, 281
Deganwy (hillfort, 88, 130, 131, 132, 140, 162, 173
Denbigh:13, 15, 70, 94, 142-144, 185, 196, 203-205,, 218, 232, 240, 250,251, 290, 297, 302, 307, 322
Dinorben (hillfort,): 52, 68, 79, 80, 129, 157, 163, 257

Fawnog Fawr (peat bog): 183, 240
Ffrith Uchaf (upland area): 181-183
Ffynnon Fair (St. Mary's Well): 89. 112-116
Ffynnon Meirchion: 103, 176
Galltfaenan (house and estate): 210, 213/4, 218, 225, 312, 334
Garthewin: (house and estate) 13, 122, 198/9, 205-207, 210-212, 235, 274, 275, 279
Gwytherin:: 16, 29, 40/1, 52, 58, 60, 72, 82, 85, 87,90-92, 94, 97, 99, 102-109,135, 148151, 159,161164-6 180-183, 185, 210-11, 241-2, 246, 263, 266,269-71 275, 278, 279-81, 289,302, 418, 320, 324
Hafod Elwy (estate): 184, 190, 205, 206
Hafodunos: 110, 198-200, 214, 223-2226, 263, 286-287
Henllan: 48, 64, 81,94,96, 103 121, 138, 151,-,152,161, 164/5, 167, 196, 218, 233, 240, 243/4, 247,249, 250, 263, 265, 305-313, 321,324, 339
Llanelwy (St Asaph) monastery: 79, 86 91, 117-118
Llanfair Talhaearn: 13, 14, 24, 51, 61, 70, 81/2, 93-96, 111-116, 120, 136 157, 159, 162, 164-168, 171, 212/4, 217 220/222, 231/2, 237/9, 243, 250/1, 253, 250, 264/5,276, 278/9, 281/1, 288- 294, 299, 302, 305, 324, 340, 343
Llangernyw: 6, 9, 16, 20, 26, 41, 52, 55, 58, 60, 64, 72, 79, 82, 85, 87, 79, 88/9, 90, 84, 93/5, 103107-111,122, 138-144 148, 152/5, 159, 162/4, 167/8, 183, 197/8, 200, 202/4, , 223/4, 231, 234, 243, 251/3, 259, 263, 2264, 266, 269, 274/279, 285-288, 302, 316/8, 324, 327
Llannefydd: 24, 37, 41, 58/9, 65/7,70, 88, 90, 93/4, , 96, 121,123-6 146, 151, 157, 159, 160/2, 164/5, 167/8, 217, 219, 221 228, 233, 240, 244/5, 263/4, 266, 271, 276, 291-300, 315, 324,

Llanrwst: 202, 232, 235, 251, 292
Llansannan: 24, 51, 58/9, 61/2, 93/5, 98, 120, 121-123, ,
    148, 159, 163/4, 166/7, 185/6, 191, 194,,
    201, 207, 235, 237, 239, 241, 243, 245, 248,
    251, 264/5, 269, 272, 274/5, 277/8,279,
    290, 298, 300-305, 321, 322, 324/5,
Llyn Aled (lake): 21, 56, 59, 174, 188, 195, 197, 206
Llyn Ales Isaf (reservoir, Mesolithic site): 35, 59, 206/7, 241
Marchaled (township): 144, 286
Meifod (township): 214, 215
Melai (house, township) 212-213, 221, 288
Mynydd Bodrochwyn: 239, 281, 288
Mynydd Hiraethog 6, 11, 16, 20, 21, 24, 26, 34/5/6, 42, 48, 51, 57,
    59, 60 97, 146/7, 148, 151/2, 163, 166/7, 176-180, 185/6
    1188/9, 190/1, 197/8, 203, 241, 242, 244
Mynydd y Gaer (hill fort): 67-71,73,113,125-129,156,180,219, 300
National Library of Wales: 285, 290, 318, 331
Old Foxhall (Iron Age enclosure, house): 38, 66, 78, 219
Pandy Tudur (village) 183, 243, 268/9, 317-318
Pennant (hamlet): 30, 183, 281,318-321
Penporchell (township): 146, 233, 294
Pentre Foelas:126, 183, 201, 205, 240, 249, 251, 302,
    313
Pentre Du (Llannefydd) (limekilns): 240
Pentre Isaf (Llannefydd0: 264, 268, 271
Pentre Uchaf (Llannefydd): 299
Perfeddwlad: 132, 134, 141, 142, 144
Plas Heaton (house and estate) 222, 225, 226, 228
Pontnewydd Cave: 12, 22, 29, 30, 35, 37
Plas Harri (house): 163, 170

Pont y Gwyddel (bridge, hamlet): 70, 249/50, 276
Pont yr Allt Goch (bridge mill): 246/7, 249
Prestatyn: 76, 78, 206, 3126
Rhaeadr y bedd (waterfall): 21, 206
Rhos (cantref): 36, 78, 128, 131/2, 143, 326/7, 334, 335
Rhuddlan: 36, 78, 131/2, 134/5, 138, 144, 147,
Rhufoniog (cantref): 128, 132, 134, 135, 138, 140, 144, 147, 158,
    168
Rhyl: 206
Ruthin: 22, 172, 200, 265, 326
St. Asaph cathedral & diocese: 41, 52, 97, 104, 112, 116-119,
    125/6.143, 164, 168, 202, 274/5, 286, 305, 326/43
St. Asaph (Llanelwy): 12-14, 20, 24, 77/8, 88, 91, 116, 120, 208
    249, 253, 263, 265, 270, 272, 273, 278, 285,
    293, 305, 326-345
Segontium (Caernarfon): 76, 78, 250
Shrewsbury: 103, 322
Tandderwen (Mesolithic site): 36
Treflech (township): 171, 300
Tremeirchion: 124
Tywysog (township) 15, 72, 166, 234, 321
Uwchaled 135, 143, 152, 203
Uwchdulas: 135
Varae or Varis (Roman settlement): 24, 76, 77/8, 81, 326
Wigfair (township, hall): 87/8, 112-116, 222, 225, 314
Wrexham: 213, 234, 237
Ysbytty Ifan: 201

LIST OF ABBREVIATIONS

Arch. Camb.	Archaeologia Cambrensis
CPAT	Clwyd-Powys Archaeological Trust
CUP	Cambridge University Press
DRO	Denbighshire Record Office (Ruthin)
GR	Grid Reference (Ordnance Survey)
NLW	National Library of Wales
OUP	Oxford University Press
PRO	Public Record Office (Kew)
RCAHM	Royal Commission on Ancient and Historical Monuments
SAC	Special Area of Conservation
SMR	Sites and Monument Record
SSI	Site of Special Scientific Interest
Trans DHS	Transactions of the Denbighshire History Society
Trans. IBG	Transactions of the Institute of British Geographers
UCNW	University College of North Wales
W.H.R.	Welsh History Review

Published by Marlston Books
115, Lache Lane,
Chester
CH4 7LT

Tel. 02144 677360